Satire and Society in Wilhelmine Germany

Satire
and Society
in Wilhelmine
Germany

Kladderadatsch

&

Simplicissimus

1890–1914

Ann Taylor Allen

THE UNIVERSITY PRESS OF KENTUCKY

PT
851
.A5
.A4
.A4

Frontispiece: Color lithograph by Thomas
Theodor Heine, 1919. Courtesy of the
Stadtsmuseum, Munich.

Library of Congress Cataloging in Publication Data
Allen, Ann Taylor, 1944–
  Satire and society in Wilhelmine Germany.

  Bibliography: p.
  Includes index.
  1. Satire, German—History and criticism. 2. German
prose literature—19th century—History and criticism.
3. German prose literature—20th century—History and
criticism. 4. Social problems in literature.
5. Kladderadatsch (Berlin, Germany) 6. Simplicissimus
(Munich, Germany) I. Kladderadatsch (Berlin, Germany)
II. Simplicissimus (Munich, Germany) III. Title.
PT851.A4 1984   837'.8'09   84-5114
ISBN 0-8131-1512-4

To my parents
Ann Updegraff Allen and
Franklin Gordon Allen

Contents

Illustrations

Preface

THIS book is a serious study of humor—a seemingly contradictory undertaking to which I was drawn because of the great importance of satirical literature to our understanding of public opinion, especially in societies which prohibit, restrict, or discourage more direct forms of protest. Wilhelmine Germany provided in many ways an ideal environment for the development of humor, not only as the passive expression of opinion but as an active force for social change. Although cultural historians have given much attention to dissent, protest, and alienation during this period, their studies have for the most part been centered on elites, whether individual authors or groups such as artists, middle-class youth, or academics. Literature such as *Kladderadatsch* and *Simplicissimus* suggests the increasing prevalence of certain skeptical, dissenting, or critical attitudes among a significant segment of the general public. To be sure, not all Germans read these magazines or subscribed to their views, nor were they the most widely circulating of contemporary periodicals. But they were genuinely popular, appealing to a diverse and enthusiastic readership and attracting widespread attention (even among nonsubscribers) through their flamboyant and sometimes scurrilous attacks on authority. Certainly the vociferous support given to *Simplicissimus* by the people of Munich (or at least a considerable number of them) in its confrontation with religious authority reflected the journal's growing importance as a symbol of antiestablishment opinion. As organs of an oppositional liberalism which had little organized political expression during this period, the *Witzblätter* provide unique and valuable evidence of the evolution of critical and self-critical attitudes among a significant segment of the Wilhelmine bourgeoisie.

Satire is such a diverse and varied phenomenon that it was necessary to focus on a few important and representative examples. *Kladderadatsch* and *Simplicissimus,* as the most conspicuous examples of the old and the new styles of satirical journalism respectively, commended themselves both by their intrinsic artistic and literary interest and by the diversity of their content. This book is purposely confined to the bourgeois satirical press, since socialist periodicals such as *Der Wahre Jakob* differed from their liberal counterparts both in their purpose (as propaganda organs for a specific party line) and in the audience to which they appealed. I have analyzed the caricature art of the two journals more for its political or social message than for its artistic style. To be sure, both journals (especially *Simplicissimus*) offer a fertile field of research to the art historian. But a full exploration of their aesthetic aspects would require another book.

I thank the College of Arts and Sciences of the University of Louisville for several research grants which helped with travel and other expenses, and the Academic Publications Committee for a partial subsidy of the costs of publication. I am also grateful to the *Journal of European Studies* for permission to publish portions of my earlier article "Sex and Satire in Wilhelmine Germany" in chapter six.

Over the long period which I have spent writing, revising, and rewriting this book, I have been supported and sustained by so many friends, relatives, and colleagues that a full acknowledgement of their valuable assistance would be impossible here. To the staffs of the Munich Stadtbibliothek, the Bayerischer Hauptstaatsarchiv, and the Stuttgart Hauptstaatsarchiv I owe appreciation. I am particularly obliged to Dr. Stukenbroek of the Hamburg Staatsarchiv for digging out the useful newspaper clipping file of the *Politische Polizei.* To Fritz Stern, sponsor of the original dissertation, I acknowledge my abiding gratitude for his rigorous and penetrating criticism and for his insistence on clear thinking and writing. As second reader, Geoffrey G. Field offered some perceptive suggestions which have been of great value to me in the revision process. For their constructive and helpful comments on the manuscript as a whole or on its various parts (including those presented as papers at professional conferences) I thank John Toews, Andrew Lees, Barbara Miller Lane, Beth Irwin Lewis, Gary Stark, Marion Deshmukh, and James C. Albisetti. Otto M. Nelson showed great patience and thoughtfulness in his painstaking evaluations of two versions of the manuscript. David Jobling provided much assistance and encouragement during the initial stages of this project. Allen J. Share was always ready with practical help, constructive criticism and good cheer during moments of discouragement. My friends in the Department of History at the University of Louisville, especially Mary K. Tachau and Arthur J. Slavin, gave me much good advice and generous support. To whatever is of value in this work, these and many others have contributed; any errors or omissions are entirely my own. My son Ian buoyed up my frequently sagging spirits with laughter, high spirits, and many welcome distractions. I dedicate this book to my parents, who first taught me the importance of a sense of humor.

A Playful Judgment: The Social Function of Humor

1

KUNO Fischer defined wit as "a playful judgment." As buffoon and as critic, the humorist performs an essential function in the development of culture. By debunking old beliefs, humor helps to clear the way for new ideas and perceptions. Thus in every society it sensitively reflects the tension between old and new, between conservatism and radicalism, between conformity and rebellion. "The antagonism between a philosophy consolidating the absolute and a philosophy questioning the accepted absolutes appears to be incurable. . . . It is the antagonism of the priest and the jester," stated one perceptive analyst, "and in almost every historical epoch the philosophy of the priest and the philosophy of the jester have been the two most general forms of human culture." The jester who questions accepted ideas is seldom popular among those in power. "By its nature," remarked Malcolm Muggeridge, former editor of *Punch*, "humor is anarchistic and implies, when it does not state, criticism of existing institutions, beliefs and functionaries."[1]

A study of German social and political satire at the turn of the century must therefore analyze humor as a vent for protest and as a force for social change. Because satire is such a highly diversified and widespread phenomenon, I have found it necessary to limit this study to a few outstanding and representative examples. Attention will be focused on the period's most famous liberal organs of political satire, *Kladderadatsch* and *Simplicissimus*. Their genuine popularity, the wide-ranging scope of their social and political commentary, and their high intrinsic literary and artistic quality commend these periodicals to the historian.

The study of a historical period through its humor is a relatively novel undertaking. Until recently, historical accounts of German popular humor were few and, in general, unsatisfactory. Although the satirical journals, or *Witzblätter,* as they were usually called, have had their place in histories of art and journalism, little serious analysis of them has been done. The recent appearance of several dissertations—most notably Klaus Schulz's on *Kladderadatsch* and Ruprecht Konrad's on *Simplicissimus*—reflects a new interest in satire as a phenomenon of social and intellectual history. But though solid and scholarly, both of these studies are somewhat limited in scope. Schulz devotes more attention to the journalistic techniques and financial policies of *Kladderadatsch* than to its more general significance as an organ of public opinion. Konrad's analysis of *Simplicissimus* concentrates almost exclusively on explicitly political content, without giving much attention to the cultural criticism which inspired the humorists' most controversial and innovative insights. Neither study attempts systematically to apply the extensive sociological and psychological research on the social function of humor to the analysis of this material. Still lacking is a thorough interpretation of the significance of popular humor as historical documentation.[2]

The neglect of the *Witzblätter* by "serious" historians may reflect their belief that humor—by contrast, of course, with such solid stuff as parliamentary debates, railway stockholders' reports, and ideological manifestoes—is frivolous, ephemeral, lacking in both intrinsic value and historic importance. But contemporary readers—politicians, courtiers, officers, trade-unionists, priests, and other members of the journals' considerable readership—would hardly have concurred in this judgment. The strength of their reactions, both positive and negative, showed that they considered joking a serious business.

The development of the satirical journals must be seen in the larger context of the evolution of the nineteenth-century press. By encouraging the exchange and wide dissemination of ideas, the Enlightenment had given a powerful stimulus to reading, transforming it from an elite to a popular pastime. By involving the masses in political activity, the French Revolution of 1789 had likewise precipitated a considerable expansion of daily and periodical journalism. In the nineteenth century the continued growth of a literate public caused a steady increase in the number, circulation, and influence of such publications. By far the greatest expansion occurred in the century's later decades when universal education and urbanization created a mass audience. In the city, social unrest intensified political awareness and the hectic pace encouraged the acceptance of impermanence and change as normal conditions of life. The daily and periodical journalism of the nineteenth century appealed both to awakened political passions and to the craving for novelty and sensation bred (or so many contemporary observers asserted) by the fast-paced metropolitan culture.[3]

In the course of the nineteenth century, moreover, reading habits changed to include fewer books and more newspapers and magazines. Not yet in competition with other media, the press at the turn of the century exercised a more potent influence on public opinion than perhaps at any time before or since. "Many people," asserted historian Rolf Engelsing, "above all simple people, but also members of the highest class, knew practically nothing that they had not learned from the press." And there was much to learn, for increased readership stimulated diversification. Among the 2,150 new magazines founded in Germany between 1888 and 1900, there were some to appeal to almost every taste and interest.[4]

In the period from 1890 to 1914 the German satirical press shared in these trends. The continued success of traditional *Witzblätter* and the spectacular rise of new ones attested to the popularity of this type of journalism. Chief among the traditional magazines was *Kladderadatsch*, which in 1890 had a circulation of about 50,000. Another popular *Witzblatt*, founded like *Kladderadatsch* in the 1840s, was the *Münchener Fliegende Blätter*, which maintained a circulation of about 20,000. Among the new magazines which appealed to a middle-class audience, the most successful was *Simplicissimus*, founded in 1896. Its circulation rose from 15,000 in 1898 to about 86,000 in 1908, and the circulation of very controversial issues could sometimes be twice as high. Another *Witzblatt* of similar political orientation, *Jugend*, founded in the same year, gained a circulation of 70,000. Several newspapers published satirical weekly supplements; the most popular among these was *Ulk*, published by the *Berliner Tageblatt*, whose circulation in 1900 was 70,000. Even larger was the circulation of the socialist *Witzblatt*, *Der Wahre Jakob*, aimed chiefly at a working-class readership; by 1908, *Jakob* boasted a figure of 230,000. None of these figures matched those of the popular illustrated papers, such as the *Berliner Illustrierte*, which by 1914 gave out a figure of 600,000. Considering their often controversial subject matter, however, the circulation figures of the satirical journals were high. Moreover, because magazines were passed around in cafes, casinos, lending libraries, and beauty parlors, one issue might often reach many people, including some who could not afford a subscription.[5]

Periodical literature provides an invaluable source for cultural history. Appearing over months, years, and decades (*Kladderadatsch* ran for almost a century), the periodical documents change in the many aspects of life which combine to constitute a culture. It records and reflects political and social attitudes, fads, fashions, and literary and artistic styles. Humor in particular has often served a documentary function recording various aspects of everyday life considered too common, coarse, or mundane to be treated by "high" art. More importantly, the periodical fulfills the need of the reading public not only to record and illustrate but to structure and interpret daily experience. Unlike the newspaper, the periodical seldom announces startling news or calls for direct action. Rather it analyzes and reflects on the current scene, often attempting to integrate diverse events, ideas, and trends. Thus a magazine such as *Simplicissimus* can come to exemplify not only specific political or social attitudes but an entire world view. Such popular materials as the *Witzblätter* can help the historian to understand one of the most important and least tangible facets of social change—the concomitant development of the perceptions, attitudes, and values of the people affected. Popular sources, suggested historian William C. Cohn, enable us to "examine and describe how people at all levels of society respond to pressures on their culture." For the years from 1890 to 1914, which many historians have seen as a period of cultural crisis, such information becomes particularly important.[6]

A discussion of satirical literature as a historical source must deal with the fundamental but difficult question of cause and effect. Does such literature create or merely reflect public opinion? One prominent historian of the German press, Rolf Engelsing, assigned to the periodical a basically passive and reflective function. A medium in which the reader "sees his own image," the periodical expresses "the sum of individual feelings which must develop before a periodical develops." Thus the birth of a new periodical—*Kladderadatsch* in 1848, *Simplicissimus* in 1896—appeared to Engelsing as a result rather than a cause of changing political, social, and cultural attitudes. But both the supporters and the critics of the *Witzblätter* often attributed to them a much more active role in the formation and spread of new attitudes, images, and stereotypes. Indeed, if satire had no formative impact on public opinion, it would not arouse the hostility and opposition of governing elites. "Against the assault of laughter," observed Mark Twain, "nothing can stand." The relationship of satirical literature to public opinion may only be understood in the context of psychological and sociological theories of the social function of humor.[7]

Humor and Society

Simplicissimus and *Kladderadatsch* contained all forms of joking, including the harmless puns and slapstick which seem simply to represent an adult form of the child's delight in nonsense. Satire, their main content, is usually defined as the type of humor which holds up some individual or social vice, folly, or error to ridicule, usually with the purpose of bringing about social reform or improvement. Robert C. Elliot has found the origin of satire as a literary form in the magical beliefs of primitive society, tracing the verbal lampoon to the sorcerer's evil spell (usually recited in a mocking or jeering tone), and the caricature to the effigy. The double face of satire has been noted time and again. The French literary critic Boileau saw its entertainment value: "For satire, ever moral, ever new / Delights the reader and instructs him too." And the Roman Juvenal noted its aggressive and hostile function: "facit indignatio versum."[8]

From ancient times, humor has been the subject of a highly serious debate. The results have been diverse and contradictory. Does humor arise from emotional sickness or health, from anxiety or confidence, from friendly or hostile feelings? Is its basic impulse intellectual or emotional? "Contradictions abound," laments psychologist Hans-Jürgen Eysenck, "and conclusions are notable by their absence."[9]

In the absence of consensus, the historian must choose from the plethora of conflicting theories those which seem best to fit the specific material and its historical context. Obviously appropriate to journals specializing in aggressive political and social satire is the large body of opinion which identifies satire as the disguised expression of hostility. Indeed, humor itself has sometimes been defined as delight in the misfortune or degradation of another person, particularly of an especially powerful or fortunate one. Thus Plato attributed the sense of humor to the simultaneous painful and pleasurable feelings occasioned by the misfortunes of an envied person, while Thomas Hobbes defined it as a "sudden glory arising from a conception of some eminency in ourselves by comparison with the infirmity of others, or with our own formerly."[10]

The most fully elaborated theory of humor as disguised aggression, Freud's *Wit and Its Relation to the Unconscious,* dates from the same period and responded to much the same culture as *Simplicissimus* and *Kladderadatsch.* Freud saw "tendency" wit (a term which he used to define all topical, satirical, or risqué jokes) as an indirect and socially permissible outlet for aggressive and sexual drives repressed since childhood. Thus joking provided a safety valve relieving the stifling pressure of civilization on individual desires: "We are now prepared for the role that wit plays in hostile aggression. Wit permits us to make our enemy ridiculous through that which we could not utter loudly or consciously on account of existing restrictions; in other words, it affords us the means of surmounting restrictions and of opening up inaccessible pleasure sources." Such disguised aggression Freud saw as directed against all forms of authority, whether political, religious, or moral: "The prevention of abuse or insulting retorts through outer circumstances is so often the case that tendency wit is used with special preference as a weapon of attack or criticism of superiors who claim to be in authority. Wit, then, serves as a resistance against authority and an escape from its pressure. In this factor, too, lies the charm of caricature, at which we laugh even when it is badly done, simply because we consider resistance to authority a great merit." In both function (the "short-circuiting" of repression) and method (displacement, incongruity, condensation, and symbolic communication) Freud saw the joke as similar to the dream. Both he described as windows on the subconscious mind.[11]

While Freud's analysis treated "tendency wit" only as the protest of the isolated individual against the pressures of civilization, other researchers have explored its function as the expression of group consciousness and cohesion. "One would not appreciate comedy," remarked the French philosopher Henri Bergson, "if one felt alone. It seems as if laughter needs an echo. . . . However spontaneous, laughter covers up the underlying agreement, one might say complicity, with other laughers, real or imaginary." "Humor," observes a contemporary psychologist, Christopher P. Wilson, "is oil in the social machine, lubricating group dynamics, easing the recurrent frictions that threaten group solidarity." While accepting Freud's basic premise, such theorists have interpreted the function of aggressive joking not merely as a "harmless" release of tension but as a positive incentive to group solidarity and thus, in some cases, to collective action. In a classic and widely quoted study of underground humor in Nazi-occupied Czechoslovakia, sociologist Antonin Obrdlík described humor as a disguised but nonetheless indispensable expression of a still unbroken will to resistance. "In a word," explained Obrdlík, "they [the Czechs] have to strengthen their hope because otherwise they could not bear the strain to which their nerves are exposed. Gallows humor, full of invectives and irony, is their psychological escape, and it is in this sense that I call gallows humor a psychological compensation. . . . Relying on my observations I may go so far as to say that gallows humor is an unmistakable index of good morale and the spirit of resistance of oppressed peoples." Even when overt resistance is impossible, joking may serve as a device for preserving inner integrity by refusing to internalize the values of the oppressor. Obrdlík further observed that the Nazis' ruthless reprisals against jokers demonstrated their own awareness of the importance of humor to the resistance movement. Thus by contrast to Freud's fundamentally conservative view of aggressive humor as a device to preserve the status quo by avoiding direct confrontation, later theories have stressed its subversive and rebellious function.[12]

Arthur Koestler added an important dimension to the interpretation of humor by exploring primarily its creative rather than its destructive aspects. Both a successful joke and a significant scientific discovery, Koestler asserted, originate in the same process, which he termed the "bisociation of matrices." Defining a "matrix" as a conventional or accepted intellectual system, he described the creative act as the discovery of an unexpected relationship between two such systems, leading to a third and original view of the world. Koestler gave the example of Gutenberg, who while observing a wine harvest suddenly realized that the press which squeezed juice from grapes might also (with modifications) print words on paper. The unconventional, even "playful" thinking which cuts through stale patterns of thought to express original insights is also apparent in the joke, which defies conventional logic and common sense to reveal truth through apparent incongruity. By the distortion of reality as conventionally perceived, the satirist makes way for new perceptions. By focusing our attention on "abuses and deformities in society of which, blunted by habit, we were no longer aware," humor leads us to discover "the absurdity of the familiar and the familiarity of the absurd."[13]

Common to both Freudian and Koestlerian theories is a stress on the importance of humor as a metaphorical or symbolic form of communication. The role of the caricaturist in creating widely recognized symbols was described by the eminent American political cartoonist Herbert Block. Alluding to such common uses of synecdoche as the fat cigar representing political corruption or the silk hat identifying the Wall Street financier, Block remarked that one could apply to newspaper readers "what Pavlov learned about dogs—that symbols alone can produce reactions, even after they've been separated from the things that they're supposed to represent. Cartoonists use symbolic devices more than most people." Such devices of verbal wit as pun, hyperbole, parody, and allegory can also, of course, create striking and unforgettable images. Sociologist Clifford Geertz has analyzed the central importance of symbolic and metaphorical discourse in the formation and propagation of political ideologies. As an influential creator and popularizer of new images, the humorist must play a crucial role, especially in periods when (as Geertz maintains) the obsolescence of previously accepted tradition forces the individual to search for new imaginative or symbolic models for the interpretation of unfamiliar conditions. Thus the contrast not only in content but also in imagery between the traditional *Kladderadatsch* and the avant-garde *Simplicissimus* will provide an important guide not only to changing aesthetic taste but to changing attitudes, beliefs, and ideologies as well.[14]

Thus the historical analysis of popular satirical literature must focus not only on its aggressive, or Freudian aspects, but also on its creative, or Koestlerian, function. It must interpret not only content or "message" but the verbal and visual imagery which provides an even more sensitive guide to changing perceptions of reality. The historian must place jokes in their social and cultural context, giving particular attention to official and public reactions, which often reflect the impact of humor as a form of antiauthoritarian protest and as a focus for group cohesion. Finally, the historian must take into account the ambiguous and many-faceted social functions of humor, which can serve either as a conservative force facilitating individual adaptation to painful circumstances or as a progressive force promoting social and political change.

Humor and Politics

As a vent for protest, as a catalyst for new ideas, the humor of the Wilhelmine period was an important means of political self-expression. Indeed, the kaiser and the society which bore his name may be said to have provided the ideal political and spiritual climate for the development of a flourishing satirical literature. As social critic, the satirist needs a target worth attacking—that is, an authority structure sufficiently solid to compel at least external respect and obedience. No pleasure can be gained by mocking institutions or values which have already collapsed. Not only the monarchical government but the class structure, the army, the Church, and the complex system of social values which supported these institutions upheld traditional authority in Wilhelmine Germany. But the successful satirist must also perceive the flaws in this structure, signs of the discrepancy between ideals and reality. And the development of the German Empire, in fact, had determined that a still outwardly impressive authority structure should appear more and more obviously clumsy and anachronistic. The Bismarckian constitution had placed a dynamic industrial state under the control of a political system still based in part on feudal values. In the absence of its architect, the inadequacy of the system became ever more apparent. As Barrington Moore described the German Empire: "The results had some resemblance to present-day Victorian houses with modern electrical kitchens but insufficient bathrooms and leaky pipes hidden decorously behind newly plastered walls. Ultimately, the makeshifts collapse." The signs of weakness, even of disintegration, behind the magnificent facade of the new Empire provided ideal material for the satirist.[15]

The freedom of the satirist, or of any other dissenter, to express controversial or critical views was limited in Wilhelmine Germany by a complex set not only of laws but also of moral, religious, and social attitudes. The Imperial Press Law of 1874, which remained in force throughout the period, provided specific penalties only for pornography, *Majestätsbeleidigung* (insults to the person of the monarch), and incitement to class hatred (a prohibition aimed chiefly at the socialist press). Such specific and seemingly limited restrictions would appear to leave the journalist ample scope, yet the political and religious establishment of the Empire was far more hostile to dissent than these comparatively mild laws would indicate. Bismarck's policy of "negative integration"—the attempt to unite a still divided nation by turning public opinion against supposedly disloyal minority groups—was continued under Wilhelm II. Denouncing all dissenters as subversives ("Schwarzseher dulde ich nicht"), Wilhelm was particularly intolerant of critical journalists, whom he often accused of undermining Germany's international prestige. "Every country," he once declared, "is, in the long run, responsible for the window which its press opens up on the world. It will someday bear the consequences of its indiscretions—the hostility of foreign lands." In the 1890s powerful conservative groups responded to innovative trends in art and literature by vehemently advocating stronger censorship laws. One such campaign, centered on the proposed "Lex Heinze," which was designed to ban any frank presentation of sexual subject matter, received vigorous support from the emperor himself. The failure of such campaigns was due chiefly to the active intervention of the artistic and intellectual community and, to a lesser degree, to the still tolerant attitude of the majority of the public.[16]

The still vivid historical memory of far more horrible regimes tempts us to trivialize the penalties meted out to dissenters, including the humorists of *Kladderadatsch* and *Simplicissimus*, at the turn of the century. To be sure, the vacillation of the responsible officials between heavy-handed condemnation and careless permissiveness reflected the inconsistency and hollowness of the Wilhelmine authority structure in general. Yet those forced to pay substantial fines, serve prison sentences (even the relatively humane six-month *Festungshaft* could be unpleasant, sometimes frightening), and spend long periods in exile did not in general take these penalties lightly. More disturbing than the legal penalties was the role of social deviant or outsider to which the critic was condemned. For historian Ludwig Quidde, the publication of a famous pamphlet criticizing the kaiser meant the ruin of an academic career. Even to independent writers and artists such as the *Simplicissimus* and *Kladderadatsch* groups, who were often well-off financially, the role of critic could bring severe psychological and emotional conflicts, as the career of Ludwig Thoma (for years editor-in-chief of *Simplicissimus*) will clearly show.[17]

The role of the humorist in Wilhelmine journalism was as important as it was difficult. Both *Kladderadatsch* and *Simplicissimus*, though formally affiliated with no political party, belonged to the liberal tradition. *Kladderadatsch* was one of the cluster of liberal periodicals founded in the turbulent spring of 1848. *Simplicissimus*, whose liberalism was of a more modern variety, still preserved the memory of 1848 as a reproach to a more passive generation. The great significance of the two periodicals in the development of liberal journalism was derived from their circulation figures, far higher than those of other, more "serious" and intellectual periodicals. Of the non-socialist oppositional journals of the Wilhelmine period, for instance, the circulation of Theodor Barth's *Die Nation* was only about 3,000 and that of Georg Michael Conrad's *Die Gesellschaft* (which published Quidde's *Caligula*) only about 1,000. Maximilian Harden's *Die Zukunft*, among the most aggressive critical journals of the era, attained in 1908 what was considered to be the very wide circulation of 23,000. The far higher circulation figures of *Simplicissimus* and *Kladderadatsch* indicate a readership which was both more numerous and less specialized.[18]

The satirists were thus popularizers who transmitted liberal ideas to a broad and diverse public. Maximilian Harden, himself a formidable critic, attributed the effectiveness of such literature to its appeal to readers of all levels of intelligence and education. "The humorist, writer, or artist," declared Harden, "who puts his art in the service of one of the great illustrated magazines is, as an individual, known only to a small circle. To the great mass of his countrymen, he is only a voice which expresses, with wit or passion, what these people think and feel and have tried to express. No other sort of publication can have such an effect on public opinion as the illustrated satirical magazine, which appeals to the most brilliant and to the simplest mind and, with its scornful challenge and raucous laughter, attracts attention everywhere."[19]

As popularizers of liberal ideas, both *Kladderadatsch* and *Simplicissimus* were designed primarily for middle-class readers (although *Simplicissimus* also gained a working-class readership). In their accounts of Wilhelmine bourgeois culture many historians have stressed conservatism, conformity, and "feudalization." "A kind of psychological support for the institution of the authoritarian state," generalized Hans-Ulrich Wehler, "was the so-called *Untertanenmentalität*. To accept the arbitrary actions of the political authorities, to react to minor everyday humiliations in silence, to doff one's hat to the lieutenant on the sidewalk, to see even the village policeman as a representative of the majesty of the state—these were its requirements. . . . In 1919 Albert Einstein declared that no revolution could overcome such hereditary servility." Critics of the Wehler school, however, have stressed the importance of dissenting trends such as literary and artistic modernism, the feminist and youth movements, the campaign for school reform, and many others. In such attempts at cultural change and renewal they see the clearest manifestation of a progressive challenge to a rigid and outmoded authority structure. The satirical journals provide a vivid chronicle of these dissenting trends, with which *Simplicissimus* was so closely identified that its very name (as in the expression *Simplicissimus-Stimmung*) came to stand for a spirit of criticism and irreverence.[20]

As an indirect outlet for dissatisfaction, humor was of great importance in a system which provided few direct avenues for antiestablishment protest. In the thoughtless exercise of his immense powers, the emperor showed not only disregard but contempt for public opinion. The elected Reichstag had few effective powers, none at all over such vital areas as foreign and military policy. The liberal parties offered few opportunities for political action—the mainstream National Liberal party, demoralized since Bismarck's triumph in the 1860s, supported the status quo and the left-wing liberal parties were in general too small and splintered to be effective. Thus the indirect device of joking provided, just as Freud and others postulated, an outlet for opinions which often could be expressed in no other socially acceptable way.

Of course, people have always enjoyed laughing at authority; political satire of the type represented by *Kladderadatsch* had been popular for a long time. But the development in the 1890s of a far sharper and more flamboyant style, exemplified by *Simplicissimus,* will suggest an increase in both the scope and the intensity of dissent. The turn of the century, in fact, was an extraordinarily fruitful period for satire. One has only to think of the works of Frank Wedekind, Heinrich Mann, and Karl Sternheim, to name but a few. Authors such as these wrote for *Simplicissimus,* which played an important role in publicizing the new satirical style. Indeed, the greatest satire of the period, Heinrich Mann's *Der Untertan,* was inspired by *Simplicissimus* and its first chapters appeared in the magazine.[21]

Not only an outlet for frustrated anger, the *Witzblätter* also provided a medium for the expression of new ideas. The comparison of *Kladderadatsch* with *Simplicissimus,* in fact, provides a vivid case-study of changing attitudes and perceptions. *Kladderadatsch,* founded in 1848, was by the turn of the century the still-flourishing product of a long tradition, exemplifying a style which in many ways had changed little over the years. In 1900 its editor-in-chief was sixty-three years of age, and the average age of its five most important staff members was forty-eight. *Simplicissimus,* founded in 1896, was a new creation, flaunting an aggressively innovative style. In 1900 its editor-in-chief was thirty and the average age of its staff members was twenty-eight. Along with the difference in age went dramatic differences in political stance, social awareness, aesthetic taste, and imaginative perception. *Kladderadatsch* focused on politics in the narrow sense of governmental activity, while *Simplicissimus* explored political attitudes and the social structure which underlay them. *Kladderadatsch* limited its attention to middle-class issues, while *Simplicissimus* showed a far greater awareness of the working class and its problems. *Kladderadatsch* respected traditional sexual morality, *Simplicissimus* aggressively challenged it. *Kladderadatsch* communicated primarily through the written word, *Simplicissimus* primarily through pictures. It will be the purpose of the following chapters to explore the meaning of these contrasts, not just for the evolution of German satire but for the development of German culture as a whole during this period of transition.

Kladderadatsch, Simplicissimus, and German History

2

Kladderadatsch

THE tavern where *Kladderadatsch* was born in 1848 was in Berlin. The founding fathers were Albert Hofmann, later publisher of the sheet, and David Kalisch, the popular author of many light comedies, who wrote the early issues almost single-handedly. It was Kalisch who named the *Witzblatt* as (or so goes the tale) a dog scampered through the room, bumping into tables and upsetting the many glasses and bottles. " 'Kladderadatsch!' cried Kalisch suddenly, in a voice which could be heard throughout the place. 'Kladderadatsch!' echoed his two boon companions as the fragments of the glasses which they had dropped in their fright tinkled among the broken bottles on the floor. 'Kladderadatsch will be the name of our new *Witzblatt*,' announced Kalisch, 'and I've already planned out the first number.' " *Kladderadatsch* may be roughly translated as "crash" or "Kerboom!" "The time's turned upside down!" screamed the first title page. "The wrath of Jehovah thunders through world history . . . Princes are overthrown . . . thrones have fallen . . . castles have been looted . . . virgins outraged . . . Jews persecuted . . . priests murdered . . . barricades erected . . . *Kladderadatsch!*"[1]

The intense and catastrophic tone of these lines exuded the spirit of the spring of 1848, when the first issue appeared. Shocked and temporarily panic-stricken by the uprising which followed the overthrow of Louis Philippe, Friedrich Wilhelm IV had withdrawn troops from Berlin, promised a new constitution, and lifted censorship. The result was the release of pent-up popular discontent in a flood of new newspapers and periodicals—one historian estimates about a hundred in the first year. Along with revolution went a revolutionary change in political consciousness. For the first time in German history the ordinary citizen felt intensely involved in political events. All the turbulent emotions of March—resentment of established authority, exhilarated surprise at its seeming collapse, wild dreams of future Utopias—emerged in the new journals. And by their topical and highly ephemeral content, these periodicals reflected a new awareness of accelerated change. "Our children," commented an editorial in the third issue of *Kladderadatsch,* "will learn world history not by the year but by the hour."[2]

Of all the techniques used by revolutionary journalists to influence public opinion, satire was the most striking. Caricatures, satirical pamphlets, posters, and speeches stirred up excitement and made complex issues comprehensible to people of all educational levels. Of the many satirical periodicals, whose titles were often inspired by the Berlin or Jewish sense of humor—*Berliner Krakehler, Tante Voss mit dem Besen, Berliner Omnibus,* and many others—*Kladderadatsch* became the most popular and the only one to survive. By the evening of May 7, when the first issue appeared, 4,000 copies had already been sold, and more were soon printed to satisfy public demand. The physical format, which was established in the first few issues, remained essentially the same throughout the magazine's history. Beneath the title *Kladderadatsch—humoristisch-satyrisches* (later *"satirisches"*) *Wochenblatt* was the peculiar statement, "appears daily except weekdays." The title page was dominated by the grinning boy's head which soon became the magazine's trademark. "The famous head grins at us impertinently," wrote a contemporary reader. "Man of the century, you need only groan or prattle or laugh, and your wisdom exceeds that of the seven wise men of Greece. How can we poor scribblers doubt your eternal life?"[3]

Although Kalisch, the real founder of the sheet, wrote the first issue single-handedly, the editorial staff soon gained two important new members, Ernst Dohm and Rudolf Löwenstein. The trio, often referred to by the public as the "Three Scholars," worked closely together, publishing their contributions anonymously. David Kalisch, born in Breslau in 1820 of a Jewish merchant family, had forsaken the business career for which he had been trained to become a successful comic playwright. Although not himself a native Berliner, he became a master of Berlin dialect humor, and his contributions gave *Kladderadatsch* the "folksy" touch which made it widely popular. Dohm, born in Berlin in 1819, took over as "responsible editor" from Löwenstein in 1849, and served several prison sentences when the *Witzblatt* offended the authorities. Löwenstein, born in 1820 of a Jewish family in Breslau, spent much of his childhood in an orphanage and was enabled through scholarship funds donated by the king of Prussia to attend the universities of Breslau and Berlin. The author of children's books, song lyrics, and "serious" poetry, he turned to journalism at first chiefly in order to finance his studies. Dohm, Löwenstein, and the future cartoonist of *Kladderadatsch,* Wilhelm Scholz, had all belonged to the liberal Rütli society during the pre-March period. As publisher of the magazine, Albert Hofmann, another former member of Rütli, did much to shape its liberal editorial policy.[4]

Both the style and the content of *Kladderadatsch* reflected not only the political views but the ethnic and cultural characteristics of its editors. As adoptive Berliners they had absorbed the characteristic Berlin sense of humor—dry, cynical, and laconic. A regular weekly feature, the dialect conversation between Müller and Schulze, two lower-middle-class Berliners, appealed to the local taste for puns and quick repartee. Not only the Berlin but also the Jewish sense of humor was reflected in *Kladderadatsch,* two of whose editors were of Jewish ancestry (although Löwenstein had been baptized). The great number of Jews who became journalists during this period may be partly explained by their exclusion from other liberal professions. The disadvantaged Jew could be expected not only to view the political system from which he had been excluded with hostility thinly disguised as humor, but to support the liberals of 1848, some of whom favored Jewish emancipation. Irony requires detachment, a stance which the Jew as outsider found congenial. Certainly an important aspect of the allegedly "destructive" role which antisemites ascribed to the Jew was his sharp sense of humor.[5]

Kladderadatsch played an active part in the clash of ideas and ideologies amid which it was born. Its intense, highly emotional style contrasted with the more relaxed and frivolous satire of contemporary periodicals such as the *Münchener Fliegende Blätter.* Its front-page editorials commented on the events of the day in a tone which was by turns fiery, sarcastic, aggressive, or pathetic. Such satirical pieces often contributed to the ongoing debate by revealing weaknesses in one party's argument which the oppo-

№ 10.   Sonntag, den 9. Juli.   **1848.**

Kladderadatsch.

Wochenkalender.

Montag den 10. Juni.
Erzherzog Johann: Reichsverweser! Das Vaterland ist gerettet!

Dienstag den 11. Juni.
Deutschland einig. Freiheit, Gleichheit, Brüderlichkeit in allen Gauen. Der Schriftsteller Saphir in Wien geht mit dem Kaiser Ferdinand auf Duzgemment ein.

Mittwoch den 12. Juni.
Friede und Eintracht. Der Patriotenverein in Berlin giebt den Studenten Saßleffel und Menecke ein solennes Festessen. Gehnheim vom Preußen-Club mit Fackelzug eingeholt.

Wochenkalender.

Donnerstag den 13. Juli.
Jeder Religionshaß geschwunden. Der Prediger Ulich tanzt mit dem Prediger Sido auf öffentlichem Markte Polka, und der Israelite Meyerbeer macht Musik dazu.

Freitag den 14. Juli.
Jede Ungleichheit des Besitzes aufgehoben. Der Banquier Rothschild leiht sich bei dem Proletarier Reich 5 Sgr., verspielt sie unter den Zelten, und wird durchgeprügelt.

Sonnabend den 15. Juli.
Die Brüderlichkeit hat den höchsten Gipfel erreicht. Der Professor Lachmann sagt zu dem Schriftsteller Held: „Bruder, heut bekneipen wir uns!"
Kladderadatsch.

Organ für und von Bummler.

Dieses Blatt erscheint täglich mit Ausnahme der Wochentage für den Preis von 1½ Sgr. Es kann jeden Sonnabend von fünf Uhr ab aus sämmtlichen Buchhandlungen abgeholt werden. Abonnements für 13 Nummern vierteljährlich werden mit 17½ Sgr in allen Buchhandlungen und bei Königl. Postämtern angenommen. **(Für die Monate Mai, Juni wird das Blatt mit 13½ Sgr. für 9 Nummern von den Königl. Postämtern geliefert.)** — Beiträge erbittet unter Adresse der Verlagshandlung **Die Redaktion.**

The *Kladderadatsch* boy (July 9, 1848).

sition could develop and exploit. In keeping with its apocalyptic title, its tone was revolutionary. "We are traitors and king-haters! We are robbers, murderers and *canaille!*" screamed one headline. Its political ideology was left-wing liberal, advocating national unification, a constitutional state, a freely elected representative body, and civil liberties. It aggressively attacked all forms of conservatism, whether represented by kings, Junkers, generals, clergy, or guildsmen.[6]

The humorists of *Kladderadatsch* were thus quickly disenchanted with the Frankfurt Assembly, where the discrepancy between ideals and reality, always a basic theme in satire, became particularly clear. In fact the image of the "professorial parliament," now a cliché of history textbooks, was first developed by the satirists of the period, who created the pretentious but timid figure of Herr Piepmayer to mock the German burgher. *Kladder-*

"The Frankfurt Unification Fair." Prince Johann of Habsburg, the "Reich Administrator," in despair, contemplates the quarrels between the German states. (Scholz, *Kladderadatsch*, Aug. 6, 1848.)

adatsch lamented particularism, another reactionary force pre-
venting unification:

Our land was to be born anew
In Frankfurt's church of Paul.
But shout and fight—that's all they do
And each state wants it all.
Protect us please, Apostle Paul,
For this looks like a nasty brawl!

Löwenstein reacted with anger to the Parliament's choice of the
king of Prussia as head of the new state:

The New German Crown

Oh, not by King or golden throne,
Can unity at least be won,
And tyranny be shattered.
The crown is but a golden ring,
The scepter is a childish thing,
The ermine robe is tattered.
So end this stupid, trifling show
And give the people freedom now![7]

Kladderadatsch reacted bitterly to the failure of the revolution
and the establishment of a military government in Berlin. In spite
of liberal protests, there was no significant popular resistance.
Two of the most popular and enduring of *Kladderadatsch* characters, the reactionary Junkers, Strudelwitz and Prudelwitz, were
shown returning from their exile and laughing at the passivity of
the Berlin population. "Around three o'clock we marched into
Berlin. Dammit, what a wonderful sight. We thought we'd find
the *cannaille* behind barricades, but the stupid oafs just stood
around, as if turned to stone." Protesting General Wrangel's ban
on the sale of the *Witzblatt* in Berlin, the editors ingenuously
declared innocence of any subversive intent. "We only laughed
at what was laughable. We have never *made* any person or thing
ridiculous—it is impossible even for the most biting and malicious mockery to *make* anything look funny, which isn't already
funny." Kalisch, Löwenstein, and Hofmann fled the city, leaving
Dohm as "responsible editor"; during this time Hofmann smug-
gled copies of the sheet into Berlin under his overcoat! But the
satirists had not lost hope. In typically Jewish imagery a *Kladderadatsch* editorial retold the story of Jacob who, cheated of his

rightful bride after seven years, worked seven more years to win her. Like Jacob, the German people would try again.[8]

Like most other German liberals, the humorists of *Kladderadatsch* found the 1850s a depressing period. Some hostile comments on the czar of Russia, reflecting the bitterness of German nationalists over the humiliating Treaty of Olmütz, brought Kalisch and Löwenstein short sentences in Spandau. But in spite of the reactionary political atmosphere, the journal's circulation figures more than tripled, from 6,000 in 1851 to 22,000 in 1858. Its brushes with the law provided useful publicity, and its ardent nationalism, expressed during this period primarily through a campaign against Napoleon III, appealed to a broad segment of middle-class opinion. But the magazine also gained popularity through changes in tone and format which sensitively responded to the changing mood. In an editorial of 1858, *Kladderadatsch* rejoiced in the increasingly cultivated, self-assured, and cosmopolitan atmosphere of German society, and promised its readers to meet their rising expectations. The respectable atmosphere of this more stable society was reflected in a new image. Gone were the screaming headlines, replaced on the front page by Löwenstein's clever and carefully crafted political verses. Gone, too, was the iconoclastic tone; criticism of the establishment, even at its most bitter, was now tempered by an increasing commitment to national solidarity. *Kladderadatsch* had found that combination of liberalism and nationalism which would be its guiding philosophy for decades.[9]

In the revived drive for unification of the 1860s, spearheaded by such liberal organizations as the Nationalverein, *Kladderadatsch* played an important role. By far the most popular political journal in the German states, it coaxed, challenged, and implored its readers to join in the liberal campaign. In order to castigate traditional bourgeois passivity it invented the satirical figure of "the good old German," whose first thought in the morning was, "What could I do for my fatherland—if I wanted to?" One of the good old German's dubious virtues was his modesty. "He never has the impertinence to say, like other people, that he has a fatherland." But the humorists' call to action was now addressed only to middle-class liberals. The socialist movement, supported by the growing urban industrial working class, was from the beginning abhorrent to these erstwhile revolutionaries. Socialist politicians, when pictured at all, appeared as wild-eyed and foulmouthed agitators. Thus *Kladderadatsch* reflected the narrowly middle-class outlook of German liberalism which deprived it of real popular support in its struggle against the new Prussian prime minister, Otto von Bismarck.[10]

With the appointment of Bismarck in 1862, the humorists plunged into a remarkable love-hate relationship which endured and developed for nearly four decades, until Bismarck's death in 1898. At first the hostile feelings predominated. Not only was Bismarck pictured as a Junker, soul mate to Prudelwitz and Strudelwitz, but more negatively still as a Francophile and disciple of the sinister Napoleon III. His conduct in the Prussian constitutional conflict seemed fully to justify these suspicions. *Kladderadatsch* conducted a shrill and impassioned campaign against the Junker statesman's illegal tactics, castigating his overweening arrogance and contempt for public opinion.

From my head to my toe, what a genius I am!
Of course I'm not modest—that's only for fools!
For the mood of the age I do not give a damn,
And for parliaments—no, I don't play by those rules.
What 'mood'? and what 'age'? What an abstract expression
Fit only for schoolbooks, so dusty and dry.
To scorn all that nonsense is my Higher Mission.
How daring! and O what a genius am I!

What's 'public opinion?' Ridiculous phrases,
How do you find out that 'opinion' and where?
I know that the masses will welcome with praises
The confident man, who can do and can dare.
Those carpers and grumblers, the Press and its minions,
To listen to them would be quite ignominious!
For only a weakling would heed *their* opinions
Well, I may *seem* rash—but then, I am a genius.

This hostile view was only slightly mitigated by the annexation of Schleswig and Lauenburg in 1864. The humorists' reaction to the outbreak of war in 1866 was wholly negative. Warning graphically of the horrors of war, they seemed almost to hope for a defeat which would topple the hated prime minister—a subordination of nationalism to political partisanship which would have been utterly unthinkable even a decade later. Certainly the magazine's tone was thoroughly defeatist. The schoolboy Karlchen Miessnick, another favorite *Kladderadatsch* figure, wrote to his friend that he was preparing for the invasion of the Slavic hordes

"The French People-Watcher." Comparing Bismarck to Napoleon III, this cartoon criticizes Bismarck's demagogic reliance on "the people" and his contempt for politicians. (Scholz, *Kladderadatsch*, 1862.)

by learning Czech. Even after Bismarck's victory in the Six Weeks' War, *Kladderadatsch* did not emulate the groveling behavior of some liberals whose admiration for the victor led them to renounce their earlier opposition. Its verse on the Indemnity Bill, a parody of the Mozart aria "In diesen heil'gen Hallen, kennt man die Rache nicht," was deeply ironic.[11]

But after 1866 the humorists were pushed toward Bismarck by the force not of positive inclination but of a greater hatred. In the growing tension between France and the new Confederation, *Kladderadatsch* saw its old enemy Napoleon III as the aggressor and Bismarck (as one cartoon portrayed him) as a "good shepherd" protecting his flock from the French "wolf." Indeed, the contents of the magazine during the late sixties attested to Bismarck's success in using foreign affairs to distract attention from internal conflict. Of thirty-one cover verses which appeared in the year 1870 before the outbreak of war, thirteen castigated Napoleon III, ten were anticlerical (an issue with foreign as well as domestic implications), and only eight concerned issues of purely domestic politics. Completely abandoning their earlier defeatism, the humorists reacted to the war of 1870 with enthusiasm, expressed especially by one of Löwenstein's verses, the "Chasse-pot-Lied," which, set to a familiar tune, became a marching song of the army. Even such patriotic verses failed, however, to mention Bismarck. In response to the founding of the Empire those loyal Berliners, Schulze and Müller, suspended their usual skepticism in an outburst of local patriotism:

> *Müller:*   Schulze, what a mood I'm in!
>   joyous and ethereal!
> *Schulze:* What a thrill to see Berlin,
>   Decked in robes imperial!
> *Müller:*   Schulze, am I still the same
>   man you see before you?
> *Schulze:* No, you're quite transfigured by
>   All our new-found glory![12]

In the 1870s *Kladderadatsch* continued critical of Bismarck, strongly condemning the feudal structure of the new Empire and the chancellor's autocratic treatment of the Reichstag. But the *Kulturkampf* was a cause which like other liberals they enthusiastically supported. Harking back to their long-standing feud against clerical reaction, the humorists urged Bismarck to crush the infamous ones. A cartoon of 1872 entitled "Radical—not palliative" depicted Bismarck standing by a tree (the German Empire) riddled with termites (Catholic priests). In the background stands a statue of Arminius, inscribed "Down with Rome." "It doesn't help to poke them," says the *Kladderadatsch* boy to the chancellor, who is attacking the insects with a walking stick, "they just bite more. You have two alternatives—either to leave them in peace or to exterminate them completely. There is no middle way." Throughout the 1870s *Kladderadatsch* used all the tried-and-true anticlerical arguments to reach many different segments of public opinion, appealing to conservatives by stressing clerical exemptions from military service, and to Jews by raising the spectre of the Inquisition. Like most other liberals far more radically anticlerical than Bismarck himself, the humorists reacted with such hostility to the phasing-out of the *Kulturkampf* in 1877 that the chancellor, who usually regarded the sheet with amused tolerance, ordered the editors condemned to a fine and twenty days in prison.[13]

As an established and popular magazine, *Kladderadatsch* reflected many important trends in liberal opinion during the 1860s and 1870s. Most apparent was the change in the image of Bis-

"Radical, not Palliative." The *Kladderadatsch* boy advises Bismarck on the *Kulturkampf*. "It doesn't help to poke them, they just get more vicious. Either leave them alone or destroy them—there is no compromise." (Scholz, *Kladderadatsch*, 1872.)

marck, from hated reactionary to respected, though still highly controversial, statesman. Also significant was the growing priority given to national goals when these conflicted with liberal beliefs. Certainly the humorists' participation in the *Kulturkampf* was motivated more by national than by liberal motives, and reflected a growing indifference to the rights of groups regarded as subversive. These developments, however, reflect not only the changes in the humorists' own point of view but also Bismarck's skill in choosing issues which would unite public opinion behind him. The *Kulturkampf* prompted the humorists of *Kladderadatsch* for the first time to portray the once-hated Junker as a hero. Thus, by stirring up hostility against minority groups, whether socialists, Catholics, or Jews, the chancellor had successfully diverted his critics' attention from the serious flaws in the Bismarckian system.[14]

The development of the humorists' point of view may also be discerned in their response to another issue, the social question. As we have seen, *Kladderadatsch* had been intolerant of socialism since the 1850s. Increasingly it spoke, not as before for the revolutionary Left, but for the middle class, now well established, which had no desire to share its prosperity with the industrial worker. *Kladderadatsch* was mildly critical of Bismarck's anti-socialist laws but chiefly because their illiberal restrictions on political activities might affect law-abiding liberals as well as dangerous revolutionaries. Thus a cartoon of 1878 showed the chancellor staggering under the burden of a huge scroll labelled "Emergency Laws," which swung to left and right, hitting socialists and liberals indiscriminately. The humorists' perception of the socialists' viewpoint was limited to sympathy with individuals banished from their home towns. A poem of 1878 entitled "Dura Lex," written by Johannes Trojan, later editor of the sheet, expressed the rather naive hope that the law, made in response to "the troubles of the time," would have a "healing effect" on its victims "and not fill them with hate or bitterness." Trojan also warned his fellow citizens against "greed, which leads cities and great states to their downfall." As free-enterprise liberals the humorists were also skeptical about Bismarck's social policies. A cartoon entitled "Experimental socialism" depicted Bismarck showing magic lantern slides of an angel conquering the fierce socialist lion. The caption reads, "What a show!—but alas, it is only a show."[15]

Thus the magazine which once happily envisaged the collapse

"The arrow is aimed at the Social Democrats, but what if it overshoots its target?" A comment on Bismarck's anti-socialist legislation, pointing out its dangers for liberals. (Scholz, *Kladderadatsch*, 1878.)

of the establishment now defended it against a new generation of revolutionaries. The move to the right resulted in a significant change of staff. In 1884 a split between the right wing of the liberal party and its left wing (thereafter known as the Freisinn) also split the *Kladderadatsch* editorial staff. Löwenstein, who supported the Freisinn, was opposed by his younger colleagues. After Johannes Trojan took over as editor-in-chief in 1886, Löwenstein retired. "Exhausted, I retired in 1887 from the editorial staff of *Kladderadatsch*," he wrote in his brief autobiography. "Weakened by grief and sickness, I was no longer able to work or to express my left-liberal beliefs, which I was the only one of the staff to hold."[16]

The change in personnel brought about another decisive change in style. Trojan represented not only a new generation but a different background. Born in 1837 in Danzig, Trojan would have been too young to participate in the 1848 revolution, which had shaped Löwenstein's political philosophy. Instead, Trojan's young manhood was passed in the decade of the 1860s, when Bismarck first emerged as a national hero. Unlike Löwenstein the baptized Jew, Trojan was born into a prosperous Protestant family. After Löwenstein's retirement the Jewish allusions and jokes which had been such an integral part of the *Kladderadatsch* "personality" all but disappeared—a change which added to the magazine's respectability but detracted from its liveliness. Trojan's decision to become a professional writer was very displeasing to his highly respectable family; in Danzig, he complained, writers were held in about as much esteem as bandits or gypsies. As editor of *Kladderadatsch,* he remarked in 1892 that among the admiring letters he received there was not one from Danzig, for he had not chosen an "honorable profession." Jew or Christian, the satirist was still an outsider.[17]

As a struggling young writer, Trojan had sent his first verses to *Kladderadatsch* in order to earn a little extra money; he was employed full-time in 1862, though not until 1866 did he earn enough to marry and support a family. The praise bestowed on his more "serious" literary work—stories, essays, poems, and children's books—by an interviewer in *Schorers Familienblatt* suggests that they appealed to a fairly conventional audience.[18]

Trojan's most important colleague on the editorial staff was Wilhelm Polstorff, who was born into the family of a Protestant pastor in 1843. As "responsible editor," Polstorff defended his journal's honor in a duel with the kaiser's close associate, Alfred von Kiderlen-Wächter in 1894. Of Polstorff, Rudolf Hofmann (son of the original publisher Albert) remarked that he had "a satirical talent and a combative nature which reminded one of Ernst Dohm, but Polstorff—unlike Dohm—adds to these qualities, which are indispensable to the editor of a *Witzblatt,* a comfortable and beneficent humor, which we often see in social life as well as in *Kladderadatsch.*" Like Trojan, Polstorff was a loyal Bismarckian. During the 1880s the *Witzblatt* also gained three gifted cartoonists: Paul Roland (born in 1856), Gustav Brandt (born in 1861), and Ludwig Stutz (born in 1865). These men, all considerably younger than the two editors, were responsible for most of the artwork, some quite modern in style, which appeared in the 1890s. Editorial policy, however, was controlled by Trojan and Polstorff.[19]

The political views of the new editors altered the magazine's picture of Bismarck. Unlike the older generation, who had never wholly lost their mistrust of the Junker statesman, the younger editors regarded him far less critically. In the 1880s his image became more and more heroic; for instance, a cartoon of 1884 which showed workmen carving an enormous marble bust suggested that even during his lifetime the great man had become a monument. As we shall see in a later chapter, the humorists' shocked reaction to the chancellor's retirement showed how dependent on his leadership they had become. With typical ironic wit, Bismarck himself found an opportunity to comment on his former critics' change of heart. Trojan recounted in his memoirs that one day on an outing to Friedrichsruh he and some friends chanced to hear the chancellor addressing a visiting *Turnverein.* Hearing that Trojan was in the crowd, Bismarck sought him out and invited him to luncheon the next day. At the end of what Trojan found a thoroughly delightful occasion, the host proposed a toast to *Kladderadatsch.* "This magazine," he laughed, "didn't treat me very well at first, but recently I've gotten better treatment." "May I take a greeting from Your Highness to my colleagues?" asked Trojan. "Certainly," replied the old chancellor, "and a very cordial one." This incident, which the flattered Trojan later described as one of the great experiences of his life, demonstrated Bismarck's skill in cultivating the loyalty of journalists who supported him against his enemy, Wilhelm II.[20]

The history of *Kladderadatsch* up to 1890 was very similar to that of the equally famous British humor magazine *Punch.* Like its German counterpart, *Punch* was founded in the tense and turbulent 1840s. When the first issue appeared in 1841, the fourth year of Victoria's reign, few could foresee the prosperous and stable era to which the young queen would give her name. Instead, the predominant mood was fear—of the Chartist agitation, of working-class unrest, and of the cities which during this decade seemed to grow ever more crowded, filthy, and menacing. Like the early *Kladderadatsch,* the early *Punch* spoke with the raucous and derisive voice of the streets. In 1848 a cartoon showed a sober old gentleman attempting to dissuade a young lady from reading *Punch.* "And besides, are you aware who are the conductors of that paper, and that they are Chartists, Deists, Atheists, and Socialists to a man. . . . The chief part of their income is derived from threatening letters which they send to the nobility and the gentry. The principal writer is a returned convict. Two have been tried at the old Bailey and their artist . . . as for their artist . . . ." Like the "robbers, murderers and *canaille*" of *Kladderadatsch,* the editors of *Punch* cultivated their outrageous image.[21]

Like *Kladderadatsch, Punch* was nationalistic. "Its radicalism," remarked *Punch* biographer R.C.G. Price, "was a robust, furriner-hating radicalism." Like *Kladderadatsch* it was sternly anti-Catholic, especially when the Oxford Movement of the 1840s raised fears of increased influence from Rome. And, like that of *Kladderadatsch,* its changing tone reflected the increasing stability of mid-century society. In response to the death of the prince consort, its once slashing attacks on the monarchy ceased. The humorists who had once championed the poor now perfected the popular "servant joke," mocking maids who imitated their mistresses. A frequent contributor, William Makepeace Thackeray, became known for his "gentleness, fun, kindly sentimental humor." Gone was the guttersnipe humor of the 1840s; Mr. Punch and the *Kladderadatsch* boy, though still intensely critical, now stayed within the bounds of middle-class respectability.[22]

The importance of *Kladderadatsch* in reflecting and, in some important cases, shaping public opinion was attested by its wide circulation. The circulation figure, which as we have seen increased rapidly during the 1850s, continued to grow during the succeeding two decades, from 22,000 in 1858 to 50,000 in 1872. Though far behind the nonpolitical family journal *Die Gartenlaube* (which in 1867 boasted a circulation of 215,000), *Kladderadatsch* was the second most popular periodical in Germany during the 1860s. Its circulation far outstripped that of most daily newspapers. Even in 1885, when newspaper readership had considerably expanded, only five had circulations of over 40,000. Until 1899 *Kladderadatsch* was by far the most effective popularizer of liberal ideas. Indeed, during these years it enjoyed a virtual monopoly of political satire; the other popular *Witzblatt,* the *Münchener Fliegende Blätter,* confined itself chiefly to social satire, most of it highly innocuous and *gemütlich.* Moreover, the reading habits of the German public, which often relied more on lending libraries and on newspaper racks in cafes and barbershops than on individual subscriptions, ensured that the actual readership was far larger than the figures alone would indicate. Müller and Schulze became folk heroes whose portraits appeared not only on German, but also on French and Danish advertising posters. Special editions of *Kladderadatsch* appeared in many foreign cities, including Paris and New York. The intense interest of readers was attested by the letters to the editor, sometimes numbering over 100, which responded to each issue. When in 1860 the magazine began to accept advertisements it was soon overwhelmed, a sign that the business community appreciated its popularity and influence.[23]

A great deal about the social composition of the magazine's

readership may be gathered from its style, tone, and content. Like most journalism of the mid-nineteenth century it appealed primarily to an educated audience. A striking and, to the modern reader, troublesome aspect of *Kladderadatsch* is its assumption that the reader is well acquainted with the Greek and Latin classics, with classical German literature, and with Mozartian opera. The heavily classical and literary style reflected the taste not only of the erudite philologist Löwenstein but presumably of the readers who understood and appreciated his contributions. Many jokes turned on classical allusions. In the 1890s, for instance, *Kladderadatsch* poked fun at socialism by imagining how the socialist newspaper *Vorwärts* might have reported the Thersites incident in the *Iliad.* Löwenstein's opening verses often parodied poems of Goethe and Schiller—mostly, to be sure, those which every schoolchild would know, such as *Erlkönig* and *Wanderers Nachtlied,* but some less known poems as well. Another important source of literary inspiration was the student song—both Löwenstein and Trojan were loyal *Korpsstudenten* who had contributed verses to their fraternities' *Kommersbücher* as well as to *Kladderadatsch.* From such content one might gather that the magazine appealed chiefly to an audience of university graduates, all male, all from middle- to upper-class families.[24]

Yet other aspects of the *Kladderadatsch* personality lend at least some credence to the editors' claim that their magazine was popular "in palace and hut." Mid-century liberalism, though most widespread among the educated and professional classes, appealed to a wide and diverse constituency, including businessmen, shopkeepers, merchants, farmers, and civil servants of all grades. By contrast to Löwenstein's elegant and allusive verses, other regular features, such as the dialogues between Müller and Schulze, the letters of the eternal schoolboy Karlchen Miessnick, and the frequent excursions into Berlin dialect humor, required far less erudition and sometimes made a conscious appeal to the "little man." *Kladderadatsch* often championed lower-middle-class people who had not benefitted from the booming prosperity of the *Gründerzeit.*[25]

The advertisements, after 1866 a highly conspicuous feature of the magazine, suggest a fairly diverse readership. At first referring only to books, the advertising supplements soon tempted the reader with almost every object or service available in an opulent and booming economy. To be sure, most of these commercials appealed to upper-middle-class wealth, snobbery, or ambition.

"Well-off capitalists," read one such announcement, "will find that the purchase of a valuable estate, only twenty minutes from Berlin, is a very good opportunity." Along with houses, estates, even castles ("in a lovely setting, with park and meadows, only 10 minutes from a railway station"), scientific papers and doctors' diplomas ("from one of the most famous universities") were offered (sometimes "discreetly") for sale. Even conjugal bliss was advertised for a price. "An educated merchant, religion protestant, 30 years old, owner of a retail business," stated one classified ad, "is searching for a life's companion with a net worth of at least 5,000 *Thaler.*" Yet other advertisements could have appealed to people of more moderate income. Patent medicines for all conceivable human ills, pipes, velocipedes, iceboxes, sewing machines, and beer were only a few of the many and diverse items for sale.

The literary advertisements also appealed to a wide range of interests, offering not only the classics but books for the whole family. *A Voyage in Pictures* and *Goethe's Women* were clearly intended for the ladies of the household, while *Familiar Stories for Young People* was described as "the best Christmas present for boys from ages 10 to 16." Such a work as *Sensuality and Its Victims: A Complete History of Prostitution* obviously appealed to a more sophisticated male taste. While geared chiefly to an educated audience, *Kladderadatsch* nonetheless probably circulated among the variety of middle-class readers. And the many references to farms and estates for sale suggest some aristocratic readership as well. We have seen that Bismarck, admittedly a highly atypical Junker, read and often enjoyed *Kladderadatsch.*[26]

Indispensable to a family magazine was a strict respect for propriety. Only in its revolutionary years did the editors of *Kladderadatsch* permit even a mildly risqué joke. After 1850 its policy was very similar to that of *Punch,* of which a British newspaper commented, "It will provoke a hearty laugh, but never bring a blush to the most innocent cheek." The policy remained unaltered by changing literary conventions in the 1890s, as the *Festschrift* which commemorated the magazine's fiftieth anniversary in 1898 asserted. "With the same firm integrity, the editors have refused to court popularity through impure or obscene jokes, or to give the slightest attention to the culture of the *demimonde.* They are not opposed to a natural and healthy heartiness, but they reject any equivocal joking or flippant remarks on decency and morals. Moreover, they avoid any seductive pictures of nudity, or of partial nudity, such as one finds in foreign magazines." This passage illustrates a crucial difference between the traditional style of *Kladderadatsch* and the modern style of *Simplicissimus*. While critical of the political behavior of the German bourgeoisie, the older *Witzblatt* remained intensely loyal to their moral and social standards. The social satire of *Kladderadatsch*, mostly dating from the 1880s and 1890s, was mild and essentially approving. Only deviations from accepted behavior were severely castigated. It remained for *Simplicissimus* to launch a more radical critique of bourgeois culture by combining political and social satire.[27]

Still another characteristic of *Kladderadatsch* which reflected the atmosphere of mid-century society was its leisurely pace. The satirical verses and anecdotes were often quite long, complex, and allusive, and required considerable effort and concentration of the reader. Moreover, the printed word was by far the most important medium of communication. Often turning on puns, dialect, and witty repartee, the jokes of *Kladderadatsch* reflect an exuberant delight in words and their unexpected possibilities. The magazine's layout, with the graphics serving chiefly to illustrate the text, emphasized verbal rather than visual messages. A long and complex verse usually appeared on the cover page under the grinning boy's head; inside pages contained regular features such as the Müller-Schulze dialogue as well as shorter pieces in verse and prose. In issues which contained an average of eight quarto-size pages, usually only one would feature a full-page drawing.

In the 1870s and 1880s the magazine also became famous for the cartoons of Wilhelm Scholz, whose caricature of Bismarck featured three hairs on an otherwise bald crown. Whatever its artistic merit, however, the cartoon was intended to illustrate the caption. In *Simplicissimus*, by contrast, the caption enhanced the cartoon, which often told its own story without the help of words. Like its literary content, the cartoons of *Kladderadatsch* were painstaking, intricate, and detailed, again demanding time and concentration of the reader. "The painstaking drawings and the leisurely captions were indicative of the time when they were used," remarked the biographer of *Punch*. "There was more time to read, and fewer magazines. There was more time to let a joke soak in."[28]

Kladderadatsch carried its traditional style into the 1890s. By 1899 it had lost its monopoly on political satire, having been superseded by two very popular *Witzblätter*, the socialist *Der*

Wahre Jakob and the liberal *Simplicissimus.* Although for reasons still to be explored it could not compete with the newer periodicals, its circulation of 50,000 was still comparatively high, especially for a magazine of its generally lofty intellectual tone. Rolf Engelsing's study of magazine readership in Bremen during this period found that *Kladderadatsch,* not *Simplicissimus,* was invariably included in the holdings of bookstores and lending libraries which catered to middle-class readers. Likewise, a typical subscription list recommended by booksellers to well-to-do customers in 1902 included *Kladderadatsch* as well as the family journals and the *Fliegende Blätter. Simplicissimus,* which by 1902 was very well known, was not on this list, probably because it was too controversial for this presumably conventional readership. This impression is confirmed by the fact that, of all the clubs surveyed by Engelsing, only the socialist clubs, founded by workers for workers, subscribed to *Simplicissimus* rather than to *Kladderadatsch.* Engelsing's evidence, though limited to only one city, does suggest some significant facts about the readers of satirical journals during this period. First, *Simplicissimus* and *Kladderadatsch* were perceived as very different in style and content, since not one subscriber mentioned received both. Another historian of the press during this period, Isolde Rieger, described *Kladderadatsch* as "a conservative and middle-of-the-road magazine which did not, like other journals of this type, stand in absolute opposition." Though *Kladderadatsch* did indeed suffer from the competition of *Simplicissimus,* it probably continued to appeal to a segment of the public which objected to the new magazine.[29]

Their allegiance to tradition shaped the humorists' political stance during the Wilhelmine period. Ranging themselves firmly on the side of the retired chancellor, they joined him in attacking the brash young emperor and his regime. Sometimes, as we shall see, such opposition could be very aggressive. The *"Kladderadatsch* affair" of 1893–94 showed the very considerable attention that satirical literature could attract, not only among the general public but among the highest officials, including the kaiser himself. A *Bismarck-Album,* a collection of cartoons and verses from four decades, became very popular in 1895. In 1897 a cartoon comparing Wilhelm to Frederick the Great resulted in a sentence of two months' *Festungshaft,* or fortress arrest, for Johannes Trojan. Trojan's amusing little book *Zwei Monate Festung* indicates that he rather enjoyed his stay in the fortress, where he appreciated the good food, free time for thought and reflection, and some quaint old characters who provided comic relief and local color. Paul Warncke, who succeeded Trojan in 1909, was a far more aggressive nationalist and patriot than his predecessors. During his tenure the magazine lost much of its original style and flavor.[30]

The contrast between *Kladderadatsch* and *Simplicissimus* illustrates the persistence of tradition—artistic, literary, and intellectual—alongside rapid change and innovation. Inevitably *Kladderadatsch* lost ground. By 1900 the circulation of *Simplicissimus* had reached 85,000, far outstripping its older rival's 50,000. In the fast-moving urban society of the early twentieth century, the subtle, restrained, and erudite style of the older magazine seemed increasingly old-fashioned. A successful periodical had to appeal to a much broader audience than *Kladderadatsch* had ever attempted to reach, by means for which the older humorists had little understanding or sympathy. The *Festschrift* of 1898 took positive pride in the differences between *Kladderadatsch* and its younger rival. "It is only to its credit that *Kladderadatsch* avoids the style of many *Witzblätter,* which are always, simply on principle, in opposition and seek to excite the reader with scandalous broadsides." When one considers that in 1900 Trojan was sixty-three and Polstorff fifty-seven, and that the average age of the five most important staff members was forty-eight (as compared to twenty-nine for the *Simplicissimus* group) it is not surprising that they reacted negatively to the tastes of the younger generation. The history of *Simplicissimus* will show the development of this newer style.[31]

Simplicissimus

The cafe which legend names as the birthplace of *Simplicissimus* was in Munich. Thomas Theodor Heine, later the magazine's most famous and prolific cartoonist, tells of the evening—New Year's night 1896—when he was sitting, solitary and desolate, over a glass of punch. Enter Albert Langen, a rising young publisher with an interest in avant-garde literature. "Ten *Pfennig* per issue," Langen proposed. "A weekly, colored illustrations!" Heine approved, the new project was discussed at the home of Thomas Mann's father-in-law, Alfred Pringsheim (Mann himself was for some time on the editorial staff), and in April 1896 the first issue appeared. The title alluded to the well-known seventeenth-century picaresque novel by Johann Jakob Christoffel von Grimmelshausen, in which the career of the naive hero, Simplicissimus, is recounted both as a realistic portrayal of contemporary customs and conditions and as a satirical allegory concerning the individual's struggle for salvation. There are many theories about the original godfather of the magazine (Maximilian Harden took credit for the choice of name, as did Otto Erich Hartleben) but the original inspiration probably came from Willy Grétor, a friend of Frank Wedekind, whom Langen had met in Paris. Grétor, a poet and a rogue, had sold Langen some forged paintings but later remarked that he had compensated his victim in full by suggesting that he found a satirical magazine similar to the French *Gil Blas Illustré.* Grétor proved to be right.[32]

Simplicissimus belonged to Munich as surely as *Kladderadatsch* to Berlin. The contributors, though most of them came from other parts of Germany, nonetheless created a humorous style which was thoroughly Bavarian—much broader, more vulgar, and less subtle than the laconic Berliner wit. Its exuberance expressed above all the spirit of Schwabing, the Munich artists' colony which flourished at the turn of the century as never before or since. "Munich shone!" exclaimed Thomas Mann. And his younger brother Viktor described Schwabing as "both a place and a way of life. . . . It was an enclave of a large and festive city, tolerant in spite of the pious Catholicism of the countryside, and the narrowness of the *petit-bourgeois,* democratic in spite of the Royal Family, and cosmopolitan in spite of its vociferous local patriotism." Both the political and the aesthetic views of the *Simplicissimus* group held up the relaxed, tolerant, and vital Bavarian culture as a creative alternative to the Prussian values of discipline, authority, and obedience.[33]

In no place but Schwabing could the concentration of literary and artistic talent have been found upon which the new weekly throve. Contributors to *Kladderadatsch,* whose pieces appeared anonymously, subordinated individual recognition to their common cause. *Simplicissimus* stood much less for a single cause, much more for the freedom of the individual to express his own personality and viewpoint. The illustrious names of occasional contributors—Thomas Mann, Rainer Maria Rilke, Richard Dehmel, Björnstjerne Björnson—attest to Langen's enthusiastic support for the modern literary trends which the editorial staff of *Kladderadatsch* had regarded with conservative distaste. The bulk of material in *Simplicissimus,* however, was contributed by its regular staff. "We were all around thirty," recalled one prominent member, Ludwig Thoma, "about the same age, we were held together by nothing but our own inclination, and the only rules were those that we made ourselves, in the interest of our common enterprise." And Jakob Wassermann, for a time copyeditor of *Simplicissimus,* fondly remembered the atmosphere of staff meetings. "We had interests, we pursued them with enthusiasm, there was comradeship and an exhilarating unity. . . . Our opposition to the existing system though passionate, was never without humor, we felt a joyous love of our work . . . all our disagreements were for the sake of our common purpose."[34]

Simplicissimus displayed the talents of so many writers, artists, and editorial staff members that only the most important can be mentioned here. Albert Langen, publisher and editor-in-chief until his death in 1909, was the son of a rich Rhineland industrialist. After attempting his own literary career, he founded the Albert Langen Verlag in the conviction that his vocation was to publish the works of others rather than to create his own. The press, which reflected its proprietor's cosmopolitan tastes by publishing many French and Scandinavian works in translation, became known for its sympathetic support of struggling young poets and writers. Langen, who wrote little for *Simplicissimus,* nonetheless until 1906 exercised a dominant influence over its artistic and political development. Arthur Holitscher described Langen's role as that of an "impresario. . . . There were a few gifted people, whom he had brought together and they were all working together, more or less as volunteers on his project."[35]

The literary content of *Simplicissimus* was influenced overwhelmingly by Ludwig Thoma, who joined the editorial staff in 1899 and became editor-in-chief after Langen's death in 1909. A former lawyer who found legal practice monotonous and confining, Thoma accepted the editorial post in order (as he wrote to Langen) "to win his spurs" as a writer. Under the pen name Peter Schlemihl he quickly developed into a tireless, resourceful, sometimes heavy-handed polemicist, reserving his most biting attacks for the clerical party, whose reactionary influence was particularly strong in Bavaria. But Thoma's major literary effort was invested in his successful series of stories, novels, and plays celebrating the culture of the Bavarian countryside. Like the "Müller-Schulze" feature in *Kladderadatsch,* Thoma's Bavarian dialect humor lent a folksy touch to *Simplicissimus.* Less advantageous for the magazine was Thoma's passionate, often provincial nationalism which led not only to disputes with the more cosmopolitan Langen but ultimately to severe internal conflicts over his own role as a satirist. Two other important members of the staff, Korfiz Holm and Reinhold Geheeb, managed much of the everyday editorial work, particularly during Langen's period of exile in Paris from 1898 to 1903.[36]

The chief glory of *Simplicissimus,* however, was the cartoon. The change from a highly verbal to a highly visual emphasis was not only the most conspicuous but also among the most important contrast between *Kladderadatsch* and *Simplicissimus.* Like most mid-century periodicals, *Kladderadatsch* had been aimed at a comfortable readership with the time and leisure to appreciate its intellectual style. *Simplicissimus,* by contrast, illustrated the development of journalism in the later nineteenth century to attract a mass readership in a faster-moving urban environment which left little time for subtlety or complexity. "The modern newspaper," remarked a 1914 treatise on journalism, "is not read in the same way as its predecessor, at a leisurely breakfast or at the parlor table by the light of an oil lamp. Think how many papers are stuck hastily into pockets as the reader leaves the house, to be read on the commuting train, the streetcar, the bus or the subway, and not studied, but just hastily scanned." Not only did *Simplicissimus* devote more space to cartoons than did *Kladderadatsch* but the visual impact of its uncluttered modern graphics was far more direct than that of the intricate, detailed, and complex drawings of Scholz. *Simplicissimus'* striking, sometimes lurid use of color contrasted flamboyantly with its older rival's sober black and white. Moreover, the imagery of the younger artists was derived less from traditional sources such as classical mythology than from everyday life—the street, the cafe, the carnival. Colorful, daring, often risqué and sensational, the cartoons of *Simplicissimus* were designed for a wider and socially more heterogeneous audience than those of *Kladderadatsch.*[37]

The artwork was furnished by a small group who worked chiefly for *Simplicissimus,* although most contributed to other magazines as well. The turn of the century saw a flowering of cartoon art, of which the *Simplicissimus* group were the foremost practitioners. The brief enumeration of the most important cartoonists here will be supplemented by the many examples of their work to be described in later chapters.[38]

Much the most productive and perhaps the most original was

Thomas Theodor Heine, who came from a prosperous Jewish commercial family in Leipzig. Despite the antisemitic propaganda which attacked the magazine for its allegedly destructive and cynical "Jewish" spirit, Heine was one of very few Jews who worked for *Simplicissimus*. Contemporary critics responded to Heine's work with a certain bewilderment as they struggled to interpret the artist's enigmatic and complex messages. To one critic, Hermann Esswein, Heine's often horrifying portrayals of slum life expressed the "restrained rage" of a compassionate and sensitive artist forced to cultivate "stoic endurance of the pain which those revelations cause him." Other readers interpreted these same pictures as simply cold, sardonic, and unfeeling. Hermann Sinsheimer, later editor of *Simplicissimus,* called Heine's pictures of lower-class life "cold-hearted and cruel" by contrast to those of the compassionate Käthe Kollwitz. "They [the figures in Heine's drawings] were only revolting and painful to see—they were themselves in the most infernal sense ridiculous—victims of society and the times, but victims hardly worth sacrificing." Whatever the truth of the matter (and a perusal of Heine's letters tends to bear out the latter interpretation of his character) both of these critics clearly found his work more grotesque and shocking than funny.[39]

Several other cartoonists contributed almost as much as Heine to the success of *Simplicissimus.* Edward Thöny was best known for his cartoons of military life which featured one of the magazine's best known characters, the silly young lieutenant. Bruno Paul, a successful serious artist as well as a cartoonist, commented on a wide range of social issues in a style even more biting than Heine's. By contrast to Heine's sharply outlined figures, Paul's were grotesquely soft and shapeless. Olaf Gulbransson, Norwegian by birth, excelled in portrait caricature in which a likeness was achieved by a few effective lines. Gulbransson's expansive and fertile wit, which could devise a cartoon at short notice around any idea or theme, was particularly valuable as the publication deadline approached. The Viennese Ferdinand von Reznicek specialized in delicate drawings of the fashionable world, often with risqué or erotic overtones. Although Thoma was constantly irritated by the artistic mediocrity of Reznicek's drawings, Langen perceived their commercial value. Langen's friend Max Halbe commented paradoxically that cartoonists such as Heine and Paul ruthlessly mocked the middle-class people who were the magazine's chief subscribers! "And how could they have made this satire palatable to those very 'Philistines' to whom they sold subscriptions if they had not offered them a little titillation? Business was business!" The wide sale of Reznicek anthologies attested to the popularity of these spicy drawings.[40]

Until 1906 Albert Langen headed the enterprise not only spiritually, but also financially, employing the staff on a salary basis. In 1906 a palace revolution staged by the chief staff members— cartoonists Heine, Gulbransson, Paul, Reznicek, Wilke, Schulz, and Thöny, and writers Thoma and Geheeb—forced Langen to establish the enterprise as a joint stock company in which he shared both the operating costs and the profits with his colleagues. The independence of the individual contributors, who had thus freed themselves from Langen's editorial authority, was manifested in the increased diversity of opinion expressed in *Simplicissimus* after 1906. The staff members' insistence on a fair division of the profits reflected the increasing success of the once-struggling new magazine. To be sure, the deaths of both Langen and Reznicek in 1909 (another popular cartoonist, Rudolf Wilke, had died the year before) caused a slight decline both in quality and in profits, for no significant new talent was found to replace them. Nonetheless, *Simplicissimus'* continuing financial success attested to its popularity.[41]

The success of *Simplicissimus* was due in large measure to its change of direction and personality from the literary weekly which Langen had first envisaged to an organ of aggressive political satire. The discovery that political satire paid was an almost accidental result of the first issue to attract really wide attention— the "Palestine" issue of 1898, whose content will be more thoroughly discussed in another chapter. The issue, a response to Kaiser Wilhelm's trip to Palestine, contained some cartoons by Heine, but the main feature was a verse by Frank Wedekind (whose contributions to *Simplicissimus* financed his yet unremunerative work as a playwright), which in addition to its mockery of the kaiser contained some most irreverent references to religious shrines and personalities. The issue was confiscated in Leipzig, where *Simplicissimus* was then published, and a lawsuit was brought against Langen, Heine, and the still pseudonymous author of the verse (whose identity was later discovered). Following the advice of his lawyer, Langen fled immediately to Switzerland and afterward to Paris, where he remained in exile for five years. Holm, left in charge of *Simplicissimus* and the press, finally persuaded Wedekind, who was most reluctant to leave the opening

"This is how I'll do my next drawing." Heine's comment on his prison sentence resulting from the Palestine issue. (Heine, *Simplicissimus*, Jan. 1899.)

night of his play *Erdgeist,* to escape from Munich. Heine served a six-month sentence of *Festungshaft,* and Wedekind was condemned to a still longer stint of seven months when he returned to Germany and attempted to exonerate himself by claiming he had written the offending verse under orders from Langen. (Wedekind later pilloried Langen in a vitriolic comedy, *Oaha.*) Though mild compared to sentences imposed by later totalitarian regimes, these penalties were not negligible—Heine's letters from prison expressed fear and anger as well as sardonic amusement, and Thoma warned Langen to remain in exile rather than risk the destruction of his health in the damp, cold fortress. Yet the disadvantages to the culprits were more than offset by the advantages to their magazine. "The fury of the Saxon authorities against the guilty *Simplicissimus,*" wrote Holm, "had the results that our circulation rose within four or five weeks from fifteen thousand to, I think, eighty-five thousand. We were happy about this, although even then we barely broke even financially."[42]

The "Palestine affair" was only the first of a long series of confiscations, trials, and legal penalties. The grounds for confiscation were many and diverse. For instance, the clipping file of the Hamburg political police, conscientiously assembled from newspapers all over Germany, contains accounts of twenty-seven confiscations in the period 1903–07. Although some of these were initiated by zealous state prosecutors, most were prompted by the complaints of groups or individual citizens to the police. A large number of such complaints, of course, were brought by Catholic and Protestant clergy on grounds of blasphemy or "immorality." To such conservative religious leaders, *Simplicissimus* became a symbol of the widespread moral degeneration which laws such as the Lex Heinze were designed to combat. "Catholic and Protestant clergy," wrote Thoma, "rushed into the bookstores and demanded the removal of *Simplicissimus* from the windows or tried to prevent its being sold." Other complaints were made by military authorities protesting insults to the army as a whole or to individual regiments, by professional groups outraged by irreverent comments on their activities or members, or by business firms protecting their reputations against some allegedly libellous attack. For instance, one cartoon implying that the Hamburg shipping firm of Woermann had charged exorbitant rates for shipping the bodies of soldiers killed in the South African colonial wars of 1906 so offended that firm that it sued the cartoonist, Olaf Gulbransson, for libel. The prison sentence imposed in the highly publicized trial was as usual commuted to a fine—indeed, the only *Simplicissimus* staff member to serve time in prison after the "Palestine affair" was Ludwig Thoma, who spent six weeks in Stadelheim fortress in 1906.[43]

Often such lawsuits resulted in the triumphant acquittal of *Simplicissimus*. The right to trial by jury enjoyed by press offenders in Bavaria made convictions hard to get, since jurors selected from the population at large were often unsympathetic to the individuals or groups bringing the complaints. Legal proceedings against *Simplicissimus* were made still more difficult by the complex and never-resolved jurisdictional dispute between the authorities of Bavaria, where the editorial office was located, and those of Württemberg, where the magazine was printed by the Stuttgart firm of Strecker and Schroeder. Finally, although some judges were so prejudiced against *Simplicissimus* that, as Thoma asserted, they "did not hesitate to circumvent or violate the law in order to get rid of the hated *Witzblatt*," others protected freedom of the press by rejecting complaints which were obviously unfounded. For example, when religious groups in Hamburg sued certain booksellers for displaying a very explicit issue on prostitution, the judge accepted the defendants' claim that they had not known of any obscene contents and further ruled that the issue was not "morally objectionable."[44]

Even hard-line conservatives ultimately realized that these legal proceedings did more to publicize than to suppress *Simplicissimus*. For, as the editors were not slow to point out, such incidents merely vindicated their picture of an inept and reactionary authority structure. When an issue was confiscated in 1904, Thoma's attorney and close friend Conrad Haussmann gleefully pointed to the publicity value of censorship. "If the issue is not released . . . I suggest that only the 'illegal' passages be deleted, either by crossing them out with thick black lines, or by removing the offending words, leaving white spaces behind. Thus the confiscation can work to the *advantage* of the magazine. . . . But hurry up, the number's very hot now, print twice as many copies!" Thus fear of defeat and loss of face made officials increasingly reluctant to take action against *Simplicissimus*. In 1914 an advisor warned the king of Bavaria against forbidding the sale of an issue which he found insulting. "The police chief has decided against prohibiting the sale of the issue or its display in shop windows . . . because in his opinion such a prohibition would be ineffective and serve as an advertisement."[45]

Thus, despite—or perhaps in part owing to—official disapproval, *Simplicissimus* increased in popularity. By contrast to the *Kladderadatsch* group, whose formative years had been passed during the exhilarating era of unification, the majority of the *Simplicissimus* group had matured during the politically repressive decade of the 1880s. After the premature death of Friedrich III had frustrated hopes for the liberalization of the monarchy, the regime of Wilhelm II seemed to its liberal critics increasingly to exemplify mediocrity combined with arrogance; *Simplicissimus* became a conspicuous symbol of a new antiestablishment mood. Sinsheimer described it as "the expression of a universal European revolt against the authoritarian state, militarism, and imperialism, against bureaucracy and the class system, against all orthodoxies religious and otherwise." Humor provided an outlet for the tensions of a transitional period when "old and new ideas dwelt uneasily together." Freud commented that caricature was popular because "we consider resistance to authority a great merit." And likewise Georg Hirth, who, as editor of another satirical periodical, *Jugend,* served as witness at the trial of Ludwig Thoma, testified to the social value of humor. "In a discussion of my magazine, Dr. Servaes of Vienna used the following words, 'Hardly any society has ever had such a strong desire to laugh as our own . . . and a great deal of anger is released through the laughter.' These words . . . sum up the value of political satire."[46]

But *Simplicissimus* became known not only for its expression of negative emotions such as anger, but for its positive advocacy of artistic and intellectual innovation. By contrast to the conservative *Kladderadatsch,* whose adaptation to modern taste was gradual and reluctant, *Simplicissimus* soon became a symbol of avant-garde and controversial artistic trends. The heavy-handed insistence of Wilhelm II that art must "contribute to the education of the people" by confining its political content to conventional dynastic and military themes had sharpened the antagonism between individual creativity and official ideology and had driven innovative artists into political opposition. Not that the secession movements of the 1890s (chief among which were the Munich Secession of 1892 and the Berlin Secession of 1898) were chiefly concerned with overtly political themes. Indeed, the naturalist style of *Simplicissimus'* portrayals of slum life was better developed in literature than in the visual arts. But the Berlin Secession's avoidance of the fashionable patriotic imagery and its concentration on realistic scenes from everyday life aroused the opposition of conservative critics, who condemned such art as politically and morally dangerous. The spiritual kinship between the satirists of *Simplicissimus* and the artists of the Berlin Secession was expressed by the inclusion of some dozen sketches by two prominent *Simplicissimus* contributors, Eduard Thöny and Ferdinand von Reznicek, in the Secession's highly controversial exhibition of 1898. The artists of the secession movements protested not only the conception of art advocated by the kaiser, but the sentimental and complacent bourgeois taste which this official ideology reflected and reinforced. Widely read and praised by avant-garde artists, *Simplicissimus* became the highly visible champion of the artist's freedom to challenge both official repression and bourgeois stuffiness.[47]

Not only in political tendency but in visual style *Simplicissimus* became a conspicuous advocate of artistic innovation. The *Jugendstil*, publicized chiefly by *Simplicissimus* and another Munich periodical, *Jugend,* showed the influence both of the French *Art Nouveau* and of the British arts and crafts movement in its emphasis on the decorative and symbolic potential of linear design. Architectural historian Nikolaus Pevsner has identified "the long and sensitive curve . . . the curve undulating, flowering and interplaying with others" as the leitmotif of the style. Not only in painting and graphics but in the applied arts such as architecture and design, this emphasis upon grace and economy was an implied protest, made explicit in Heine's savage caricatures of the bourgeois home, against the clumsy and overly ornate conventional taste of the period. But the strong linear contours of the *Jugendstil* could reveal deformity as well as grace, the grotesque as well as the beautiful. "It is a line that hurts!" remarked Eugen Roth of Thomas Theodor Heine's mercilessly outlined figures. The cartoons of *Simplicissimus* often derived their emotional impact from the striking and economical use of a few lines to illuminate an entire personality or situation.[48]

To what groups of readers did the new style in satire predominantly appeal? In the absence of statistical readership analyses, the historian must rely on contemporary accounts and impressions. The geographical distribution of *Simplicissimus* grew steadily wider. Dissatisfied with the magazine's chiefly Bavarian circulation, Ludwig Thoma embarked in 1900 on a vigorous advertising campaign in the many German cities where it was not yet well known. Thoma suggested the hiring of street vendors in towns where conservative booksellers hesitated to display the magazine, and a systematic marketing effort aimed at barber-shops, taverns, and cigar stores. During a visit to Berlin, Thoma urged Langen to "take the North Germans more into considera-tion. . . . This is a small reform because we should never lose our South German character . . . it's our biggest asset." A 1901 police report on the magazine's circulation showed that the larg-est shipments went to Leipzig, Frankfurt, and Stuttgart, and a substantial number were also sent to Berlin. Thus, although prob-ably most popular in South and Central Germany, *Simplicissi-mus* gained a national reputation.[49]

All observers, whether friendly or hostile, noted the appeal of *Simplicissimus* to middle-class youth. "My fondness for *Simpli-cissimus*," recalled Viktor Mann, then a secondary school stu-dent, "was a youthful love at first sight, to which I was faithful until the last issue of 1933." An editorial in the right-wing *Augs-burger Postzeitung* complained of the magazine's popularity among gymnasium students, and warned that "such shameful insults [a caricature of a local headmaster], displayed openly in hundreds of Munich shop windows, are a real danger to school discipline." A Center deputy to the Bavarian Landtag quoted a patriotic Ham-burg bookseller who, shocked by the popularity of *Simplicissi-mus* among university students, appealed to German professors to "admonish their students, as did Fichte, Arndt and other men," against the magazine which "physically and spiritually poisons our youth." Another group of enthusiastic young readers were junior officers, many of whom came from middle-class back-grounds. The *Allgemeine Rundschau* asked with surprised dis-approval how a magazine which so systematically "treads the au-thority of the state . . . into the mud . . . and insults the officer class in each issue should be the most popular reading matter in casinos?" Not all authority figures considered the magazine un-suitable for young readers; the *Allgemeine Rundschau* further complained of a gymnasium teacher who had actually recom-mended it to his class because of its artistic merit, "and it wasn't even the drawing teacher but the Latin teacher (who has since been fired)." Although exact data are lacking, one can speculate that the avant-garde *Simplicissimus* attracted a younger reader-ship than the traditional *Kladderadatsch*.[50]

But *Simplicissimus* did not lack for readers among the older generation. Right-wing politicians and journalists ceaselessly complained of the magazine's popularity among precisely those "pillars of the community" whose duty it was to set an example!

What were foreigners to think of Germany, expostulated one editorial, when "everywhere in foreign stations, in foreign resorts, they see *Simplicissimus* in the hands of well-dressed Germans?" The very judges who conducted trials for *Majestätsbeleidigung,* lamented another article, commended the magazine as "an outstanding sheet which [they] like to read." Other hostile observers complained that *Simplicissimus* was to be found in clubs and in government offices and on the coffee tables of liberal deputies. Although these reports, bristling with right-wing hysteria, were probably exaggerated, they do suggest that *Simplicissimus* appealed to many members of the business and professional elite.[51]

Though particularly appealing to these elite readers, however, *Simplicissimus* seems also to have been widely distributed among the general public. The *Allgemeine Rundschau* remarked on its ubiquity in railway magazine stands, and a Bavarian Landtag deputy complained of "its extraordinary popularity among young people and among female servants because of its sale in dairy stores, stationery stores and all such small businesses." Although not primarily intended for blue-collar workers, who had their own widely circulating socialist *Witzblatt, Der Wahre Jakob,* the magazine was increasingly appreciated by the more politically sophisticated segments of the socialist working class. In 1904 socialist newspapers in Chemnitz, Dresden, and Frankfurt reported on a new and painless form of political education, the "*Simplicissimus* evening," sponsored by local trade-union organizations for their members. "The program includes readings of the best and most typical items from our most artistically outstanding *Witzblatt,*" read the announcement of one such event. "The *Simplicissimus* evening . . . was a first-class attraction," reported the *Chemnitzer Volksstimme.* "At least 1,600, perhaps more people filled the hall and spilled out into the corridor and the adjacent rooms. The name *Simplicissimus* exerts an enormous suggestive power over public opinion, and the Munich *Witzblatt* has gained immense popularity." *Simplicissimus'* growing concern with working-class and socialist issues was probably partly motivated by the desire to appeal to this large and politically active readership. "Who would deny," asked the editor of the socialist newspaper *Frankfurter Volkstimme,* "that there is no more receptive audience for the sharp, well-aimed satire of *Simplicissimus* than the organized working class? Politically mature, economically knowledgeable, socially disadvantaged, the workers have a doubly and triply keen sense of their oppression in this Holy

Roman Empire, and of the hypocrisy, bureaucratic arrogance, and police repressiveness which pervade public life." The major role played by socialist newspapers in both publicizing and protesting *Simplicissimus'* brushes with the law showed the party's willingness to join progressive liberals in a common opposition to political repression and religious intolerance.[52]

But despite its significant working-class audience *Simplicissimus,* like *Kladderadatsch,* depended chiefly on the support of the educated middle-class reader. And the success of *Simplicissimus* in supplanting *Kladderadatsch* as Germany's foremost satirical magazine may be attributed to the growing preference of at least a portion of this traditionally conservative readership for an avant-garde and oppositional style over a cautious and respectable one. Thus the contrast between *Kladderadatsch* and *Simplicissimus* will reflect important changes both in political and social attitudes and in aesthetic taste, which will be explored in the following chapters.

Politics as Theater:
The Satirical
Portrait of
the Kaiser
and His Subjects

3

Setting the Scene

W ILHELM II opened the era which was to bear his name with the promise to lead his subjects "onward to glorious days." The winter of German discontent, he asserted, was made glorious summer in an Empire now prosperous and stable, secure and splendid. "What our fathers struggled for, what dreaming German youth has hoped and sung, has now come to pass. . . . Germany has become a world Empire.. . . . German knowledge and German industry are now spread around the world. . . . I lift my glass to toast our beloved Fatherland. . . . Long live the Empire!" Some received such words enthusiastically, others skeptically. Aware of the Empire's vast unsolved political and social problems, thoughtful citizens were increasingly inclined to doubt the power of flowery rhetoric to unite a still divided people. In 1913, on the twenty-fifth anniversary of the kaiser's accession, *Kladderadatsch* published a cartoon of the German "Michel" as a child with one hand in his royal "father's" and the other pointing to a signpost reading "to glorious days." "Is it much farther, Papa?"[1]

The wry tone of this cartoon was indeed far from the unquestioning enthusiasm encouraged by the official molders of public opinion. Critics of the monarchy were many and diverse, including in their number not only socialists and disgruntled intellectuals but many people of solidly conservative, even monarchist persuasion. The history of the satirical journals demonstrates the failure of censorship laws to deter dissenting journalists. Indeed, such laws served chiefly to enhance the importance of satire as a device for disguising a politically controversial message in the symbolic form of a joke, anecdote, or fable. The satirists criticized not only the monarch's own Exalted Person, but the entire political system of which he was the nominal head.

Many of the problems of which the satirists complained could be traced to the strange and conflict-laden beginning of Wilhelm's reign. The premature death of Friedrich III, who had been expected to liberalize the monarchy, had disappointed liberals. The succession of a very young to a very old man seemed abrupt and unnatural, and Wilhelm's dismissal of Bismarck, for years the personification of stability, seemed to many to forbode disaster, for the departure of its architect highlighted the weakness of the structure which he had created to suit his own personality and political convictions. The Bismarckian system rested on an unequal compromise between the old aristocratic and the new industrial elite, whereby the former retained political power and social prestige and the latter gained economic power and prosperity. Thus the new Germany, in which a still feudal governing class attempted to rule a dynamically modern industrial society, was (in the words of one recent historian) "hallmarked by a pervasive institutional incongruence." By uniting the aristocracy and the upper bourgeoisie against the socialist movement, portrayed as their common enemy, Bismarck succeeded only in postponing, not in avoiding, class confrontation. When, in the absence of his prestigious leadership, the far less resourceful Wilhelmine authority structure faced militant left-wing pressure, many Germans were forced to the same conclusion as Max Weber, who lamented in 1890 that Bismarck's "life work should have led not only to the outward but to the inward unification of the German nation . . . and we all know that this has not been accomplished." German unity itself was a facade covering serious division and social conflict.[2]

The governing classes, moreover, responded to the pressure for change not, in general, by modifying but by arrogantly affirming their neofeudal stance. The young emperor's initial interest in social reform soon gave way to a reactionary insistence on neomedieval absolutism which reflected an arrogance bordering on delusion. His profoundly unstable personality, expressed through impulsive and irresponsible decisions, endangered not only himself but the institution of monarchy itself, for, despite its glam-

"To Glorious Days." "Is it much farther, Papa?" (Brandt, *Kladdera-datsch*, June 15, 1913.)

orous image, the monarchy lacked a solid tradition. Hailed as a symbol of unity, the office was in fact held by a Prussian dynasty foreign to most Germans and resented by many. "Men may obey *their* King," remarked A. J. P. Taylor, "even in an age when monarchical sentiment is declining—they will not obey someone else's King, and the King of Prussia was the King of others for the majority of Germans." *Simplicissimus* expressed not only liberal opposition to absolutism, but Bavarian resentment of Prussian domination. By giving the monarch immense powers, especially over foreign and military matters but also, through the chancellor whom he appointed, over internal politics as well, the imperial constitution had done much to insulate him against opposition. But in a modern state the continued survival of monarchy depended in the last analysis upon that public opinion which Wilhelm alternately courted and scorned. Thus the satirists' campaign for the reform of the monarchy sometimes had substantial impact, especially upon Wilhelm's influential advisors, who often responded to critical journalism with genuine anger and even panic.[3]

The same incongruous use of patriotic rhetoric to justify social privilege was characteristic of the monarch's chief supporters, the Prussian Junkers. Through their control of the army and of the Empire's largest state, the Junkers exercised virtually unchecked political influence. The Bismarckian coalition had encouraged a political and social rapprochement between aristocracy and bourgeoisie which was celebrated in the art, literature, and popular culture of the 1880s. In the 1890s the popular image of the Junkers as patriotic, brave, and public-spirited was increasingly discredited by their ruthless and demagogic pursuit of their own economic interests at the expense of the public. Particularly objectionable was the system of protective tariffs instituted by a coalition of agricultural and industrial interests which, by raising food prices, inflicted great hardship on the middle- and working-class consumer. The satirists' disgust at the degeneration of the aristocratic ideal into crass selfishness was shared even by such perceptive aristocrats as the Baroness von Spitzemberg, who complained that at a meeting of the Agrarian League (the Junkers' pressure group) she heard "blustering, cheap jokes, political commonplaces and inflammatory slogans. . . . I hate this kind of demagogic speech."[4]

The kaiser and the aristocracy gained the support of the middle class through appealing to social ambition on the one hand and fears of socialism on the other. The "feudalization" of the German bourgeoisie was described by historian Eckart Kehr as "a new society . . . a bourgeois-noble neo-feudalism . . . which banded together as tightly against the proletariat and against the unfeudalized bourgeoisie as earlier the officer corps against the liberals." The conservatism of the imperial bourgeoisie led to the emasculation of its historic political party, the National Liberal Party, which during this period almost totally forsook its earlier libertarian and constitutional ideals to become the spokesman for conservative business interests. Conservatism was encouraged by civil-service recruiting policies (the so-called Puttkamer system) which required Reserve-officer status and discriminated against candidates of known liberal views. But even among this prosperous and complacent class there were signs of change. New trends in art and literature patronized by at least a segment of this class advocated (as we have already seen) social as well as artistic innovation. In contrast to the cautious National Liberals, the programs of left-wing liberal parties such as the Progressive party or the National Socialist union, founded by the pastor Friedrich Naumann, showed more openness to social change. Left-wing liberals had always defended traditional liberal causes, such as the strengthening of parliamentary institutions and the defense of civil liberties. At the turn of the century, however, such intellectuals as Naumann, Friedrich Meinecke, and Theodor Barth advocated a modification of the traditional insistence on economic individualism to provide for the welfare of the poor. In 1901 the progressive liberal parties, usually unsuccessful at the polls, sought an alliance with the Social Democratic party to combat such remnants of feudalism as the Prussian three-class voting system. The liberal-socialist alliance, always shaky and problematic, nonetheless encouraged an increased sensitivity to working-class issues among some liberals—a trend which *Simplicissimus* also illustrated. In the prewar years the Bismarckian coalition of aristocracy and middle class began to disintegrate as many middle-class citizens showed increasing impatience with an inflexible system in which they were grossly underrepresented.[5]

Much the most powerful force for social and political change during the imperial period was, of course, the Social Democratic party. The lapse of Bismarck's anti-socialist law—which, far from destroying the party, had actually increased its electoral mandate and revolutionary zeal—ushered in a period of great activity and growth. The Erfurt Program of 1890 reflected the conflict between revisionist and revolutionary elements within the party by prefacing a reformist program with a thoroughly militant and Marxist introduction. Certainly most party members, especially tradeunion workers, increasingly favored an evolutionary path to social change through the processes of political democracy. Yet the hard-line revolutionary rhetoric of some leaders continued to alarm not only the government but many middle-class liberals. The party presented German society with its most important challenge— the integration of the worker, now increasingly educated and law-abiding, into the political process. But unlike the British system, which during this period peacefully incorporated many working-class demands, the German system remained inflexible. Having failed to wean the workers away from Marxism through social legislation, the kaiser changed his tactics and advocated sternly repressive measures such as the Umsturzvorlage of 1894 (punishing "subversive" activity) and the Zuchthausvorlage of 1897 (penalizing striking workers). His admonition to working-class recruits that they must be willing if necessary "to shoot (their) fathers and mothers" articulated his obsessive fear of social disorder. The tremendous socialist electoral victories of the prewar years merely strengthened the governing classes' hard-line resistance to change.[6]

The central conflict in Wilhelmine society, in the words of one recent historian, arose from "the defense of the status quo against the democratization which results from industrialization and against the gradual political mobilization of previously inarticulate citizens." The German constitution provided few legal or constructive channels for political opposition. Even political parties with enormous electoral strength such as the prewar Social Democratic party were virtually powerless to bring about change in a system which gave the elected Reichstag few powers and placed most of the important decisions in the hands of an irresponsible executive. The popularity of political satire resulted in large measure from the lack of more direct and effective outlets for dissenting or oppositional impulses. Frustration with the status quo, the mobilization of public opinion, the search for new solutions—these were to be the central themes of *Kladderadatsch* and *Simplicissimus.*

The Royal Actor

The monarchy, the court circle, the aristocracy—these were the principals in an ever more lavish pageant of imperial grandeur.

The attack on the most conspicuous figure of all, the emperor himself, bore witness to the satirists' versatility and cleverness. Among the profusion of images, one predominated, that of the theater. By the use of this suggestive metaphor, the satirists, in the best tradition of their craft, penetrated a host of external phenomena to a basic truth. In this case the truth lay in incongruous contrasts—between the impressive trappings of monarchy and its real weakness, between the monarch's boastful demeanor and his inner insecurity, between the appearance of unity and the reality of social conflict. The contrast, in short, between the world of reality and that of illusion, in both of which the royal actor lived.

Wilhelm's absurdly pompous behavior made him a favorite butt of satirical comment, both at home and abroad. The satire of *Kladderadatsch* and *Simplicissimus* may be compared to that of many other journalists and authors, who likewise avoided censorship by the use of metaphor, allegory, or symbol. One of the most famous of many such works was a satirical pamphlet entitled *Caligula,* by the liberal historian Ludwig Quidde, first published in 1894 in the socialist periodical *Die Gesellschaft.* Though presented as a scholarly biography and copiously footnoted to ancient sources, the article was in fact a transparent attack on the mad Caesar's modern counterpart. Quidde began by recounting how after the death of his virtuous father, Germanicus, with whom the hopes of an entire generation went to the grave, Caligula dismissed the "leading statesman" and began a personal rule which expressed his "intoxicating feeling of power, of being on top for once." Caligula, the main motive of whose actions was "not to do good but the ambition, as an advocate of popular causes, *to be admired,"* had also a "fantastic ambition to rule the sea" and a "comedian-like manner which is among the symptoms of megalomania." The wide success of this pamphlet, which sold half a million copies, seriously impaired Quidde's advancement in the conservative academic establishment.[7]

Another prominent critic, Maximilian Harden, a loyal supporter of the retired Bismarck, used the theme of theatrical politics to attack the young kaiser. It was Harden who mocked the monarch's fondness for travel as a publicity stunt by nicknaming him "Filmhelm" and the "Reisekaiser." A fable of 1892 entitled "King Phaeton" used the high-flying hero of the Greek myth to warn against illusions of grandeur. Another fable, like the first published in Harden's journal *Die Zukunft,* recounted the story of a prince who, condemned by an evil spell to spend half of his life as a dog, learned from this humbling experience the folly of pretensions to a "tyrannical power which only the wisest, no-blest and shrewdest of men could exercise. . . . I am not a demi-god and I am satisfied with the role of first servant." Convicted and sentenced to a short prison sentence for *Majestätsbeleidi-gung*, Harden reaffirmed the message of his transparent fable by urging Wilhelm to throw off role-playing and recognize his hu-man limitations lest he, like Louis XVI, to whose fate Harden pointedly alluded, destroy the monarchy as well as himself.[8]

Simplicissimus spread the satirical attack on the kaiser to a far wider audience than "serious" journalists were able to reach. Un-like *Kladderadatsch,* whose editors were deterred by one prison sentence (served for a cartoon to be described in chapter 4) from further direct attacks, *Simplicissimus* made the *Kaiserwitz* its specialty. As in *Caligula* and Harden's fables, the devices used to avoid censorship added to the psychological impact of the joke. Seldom directly caricatured (at least until 1908), Wilhelm was often depicted as a fairy-tale prince, a nameless *Serenissimus,* whose identity was revealed only by his telltale mustache. The aim of the caricaturist—to expose in one feature the essence of a personality—was well served by the kaiser's turned-up mus-tache which, as a flamboyant effect laboriously created, became the true symbol of his basic weakness. The tension between high-flown pretensions and real human inadequacy was the theme of even the lightest of these cartoons. Wilhelm's thoroughly dilet-tantish dabbling in art, literature, and social reform, on all of which he considered himself an authority, was mocked by a cartoon which showed a bewigged and powdered prince clutching his brow in a rococo throne room. "The common people don't know how difficult it is to rule. Every day the same worry—should I paint, or write, or solve the Social Question?" "Caligula," too, as Quidde recounted, revealed his emotional instability by the "ner-vous haste" which drove him from one project to another "in erratic and contradictory fashion." The royal actor, playing many parts at once, was out of place in an increasingly specialized so-ciety, and his claims to talents which he did not possess revealed the emptiness of his role.[9]

Like Quidde, *Simplicissimus* sometimes hinted at actual in-sanity. In 1897 it showed a fairy-tale prince sitting on a throne, with his court jester (perhaps *Simplicissimus* itself) beside him. "I am plagued by doubts," says the monarch. "Am I really the king or am I just suffering from megalomania?" "Maybe both, Sire," replies the jester. A cartoon of 1898 showed the prince in rococo dress receiving the tribute of his courtiers. "Your Majesty's most

"Reaction." "Serenissimus" rejects New Year's greetings. "But I ordered that time should go backward!" (Heine, *Simplicissimus*, Jan. 1898.)

humble servants beg to lay their best wishes to your Serene Highness for the year 1898 most obediently at your feet." "1898?" exclaims the prince. "But I thought that I had ordered that from henceforth time should go backwards!" Despite its light-hearted spirit this picture of a prince who, not content with controlling the most powerful empire on earth, aspires to control the universe, expressed very serious misgiving. In a figurehead monarch arrogant caprice might be merely amusing; in an absolute monarch it was dangerous. This cartoon was punished by a temporary ban on the sale of *Simplicissimus* on railway newsstands.[10]

As royal actor on the world stage, Wilhelm needed a grandiose script. In 1899 a *Simplicissimus* cartoon showed three Berliners looking at a Dutch portrait in an art gallery. "Who's that?" "William the Silent." "Nonsense—impossible!" While more timid journalists, embarrassed by their garrulous kaiser's ill-advised utterances, insisted feverishly that he had not really meant them, the humorists took him at his word, sometimes transforming his highly pictorial phraseology into verbal or cartoon pictures. An early example was a verse by Frank Wedekind, who responded to Wilhelm's ringing challenge, "Germany's future lies on the water" (a slogan of the naval building program) by observing that Germans had indeed become a race of reptiles:

> In the water grows the water-lily
> Which is white and innocent as we,
> Where the atmosphere is dark and chilly,
> Toads and reptiles also love to be,
> We, who are obedient from birth
> Lick his boots as loyal subjects should,
> And, forgetting that we walked the earth,
> Turn to reptiles crawling in the mud.[11]

To Wilhelm's arrogant rejection of criticism, "Schwarzseher dulde ich nicht!" ("I won't tolerate pessimists!"), *Simplicissimus* responded with an entire issue on the theme of pessimism, or "seeing black." Chancellor Bülow was shown as huckster for a sordid sideshow: "Come on in, ladies and gentlemen! Here you can see the glorious German Empire, just as it has been for twenty years. For just a penny you can rent pink spectacles so that everything looks much prettier!" Another cartoon showed a worker speaking to the kaiser, whose oversized crown covers his eyes. "Everything looks black," complains the worker. "Everything looks golden to me," replies the monarch, enclosed in his glittering

A magician named Bülow, who has transformed a too-talkative king into a fish, is carried away by an eagle, and the fish regains the ability to speak. A comment on the fall of Bülow. (Heine, *Simplicissimus*, Dec. 19, 1910.)

world of fantasy. Like Harden, *Simplicissimus* warned the deluded monarch that his continued indifference to the grievances
of his people might have disastrous consequences.[12]

Such a day of reckoning seemed at hand in 1908 when the
London *Daily Telegraph* published an interview granted by Wilhelm to a personal friend. Apparently through negligence Chancellor Bülow, to whom the manuscript had been sent for pre-
publication approval, had failed to delete many thoroughly ill-
advised, often untrue remarks about German foreign policy. Potentially offensive both to Britain and to neutral nations such as
Japan, the interview caused a storm of protest abroad and at home.
From conservatives to Social Democrats, Germans were embarrassed by their monarch's indiscretion and deeply appalled at its
possible consequences for Germany's already precarious international position. "It is the most shameful, deplorable, indiscreet
and improper thing that he has ever done!" exclaimed that thoroughly conservative commentator, the Baroness von Spitzemberg. "The Kaiser is ruining our political position. . . . These
days you are really never sure whether you're in a lunatic asylum
or not!" The *Daily Telegraph* affair had borne out the humorists'
warnings of the effect of absolute power on an unstable personality, and proved the baneful impact of theatrical politics on the
real world. *Simplicissimus* and *Kladderadatsch* joined the vast
majority of German publications in calling for constitutional
changes which would limit the kaiser's power. *Simplicissimus*
presented its own version of a painting which Wilhelm had commissioned to warn of the "Yellow Peril" by placing Wilhelm in
the place of the menacing orientals. Retaining the painting's original title, "People of Europe, defend your most treasured possessions," the satirists portrayed royal irresponsibility as a greater
danger than foreign aggression. But the protest came to nothing;
Wilhelm was not called to account for his actions or forced to
behave more responsibly. *Simplicissimus* angrily protested:

Anger, disbelief, dismay
Seethes throughout the Press today
"Who will save us?" they all say,
But from WHOM is never said.
We all know who is to blame
But we dare not speak his name.
So "the System's" blamed instead.[13]

The satirical picture of Wilhelm as an actor absorbed in his
role showed great psychological insight, for, as many observers

agreed, Wilhelm was compensating through an arrogant exterior for intense feelings of insecurity. One can see in his physical deformity—an obstetrical blunder had left his arm permanently withered—a cause of such feelings. More importantly, his job of leading a great empire was far too demanding for one with his mediocre talents. Walter Rathenau remembered from an audience with Wilhelm not an overwhelming personality but an ordinary, well meaning man trying desperately to live up to his part. He was "a real prince; always thinking about his image, always struggling with himself to keep the necessary poise, strength, control. Hardly a relaxed moment." Such role-playing, one biographer noted, caused a tension so acute as to bring on psychosomatic illness. "The strain of forcing himself to act as he thought he should do had physical consequences in bouts of acute neuralgia. At critical moments, as in 1907, 1908, and 1918, this lack of confidence and staying power became a complete loss of nerve, accompanied by such symptoms as giddiness and shivering." Though on one level Wilhelm's role was a publicity stunt, on another it was an escape from intolerable tension into a fantasy world of his own making. Though not, as Quidde sometimes implied, actually insane, Wilhelm was, as the satirists perceived him, a dangerously unstable, sometimes deluded man.[14]

Though by far the most powerful, Wilhelm was by no means the only reigning monarch in the German Reich. From 1909 to 1914 *Simplicissimus*' criticism of the Wittelsbach dynasty attracted as much attention in Bavaria as did its lampoons on the kaiser. Again *Simplicissimus* emphasized the incongruous contrast between ideal and reality, between the monarchs' high-flown pretensions and their real human inadequacy. A controversial cartoon in the 1909 "Manövernummer" (Maneuver Issue) portrayed a fierce-looking Kaiser Wilhelm instructing Ludwig III of Bavaria, depicted as senile and feeble-minded. "Prince Ludwig and the Bavarian generals are presented as the purest stereotypes of intellectual and moral degeneracy—in short, it's the worst possible insult!" thundered one right-wing newspaper, while another protested the "incredibly insulting caricature which ridicules Prince Ludwig of Bavaria by showing him next to the impressive German Emperor." Actually, the cartoon, captioned "the Kaiser shows the King of Bavaria the enemy positions," mocked both monarchs, the fierce and the feeble, for their pompous affectation of military valor in this thoroughly imaginary war game.[15]

The most notorious of the anti-Wittelsbach issues criticized

Ludwig III for selling the magnificent royal art collection housed in the Pinakothek to the Bavarian state for a considerable profit. Ludwig's alleged betrayal of the dynastic tradition of patronage of the arts was lampooned in a cartoon showing the ghost of his grandfather, Ludwig I, warning the Bavarian minister of culture, von Knilling, "Now see to it that my temple of art does not become a milk-market for Leutstetten." A verse by Edgar Steiger in the same issue similarly deplored the reigning king's refusal to support the Prinzregententheater, founded by Ludwig II and famous for performances of Wagnerian opera. The concluding stanza strongly implied that the king's refusal to purchase the theater from the real-estate firm of Heilmann was a selfish abandonment of his responsibility for the welfare of the arts in Bavaria. His calculating parsimony was contrasted to the lavish generosity of his forebears.

> And Richard Wagner? Götterdämmerung!
> Forget about him! chortle old and young.
> He's lost amid the crafty bargaining,
> Of Heilmann's agents and our Lord the King.[16]

On June 2, 1914, three *Simplicissimus* staff members, Ernst Freissler, then "responsible editor," Olaf Gulbransson, who had created the cartoon, and Edgar Steiger, author of the jingle, were brought to trial on a charge of *Majestätsbeleidigung* for an issue of which (in the words of the prosecutor) "the intention and the content, the purpose and the meaning injured the honor of his Majesty, in the most serious possible way." Freissler defended the cartoon on the grounds that it merely contrasted the "exaggerated artistic enthusiasm of Ludwig I" with his grandson's "interest in practical things," especially agriculture (hence the reference to the "milk market") with no intent to insult either the former or the latter. While Gulbransson protested that he had not been consulted about the caption to be placed under his cartoon, Steiger likewise claimed that the meaning of his verse had been altered by a misprint in the final line, where the substitution of "and" for the intended "with" had accidentally implicated Ludwig in a critical remark directed only at Heilmann. The prosecution quite rightly dismissed these thoroughly unconvincing arguments and referred the case for jury trial—never held because of the outbreak of the war, when *Simplicissimus'* patriotic response moved the Bavarian government to pardon its old offenses.[17]

By drawing a contrast between irresponsible reigning monarchs, whether Hohenzollern or Wittelsbach, and their more respected forebears, the satirists protested not so much the institution of monarchy itself as its deterioration in a modern society to which it was no longer appropriate. This view of monarchy was not lacking in nostalgia—indeed, *Kladderadatsch* wistfully recalled an age in which monarchs (in this case Wilhelm I) had enjoyed the genuine confidence of their subjects:

> We didn't drink too much, or sing
> And speeches weren't expected,
> But every word of our great King,
> Was treasured and respected.
> And all the words our Kaiser spoke,
> He spoke for all the German folk.

But contemporary monarchies sought to compensate for their loss of genuine authority through theatrical sham. Not only the political but the aesthetic instincts of the satirists were repelled by the debasement of the once-cherished language and symbolism of patriotism through melodramatic and artificial overuse. In a scathing review of a rather too complete edition of the kaiser's speeches, Ludwig Thoma protested that the stirring words of a royal after-dinner speech might have been appropriate on a battlefield, but "when the death-defying officers are expected to do nothing in response except to shout 'Hurrah!' and empty their glasses, there is a gross contrast—incidentally profoundly unaesthetic—between inspiring phrase and meaningless action. It is noise, and nothing else." That an increasing segment of the public had begun to share Thoma's opinion was pointed out by Maximilian Harden on the tenth anniversary of Wilhelm's accession. "You have been lied to for years, Herr Kaiser," he warned. "Contrary to what has been told you, the popular mood is a growing source of anxiety even to the warmest supporters of monarchy." As artists, the *Simplicissimus* group perceived the tasteless artificiality of the lavish display of royal magnificence before an increasingly disaffected audience. But theatrical politics was not only absurd but dangerous. "None of us was so clairvoyant," wrote Ludwig Thoma, "as to see the consequences of these musical-comedy politics, but we knew it was ridiculous, and behind our mockery lay a very lively discontent. And it was natural that artists, especially, should be repelled by the whole show."[18]

Behind the Scenes: The Aristocracy

Wilhelm's flamboyant public image provided a facade of authority for a government which the fall of Bismarck had plunged into a permanent state of crisis. Unable himself to exercise effective leadership, Wilhelm was often perceived as the tool of his aristocratic entourage, who ruthlessly pursued the narrow interests of their class. As important as the attack on the kaiser himself was the exposure of dishonest, corrupt, or incompetent advisors. "The audience to whom theatre is presented as reality," notes Harry Pross in his study of Wilhelmine political literature, "develop an insatiable need to see into the wings. They want to know *who* pulls the strings, where the lighting comes from. And the longer the person remains in the role of spectator the stronger the desire becomes." There were urgent political reasons for such curiosity. Seldom reading newspapers, learning of current events only from biased advisors, Wilhelm was isolated from public opinion. He listened, or so his critics maintained, only to flatterers. "No one forces his rambling fantasy into the narrow limits of plain reality," complained Maximilian Harden. "No one dispels the charming illusions or warns against the overestimation of the power of the Reich." "Court etiquette and, even more, the cringing adulation of everybody who flocks around the ruler," charged Quidde, "gives him the idea that he is exalted above all other men . . . whatever he does, he never confronts an open and courageous opposition." Deprived of legitimate political influence over the kaiser's entourage, frustrated critics often tried to discredit influential aristocrats by scandal. Such scandals, given wide publicity by satirical magazines, sometimes achieved substantial public impact.[19]

The most elaborate of these was the so-called "*Kladderadatsch* affair" of 1893–94. On December 24, 1893, *Kladderadatsch* published a seemingly innocent little fable entitled "A Fourth at Skat," asserting that a "permanent diplomatic Skat" game had been held for the past year in Berlin. The "game" had three permanent players: "Privy Councellor Oysterfriend . . . who stays in the background but has already outplayed chancellors and ambassadors," Privy Councellor Sparrow, "a droll fellow . . . who gets people into a good mood and then finishes them off," and "Count Troubadour." Those acquainted with the court circle easily recognized the three players: "Oysterfriend" as the gourmet Friedrich von Holstein, an enigmatic and immensely powerful official at the Foreign Ministry; "Sparrow" as the gossip-loving Alfred von Kiderlen-Wächter, later to become foreign minister; and "Troubadour" as Philipp zu Eulenburg, Wilhelm's closest personal friend. The "fourth" who had been added to the game was Baron Varnbüler, a close personal friend of Eulenburg who had just been awarded a diplomatic post. Political appointments, the fable implied, depended on cronyism and intrigue. Moreover, the appointment of Varnbüler continued a trend toward the removal of officials still loyal to Bismarck and their replacement by royal favorites. Thus when *Kladderadatsch* attacked Wilhelm's new advisors, knowledgeable people at once suspected Bismarck's connivance.[20]

In ever more obvious ways the attacks on the so-called "Camarilla" continued in subsequent issues. Harden, who probably wrote some of the articles, later gleefully described the court's reaction. "The situation," he remarked, "soon became more serious; giggles and whispers were suppressed and the mood changed from malicious amusement to astonishment. . . . It was a triumph for *Kladderadatsch* and actually a most convincing proof of the truth of the accusations that in spite of the disguised names the principal characters were recognized at once by anyone who was at all familiar with the situation."[21]

The reactions of the three men reflected their different personalities. Holstein immediately suspected an inside source, perhaps Bismarck or his son Herbert, and angrily rebuked the kaiser for not publicly defending him. Kiderlen, a less morose character, was at first amused but then seriously alarmed as he joined in the search for the informer. Eulenburg had probably discovered the villain, for the attacks against him suddenly ceased, presumably because of some secret agreement. But Eulenburg warned Wilhelm of a Bismarckian plot to oust the three advisors and to regain control at court. Was Bismarck trying to stage a comeback?[22]

On January 21, 1894, *Kladderadatsch* published another fable, this one concerning a king who, learning of the treachery of three unfaithful servants (whom *Kladderadatsch* called "Intriguans, "Insinuans," and "Calumnians"), threw them into a fiery furnace. When, a month later, neither Holstein nor Kiderlen had resigned, the humorists finally named them directly. "In high government circles it has always been known *exactly* against whom our attacks were directed. Nevertheless these two [Holstein and Kiderlen, for by this time Eulenburg was no longer a target] have neither sued us nor handed in their resignations. There is no fun in attacking such passive gentlemen."[23]

Holstein and Kiderlen, who had indeed considered a libel suit, had decided against it, for such a suit, they concluded, would do more to publicize *Kladderadatsch* than to clear themselves. Another means of redress was the duel which, though theoretically illegal, was still a widespread custom among upper-class Germans. Holstein sent his seconds to Herbert Bismarck, who then publicly denied any role in the "affair." Kiderlen actually fought Wilhelm Polstorff, the associate editor of *Kladderadatsch,* who was wounded in the arm.[24]

The fact that the editors of *Kladderadatsch* were willing to risk their lives to defend their accusations showed that satire was a serious business. At least in the short-term sense *Kladderadatsch* had failed, for none of the three men actually resigned. Yet because of the substantial public reaction which it provoked, the "affair" served the long-term purpose of undermining the prestige of the kaiser and his government. The angry reactions of Holstein and Kiderlen showed that even the haughtiest aristocrats now feared the might of public opinion. *Kladderadatsch* ceased its campaign after three months. Polstorff, nursing a wounded arm, was living proof that attacking high officials was risky.[25]

Another blow against the court clique was Maximilian Harden's campaign against Eulenburg. In the hard-hitting editor's exposure of Eulenburg's bisexual tendencies, the satirical journals played an important though subordinate role. Harden, who had cogent political reasons for his opposition to Eulenburg, used the sexual scandal chiefly as a lever to pry him out of office. To the public, however, homosexuality was the main issue. *Simplicissimus* used the case as a convenient pretext for two issues packed from cover to cover with homosexual jokes. It noted the immense public interest in the sensational evidence at the trial of Eulenburg's libel suit against Harden:

> Everybody wants to know
> Is he homo? Hetero?
> Is he nice? And well bred?
> Just what *does* he do in bed?

. . . .
Interesting? Fascinating!
Hear the ladies speculating
As they sit and watch the show
Is he homo? Hetero?[26]

While thus publicizing the scandal, however, the humorists of
Simplicissimus gave more than merely perfunctory consideration
to its sordid, even tragic aspects. In general the humorous magazines *Simplicissimus, Jugend,* and *Kladderadatsch* showed little
fondness for the more vicious kind of personal attack. Indeed,
the only defense of Harden's methods was that they worked, forcing the kaiser to repudiate his friend and thus terminating Eulenburg's political career. In the absence of legitimate avenues for
political dissent, frustrated protestors often turn to illegitimate
means. The Eulenburg case revealed the sordid realities concealed behind the glittering facade of the imperial court.[27]

With the smooth Eulenburg and the subtle Holstein the ordinary country Junker might seem to have little in common. Indeed, by their constant jibes at his crudity and ignorance, the
Witzblätter deflated the Junker's claims to the tradition of aristocracy. The countrified squire's lack of cultural sophistication
had been lampooned since 1848 in a favorite *Kladderadatsch* feature, the correspondence of Prudelwitz and Strudelwitz. "Don't
really know why a bunch of broken bits of marble have to be kept
in a special building," remarks Prudelwitz after a visit to the Per-
gamon Museum. "Anyway the most interesting parts of the stat-
ues are busted. If we really must have them around, let's keep
them in the packing room." What *Kladderadatsch* had expressed
verbally, *Simplicissimus* suggested pictorially through a cartoon
entitled "The Agrarians in Berlin," in which two fat pigs, be-
decked with iron crosses and monocles, wallow in a rose garden
(the image referred to both the Junkers' alleged personality traits
and their obsessive concern with livestock prices). Thus the satirists expressed an opinion similar to that of Max Weber, who
reproached the Junkers for their lack of the cultivation and ef-
fortless gentility which marked a long-standing aristocracy such
as that of England.[28]

Both the sophisticated courtier and his coarse country cousin,
however, were accused of deviousness, trickery, and irresponsible self-interest. Again, the satirists' judgment resembled that of
Weber, who argued that the Junker's pretentious self-image as "an

aristocracy, replete with feudal gestures and pretensions" was but a masquerade covering his true identity as businessman and entrepreneur. The Junker as parvenu, justifying his ruthless pursuit of commercial self-interest through patriotic rhetoric, was bitterly denounced by both *Kladderadatsch* and *Simplicissimus.* A *Kladderadatsch* verse, "Song of the Agrarians," protested a new round of protective tariffs.

> Our goal is just our country's good,
> All greed we do decry.
> As long, that is, as prices rise
> On spirits, wheat, and rye.
>
> For liberty our hearts beat high
> Free labor, competition,
> As long as tenant farmers can't
> Improve their own condition.
>
> "The Press is free!" we loudly cry
> "To speak and write the truth."
> But anyone who bad-mouths *us*
> Had better shut his mouth.[29]

A *Simplicissimus* verse entitled "The East Elbians" commented still more sharply on aristocratic scheming:

> For he's an aristocrat
> Loyal to his King
> Who will grab what he can get—
> All and everything.

Thus, like that of their royal master, the Junkers' histrionic bombast debased the tone of public life. A contemporary historian, Hans Rosenberg, remarked on the Agrarian League's use of "the lie as the handmaiden of power. . . . The resulting confusion and disorientation of political values led to objective dishonesty, hollow rhetoric and crass cynicism, functional qualities of a group which in real life could often be combined with subjective honesty and personal decency."[30]

Moreover, the Junker's role as feudal landlord was increasingly artificial in the modern age. The picture of an idyllic village life publicized by the Agrarian League was discredited by the flight of peasants from the land to a better life in the cities. In a heavy-handed attempt to preserve their labor supply, landlords often attempted to prohibit publications which might spread dangerous ideas in rural communities. Such repression under the guise of paternalistic concern was mocked by *Kladderadatsch*:

> My friend, you're finished with the weeding,
> Why don't you rest and do some reading?
> For fun or education?
> But don't go down to the café,
> And read the Liberal press today
> That's an abomination!
> But ask the *Landrat* if you can—
> That upright, patriotic man!—
> What he would recommend.
> If you obey him piously
> An anarchist you'll never be,
> But happy to the end.[31]

Simplicissimus criticized another aspect of the Junker's feudal ideology—his oppression of the Polish population of East Prussia. Unlike *Kladderadatsch,* which shied away from this controversial topic, *Simplicissimus* responded to the Polish school strike of 1906, a protest against regulations enforcing the use of the German language in schools, with a cartoon entitled "The Descendants of the Teutonic Knights." It showed Prussian policemen with drawn swords chasing Polish children to school and snarling, "You lousy Poles, of course you have to learn German— *we* had to!" *Simplicissimus* thus accurately perceived the harmful effects of aristocratic neofeudalism as a doctrine not only of class ascendancy but of national and racial superiority as well.[32]

Thus by revealing the ineptitude and self-seeking which lay behind the pompous facade of monarchy, the satirists made a strong case for reform. Max Weber refuted the common objection to democracy—its dependence on the presumably uninformed and emotional "masses"—by pointing out that the masses could hardly be more guilty of these faults than their leaders. "A monarchy ruling by a system of class suffrage," Weber concluded, "holds the record for purely personal emotion and irrational mood influencing leadership." Like Weber, the satirists hoped to achieve a more stable government by placing power in the hands of a presumably more sober and responsible middle class. But was the middle class capable of assuming responsibility?[33]

The Ugly Little German

Simplicissimus and *Kladderadatsch* urged their middle-class readers not only to criticism but to activism. Unlike the incompetent monarchs and aristocrats, the middle class—educated, industrious, enterprising—was equipped to exercise a genuine authority based not on inflated pretensions but on real skills. But much to their frustration the satirists perceived the Wilhelmine bourgeoisie not as critics but as avid spectators at the royal pageant, preferring this vicarious fantasy of power to the real power of which they had been deprived. Thus in tones which combined sympathy, contempt, and exhortation, the satirists called on the German middle class to throw off its artificial feudalized and monarchist "personality" and return to its true heritage, the liberalism of 1848. By contrast to the simple upper- and lower-class stereotypes, the *Witzblätter* portrayed a great variety of middle-class types, revealing the satirists' more complex and subtle view of the class from which they themselves originated.

Middle-class *Untertanengeist* was a frequent and fruitful theme for humor. *Simplicissimus* summed up the basic problem in a cartoon entitled "We are too much governed," showing the German body politic as an emaciated donkey vainly attempting to carry a priest and a soldier over a threatening abyss:

I passively bend to the blows
Of the merciless bridle and reins
What a long-suffering beast!
What a long-suffering beast!

A dutiful ass always shows
The patience to bear his pains
To everything I say "Ja-a-a!"
To everything I say "Ja-a-a!"[34]

Another cartoon showed the complacent citizen as a beer-drinking baby, blissfully oblivious to the shaky bridge over which his policeman-angel-nursemaid wheels his perambulator. One of Ludwig Thoma's verses (under his pen name, Peter Schlemihl)

"The Germans' Guardian Angel." "Whatever may betide me, my angel is beside me." (Heine, *Simplicissimus*, Oct. 18, 1909.)

presented the monarchist ideology as a lullaby for docile and sleepy children.

Subjects are like little children
Needing a restraining hand,
Sometimes firm and sometimes kindly—
So we serve the Fatherland.
Michelchen, now you be good!
Michelchen, now don't be rude!
Michelchen, now stop that, do!
I'll tell Grandpapa on you!

Images of docile animals and small children implied not only passivity but regression. For all its wealth and education, the German middle class, or so the satirists charged, had retreated from the responsibilities of adulthood into an artificial state of dependency.[35]

Certainly one major motive for middle-class conformity was economic greed. In a system based on a coalition of aristocrats and industrialists, conservative rhetoric could be very good for business. Like the Junker, the industrialist concealed crass economic motives under a patriotic facade:

Our Fatherland we do adore
And yet we love Another more
Our love is strong and sweet as honey
For all our money!

Long live the King! Long may he reign!
We toast him in our fine champagne,
And yet we will break still more lances,
For our finances.

For God and for the Church we strive,
We hope religion will survive,
For without God things might go worse
For our fat purse!

Kladderadatsch condemned the irresponsible self-seeking of the old and new elites by picturing a tiny figure labelled "middle class" crushed between two figures representing the Agrarian League and the Central Association of Industrialists.[36]

Yet the charge of ambition and mindless conformity was directed not simply against the very rich but against all segments of the bourgeoisie—lawyers, politicians, professors, clergy. The tendency of these professionals to political conservatism had been reinforced by the recruiting and promotion policies of the government bureaucracy, to which many belonged. Discrimination against liberal officials belied the ideal of the "unpolitical" bureaucrat and discouraged innovation and creativity by penalizing any manifestation of nonconformity.[37]

Both *Kladderadatsch* and *Simplicissimus* mocked the frantic struggle of civil servants to avoid the least suspicion of disloyalty. One such anecdote concerned a solid citizen who had (by mistake, we presume) bought a parrot previously owned by a socialist. One evening, during a large and important dinner party, the parrot joins the conversation and says "things—well just hearing them everyone turned white as chalk, their hair stood on end, and goose pimples rose on many a bald crown. Malicious observers, of course, thought the parrot had learned these shocking things from the Privy Counsellor. The unfortunate host, mad with fear, ripped the tablecloth with everything on it off the table and threw it over the cage to silence the bird. When he looked around he saw that he was alone in the room. He could still hear the last guests as they thundered down the stairs as if they were escaping from a fire. . . . The big mirror in the hall was broken— no doubt one of the guests had mistaken it for an exit and had run into it. On the stairs were many medals which had been ripped off in the mêlée. The professional and social position of the unfortunate man is said to be very badly damaged. He's lucky not to fall into the hands of the prosecutor!" The role-playing required by the civil service must have imposed considerable emotional stress, and it would perhaps not be too fanciful to see the parrot as the repressed wish which breaks through the rigid controls.[38]

But along with blind obedience to superiors, the civil service encouraged a no-less-rigid contempt for social inferiors, particularly evident in the legal profession. Ludwig Thoma, who had been trained as a lawyer, criticised the pedantic bookishness of legal education which estranged lawyers and judges from the real-life problems which caused crime. "It was offensive and rather funny," recalled Thoma, "how little the experienced jurist knew of the people among whom he lived." Such ignorance, combined with the political conservatism required by the Puttkamer system—especially of the elite who held the prestigious position of *Staatsanwalt,* or state prosecutor—produced a harsh and prejudiced judicial mentality. In a special issue entitled "Our Judges," Thoma described the attitudes of ambitious young prosecutors:

With prejudices unabated
They view "the people" with suspicion,
From common folk they're separated,
By titles, honors, high position.

For God, for King, as is the fashion,
They hand down judgments stern and hard,
They shun remorse and "false compassion"—
Such loyalty has its reward.

The middle-aged judge still showed the influence of his training. In spite of constitutional provisions for equal justice, the Wilhelmine court system often discriminated against lower-class defendants. *Simplicissimus* exposed such class prejudice in two cartoons. The first portrayed an obese judge snarling at an old beggar woman. "Oh, you begged because you were hungry, you say? Well, I know all about that!" The second, entitled "Experienced Judges," showed one judge saying to another, "Today we've handed down one hundred and thirty years of prison sentences. You know, I'd almost like to go and look at one of those jails." Thus by contrast to *Kladderadatsch,* which portrayed the successful bourgeois chiefly as lackey to the upper classes, *Simplicissimus* revealed another dimension of the *Untertanengeist* by showing him as oppressor of the lower classes as well.[39]

Such satirical comments reproached the German bourgeoisie for having made a very shoddy bargain. Having renounced the real political power which was their right, they now frantically pursued the baubles handed down by the ruling class—titles, decorations, and what Max Weber called "a kind of second-class reception at court." Observing the frantic and undignified struggle for advancement at the price of integrity, many satirists regarded the pursuit of conventional "success" with skepticism, even contempt. Ludwig Thoma forsook a legal career which he found stifling and confining for a far less secure future as a journalist. In a piece entitled "The Class Reunion" the well known satirist Karl Kraus reminisced, "Bald-headed men sit together and remember the time when they had done nothing, but had the potential to do something. Now they've done something but they've still done nothing. Nevertheless, they've spent twenty-five years acquiring spectacles, beards, and bellies." Here again, by implication, is the theme of role-playing and masquerade—the outward signs of success covering the inner emptiness.[40]

The kaiser cult was the most extreme expression of middle-class *Untertanengeist.* Even his severest critics were forced to ad-mit the extraordinary appeal of the kaiser's personality for the German public. One observer, Walther Rathenau, saw the emperor as the embodiment of an insecure generation's fantasies of power and virility. "The people of his time," explained Rathenau, "consciously and unconsciously wanted him as he was, and not otherwise, and themselves wanted to be what they saw in him. In the indescribable drama of history Clio had decided, in one great figure, to show the German people their own nature, their alienation from themselves, their idol, and their ruin. Never before had a living human being so perfectly mirrored an epoch, nor an epoch a man."[41]

While *Kladderadatsch* drew back from direct comment on the kaiser cult (presumably because of possible legal difficulties), *Simplicissimus* attacked it with considerable relish. Some jokes on the kaiser cult were light, but others were scathing, using concrete images of physical degradation to dramatize psychological realities. A *Simplicissimus* cartoon entitled "The Cigarette-Butt, or True Popularity," showed a writhing heap of well-dressed citizens fighting over the butt which the prince on parade had carelessly discarded. Leaving nothing to the imagination, *Simplicissimus* graphically described the retrieval of the precious object:

> It fell upon some horse-manure,
> Just as our Prince came riding by,
> The whole crowd stepped on it, I'm sure,
> And horses pissed on it, but I
> Was mad to get it, come what may,
> So undeterred by horses, men,
> And filth, I ran to where it lay,
> And gladly licked it clean again.

Even without exploring the possibly Freudian implications of such imagery, one can see that the theme is masochistic. The satirists portrayed a citizen who so lacked a sense of his own identity that he strove even at the cost of extreme degradation to identify himself with a powerful and domineering figure.[42]

Much the deepest and most perceptive picture of the kaiser cult was Heinrich Mann's *Der Untertan* (*The Subject*), the first few chapters of which appeared in *Simplicissimus*. A comparison between Mann's characters and those of *Simplicissimus* confirms his nephew Golo's assertion that the book was inspired by the magazine. The name of Mann's hero, Diederich Hessling—roughly translatable as "The Ugly Little German"—leaves little doubt as to the parabolic significance of the tale.

Mann's account of the education of an *Untertan* through family, school, university, and military service reaches a climax in a chapter entitled "The Riot" (*Der Krawall*), which describes the hero's first sight of his royal idol. Setting the scene for this significant chapter, Mann skillfully highlights the political and psychological roots of the kaiser cult. At the beginning we find the impressionable Diederich listening raptly to the political harangue of one of his fashionably conservative student fraternity brothers who denounces liberalism (identified as a subversive Jewish doctrine) as "the precondition of socialism," and advocates a society based on a class system, "as in the Middle Ages." Still bemused by this thoroughly romantic and artificial ideology, Diederich on his way home accidentally finds himself in the midst of a mass demonstration of unemployed workers, overwhelmed by "the slow-moving flood . . . this sad and discolored sea of the poor." Unequipped with personal courage or with real political convictions, Diederich feels hostile, confused, deeply frightened by social problems which he does not understand. But suddenly he catches sight of a figure on a white horse, riding into the crowd. "It's Wilhelm!" gasps a nearby onlooker. Now the demonstration has no further terrors for Diederich. "If it were up to me, we'd wipe out these subversives right away! We've got our Kaiser!" A man in "an artist's hat" remarks cynically that the kaiser's dramatic but meaningless gesture is "theater, and not even new!" A veteran of Sedan recalls more genuine triumphs. "This is just as good as Sedan!" cries Diederich, unable to distinguish between theater and reality. "Ecstasy," remarks Mann, "higher and sweeter than he got from beer, raised him onto his toes and carried him through the air, on a cloud of hectic enthusiasm, in a heaven of exalted feelings! On that horse there, under the triumphal arch, rode Power! Power! which tramples us and whose hooves we kiss! . . . Which we have in our blood, because servility is in our blood! . . . Each individual a nonentity, we line up in disciplined ranks, as army, bureaucracy, Church, and school, right up to the top where Power sits stony and flashing! We live, move, and have our being in it, crushing those who are farther from it!" As usual, the fantasy of power is contrasted with the reality of physical and psychological degradation. Pursuing the kaiser through the streets, Diederich slips and falls full length in a mud puddle. "A real monarchist!" laughs the kaiser, and turns once again to his companions.[43]

Lacking a well-developed personality of his own, Diederich strives to imitate the aggressive and flashy manners of his idol.

In the later chapters of the novel (not published in *Simplicissi-mus*) Mann deplored the widespread imitation of the kaiser's rhetorical style among his subjects. "Public life," declares one of the novel's liberal characters, "has taken on the atmosphere of a second-rate comedy. Loyalty must dress up in a costume; the manufacturers of tin and papers speechify like Crusaders and draw their swords for an idea such as 'Majesty' which no one believes in anymore, not even in fairy tales." Perceptive observers attrib-uted this elaborate role-playing to the lack of confidence of a na-tion without a secure sense of identity. "In Germany," lamented Walther Rathenau, "even the love of country has not found a cul-turally valid form of expression. Servile devotion and the noisy patriotism of business societies are not balanced by a secure na-tional consciousness."[44]

The humorists thus called upon the bourgeoisie to return to itself—to forsake the theatrical trappings for the reality of polit-ical power. The revolution of 1848 was constantly commemo-rated, especially by *Kladderadatsch* on its sixtieth anniversary in 1908. On that occasion *Simplicissimus* reproached Germans for denying the revolutionary tradition.

> You glorious heroes! Death was nought
> To you, for you still saw the vision
> Of the free future you had wrought,
> But now, they hold you in derision.
>
> They deck themselves with decorations
> And laugh at you, "Blind fools!" they say,
> Oh, how much greater is our nation,
> And how much smaller we today.

In March 1908 a cartoon contrasting the red-capped and warlike "Michel" of 1848 with his passive and sleepy descendant com-plained that "the red cap has faded so much over sixty years that one could almost mistake it for a sleeping cap." The same com-plaint was echoed by progressive liberal spokesmen such as Fried-rich Naumann. "For contemporary liberalism," he remarked, "it is of great value never to forget what 1848 meant to our histo-ry. There are liberals today to whom it seems almost unpleasant to remember the heroic days of their own movement."[45]

In ironic contrast to the militant of 1848, both *Kladderadatsch* and *Simplicissimus* portrayed the cautiously opportunistic lib-eral of the Wilhelmine period. A *Simplicissimus* cartoon entitled "The National Liberal" showed one such earnest and bespectacled politician orating solemnly, "Here I stand. I could also do otherwise. God help me. Amen." The Bülow bloc of 1907—a parliamentary coalition of the Conservatives, National Liberals, Progressives, and several other parties, which the crafty chancellor had precariously brought together by appealing to their common fear of socialism—inspired bitter comments on National Liberal spinelessness. *Kladderadatsch* portrayed Bülow as a high priest attempting the impossible task of conciliating a ferocious Janus, one of whose faces is labelled "Progress" and the other "Reaction." *Simplicissimus* tirelessly castigated the liberals and progressives for their sellout to conservative interests. "Now our little tree should grow right up to the sky," one liberal is shown saying to another. "We've certainly fertilized it with enough bullshit." The failure of the bloc and the subsequent conservative-clerical alliance once again confirmed the triumph of reaction over progress. *Kladderadatsch* turned a dirge for the Bülow bloc into a totally pessimistic indictment of the decadent modern age:

Everywhere I turn my gaze,
Naught but emptiness I see,
Glory of the olden days,
Now has turned to misery.
Weakness, cowardice I spy,
Impotence and selfishness.
"Backward!, Backward!" is the cry—
We'll all go along, I guess.[46]

Criticism of the sham parliamentary system of the Empire could often turn into an indictment of party politics itself. Fritz Stern has described the "unpolitical" spirit of the German middle class, which viewed parliamentary politics as divisive, self-seeking, and undignified. This "unpolitical" ideal emerged in a *Kladderadatsch* verse commemorating the liberal politician Rudolf Bennigsen and mourning the alleged deterioration of contemporary politics.

The parties squabble now in wild confusion,
All waving in the market-place one banner—
Self-interest! The people are bamboozled
By flatterers and crafty charlatans.

But such fastidious idealism ignored the function of the parliamentary process—to provide legitimate expression for the inevitable conflicts between interest groups. The mistrust of political controversy, the longing for what Hans-Ulrich Wehler has described as a "conflict-free Utopia," also reflected the example and legacy of Bismarck. "The scorn with which Bismarck regarded the professional politician," stated progressive leader Friedrich Naumann, "was accepted as if it were an eternal and universal value." The work of the satirists often showed the conflict between the activism of liberals and the aesthetic revulsion of artists against the day-to-day realities of politics.[47]

The full ambivalence of their attitudes toward parliamentary politics emerged in their response to the *Daily Telegraph* affair of 1908. In addition to angry comments on Wilhelm's character, the affair at last provoked a massive demand for parliamentary controls on his power. *Simplicissimus* commented ironically on the most unusual behavior of respectable citizens.

> What has happened? Can you guess?
> Lord, what a disgusting mess!
> Liberals are in distress,
> But the cunning Reds just smile.
> Privy Counsellors, they say,
> Now commit lèse Majesté
> In most unaccustomed style.

But while publicizing public outrage, both *Witzblätter* also encouraged citizens to avoid their own political responsibility by placing the blame for the incident squarely on Wilhelm himself. For Wilhelm had behaved constitutionally in submitting the text of the interview to Bülow for approval. In this case, therefore, the fault lay not with the leader himself, who for once had behaved responsibly, but with the system which allowed any one individual power without accountability.[48]

To be sure, the satirical journals joined other organs of public opinion in advocating constitutional checks on the emperor's power. But *Kladderadatsch* expressed continued dependence on leadership by urging not the elected Reichstag but the thoroughly unreliable Bülow to take the constitutional initiative:

> We hope amid this sad confusion,
> That Wilhelm *Imperator Rex,*
> Will not persist in the delusion,
> That he is our *Suprema Lex.*

Well, Bülow, tell us—tell us true,
You share our hope and our ambition?
We trust that if you really do,
You'll bring our hope to its fruition.

And when the slippery Bülow, who probably never considered constitutional change, proved predictably inadequate to the task, *Kladderadatsch* lamented not the passivity of the Reichstag but the absence of Bismarck, who would never have allowed such an incident to occur.[49]

Simplicissimus by contrast deplored the servility of the German people, who had not seized the opportunity to change the system. Again, the German "Michel" was portrayed as a colicky baby, soothed by its royal father, or as the castrated ox:

Oxen can't turn into stallions,
Some are strong and some are weak,
So don't worry, all you Germans,
Shut up, let your betters speak.[50]

In their satirical treatment of the bourgeoisie the humorists thus attempted to create not only negative or critical images but positive ones as well. Both by mocking undesirable behavior (the "feudalized" manners and attitudes of the upper middle class) and by encouraging more constructive alternatives (the revival of the militant liberalism of 1848), these jokes were intended to forge a new sense of solidarity and purpose among the group to which they primarily appealed. Indeed the often noted popularity of *Simplicissimus,* especially among the very "solid citizens" whom it unmercifully lampooned, suggests the growth of critical and self-critical attitudes among the middle class. But the satirists' attempt to replace the false idols of the kaiser cult with more genuine heroes reflected a central problem of German history, which had produced few examples of middle-class political activism. Even the revolutionaries of 1848 were not the fearless and committed militants wistfully portrayed by *Simplicissimus.* Thus by contrast to the vivid and telling negative stereotypes—the noisy patriot, the greedy industrialist, the stuffy bureaucrat—the positive message remained confused and ambiguous, combining exhortations to political participation with traditional aversion to the parliamentary system. One could object that caricature is in itself a negative art, more effective in debunking than in glorifying its subject. But the failure of the liberal *Witzblätter* to pre-

sent a convincingly positive liberal ideal attests also to the sense
of political impotence which haunted the German middle class.

The Social Question

The theatrical spectacle staged by the ruling class for its bemused audience could not remain undisturbed. The socialist
movement relentlessly called attention to social problems which
could not be solved by flashy rhetoric. The ruling class, to be
sure, resisted such invasions of their fantasy world. A *Simplicissimus* cartoon entitled "Jaurès Rejected" depicted the French
socialist leader confronting a gaily costumed band of armored
knights, courtiers, and clergy. "Although guests are often and
lavishly received in Berlin," read the caption, "Jaurès was rejected. How understandable! He came as a representative of the
people, in a simple suit. But politics in Berlin is a fancy-dress
ball, where only those in costumes are admitted." Nonetheless
as its electoral support grew, the socialist movement could be
neither suppressed nor ignored. The movement, and the social
problems to which it called attention, were major themes of both
Kladderadatsch and *Simplicissimus.* Although in basic agreement in their views of the upper and middle classes, the two
magazines diverged sharply in their images of the worker. The
contrast between the doctrinaire, laissez-faire views of *Kladderadatsch* and the social activism of *Simplicissimus* will illustrate
an important trend in the evolution of German and indeed of European liberalism. But despite the wide variance in both attitudes
and style, both magazines also expressed the very ambivalent,
often fearful, reaction of a privileged middle class to the workers'
demand for economic and social equality. The liberal, in fact,
found himself in a vulnerable position, crushed between two
powerful and alien forces—an inflexible governing class and a
militant workers' movement. In the humorous treatment of social
antagonisms we can often perceive the frustrations of a moderate
attempting to cope with an increasingly polarized political situation.[51]

The *Kladderadatsch* of the 1890s adhered unswervingly to the
traditional idea of free enterprise supported by the majority of
the National Liberal party and most eloquently voiced by liberal
spokesman Eugen Richter. The satirists of *Kladderadatsch* reacted to Wilhelm's early attempt at welfare legislation much as

they had responded to Bismarck's social insurance program a decade before. During the 1890s a powerful advocate of Bismarckian social policies was Wilhelm's chief economic advisor, the industrialist Freiherr von Stumm-Halberg, whose own labor relations policy combined wide-ranging welfare provisions with a ruthless suppression of trade union or socialist activity. Not wholly without reason, *Kladderadatsch* lampooned such politics as a return to feudal paternalism, as in this alleged list of "New Factory Regulations from the Kingdom of Stumm."

Each of my workers has the right to be born, live and die for Me. His birth and death, of course, will be at his own expense.

The worker is a human being, so to speak.

Whoever marries without sufficient years of service, and without My consent, will be dismissed.

Besides My welfare provisions for the old age, disability, and sickness of the workers, I have ordained that every morning the sun will shine on the just and the unjust alike.

I furthermore promise to make it rain once a month on the average. . . .

Whoever commits a crime should simply report it to Me, so that I can determine the sentence and save the court some work.

Likewise the kaiser's own proposed workers' protective legislation was held up to ridicule as the first step toward a decadent Utopia where workers, comfortably supported by the state, would be required to work four hours a day for the sake of their health. Often accurate in its perceptions of the very real reactionary implications of such government-sponsored programs, *Kladderadatsch* gave almost no attention to the social problems which they were designed to alleviate.[52]

In its view of trade-union activity, which during this period gained in both strength and militancy, *Kladderadatsch* remained narrowly middle class. It condemned trade unions for encouraging laziness and discouraging individual initiative. "Citizen O., who is in the building trade," read one supposed article from the *Vorwärts* of 1920 (thus twenty years in the future), "is said to accomplish twice as much as his comrades if he uses his time efficiently. They have therefore accused him of insulting and ridiculing them. After examining the witnesses the judge lectured the accused in very strong terms on the depravity of the offense, and sentenced him to four weeks in solitary confinement." The German *Witzblatt*'s image of the idle and irresponsible worker bore a marked resemblance to that of the British humor magazine *Punch,* which during this same period published a cartoon showing one of these disreputable figures consoling another. "Wot cheer, Alf?" "Work, nuffink but work, from morning until night!" " 'Ow long have you been at it?" "Start tomorrer."[53]

The reaction of *Kladderadatsch* to the increased strike activity of the 1890s likewise reflected a narrowly middle-class viewpoint. Often striking workers were blamed for the rise in prices which distressed the middle-class consumer. An example is this verse from a series entitled "The sorrows of a Privy Counsellor."

> Every day I sadly look into the
>   paper's gloomy pages,
> There's a meeting, there's a walkout,
>   a demand for higher wages,
> And what happens then? Why, after
>   that, I very shortly hear
> Food and clothing, coal and wood
>   have once again become more dear!
> And while all around me prices
>   are increasing like the devil,
> My salary—alas!—remains
>   right at the same old level!

The almost wholly erroneous attribution of price rises to workers' demands instead of to the protective tariffs imposed by the agrarian-industrial alliance bespoke a powerful, indeed unreasoning anti-union bias. And Müller and Schulze, those two paragons of middle-class respectability, speculated fearfully on the dire consequences of working-class "selfishness."

> *Schulze:* This Social-Democratic thing is getting worse and worse.
> *Müller:* I thought the strikes were about over.
> *Schulze:* Don't you know the story about the lion who has tasted blood?
> *Müller:* Yes, from then on he refuses to be a vegetarian.
> *Schulze:* Of course—and that's how it will be with the workers. The more they get, the more they'll want.

Müller: Well, I really don't blame them.
Schulze: Now listen here! Every minute they get more money and do less work. Where's that going to lead? Why, soon they'll be getting five marks an hour! And when the employer can no longer give any work at that price, what will the workers do?
Müller: Well, if he won't give them work, I suppose they'll just have to take it!
Schulze: Quit joking!
Müller: But Windthorst says in the Reichstag that if the Center were in power there wouldn't be any more Social Democracy.
Schulze: Oh boy! That's really the answer![54]

The hostility of *Kladderadatsch* was aroused by the presumed socialist threat not only to the economic status but to the moral values of the middle class. Foremost among these was the elaborate cult of nationalism, disparaged by the socialists as a device for maintaining the monarchical system and crushing dissent. In 1895 socialist leaders urged their followers to boycott Sedan Day celebrations on the grounds that German unification had benefited only the ruling classes. The response of *Kladderadatsch* combined conventional patriotic ardor with one-sided vilification of the socialists.

As long as praises ring
For noble deeds of glory,
Mankind our praise will sing
And tell our Empire's story.
They'll praise our courage too
That won the bloody fight
When you, you loud-mouthed crew,
Have vanished into night!

An accompanying cartoon showed the socialist leaders Liebknecht and Singer as hyenas befouling the graves of the dead of Sedan. The fear and anxiety exuded by these comments were highly exaggerated, for the patriotism of the German worker, already well established in the 1890s, increased after the turn of the century.[55]

Even more fearful was the threat of revolution which the lapse of the anti-socialist laws aroused. In spite of the reformist tone of the Erfurt program, many still feared that the growth of the socialist party might bring violent consequences. An anecdote of 1890

entitled "What happened to Schmidt" looked into the fantasy
world of the middle class, where mingled fear, anger, and guilt
combined to produce a nightmare of revolution. After an evening
of beer and skat, the *rentier* Schmidt was troubled with a horrible dream: "The workers were coming! They had burnt down the
factories and were now marching through the streets demanding
bread! . . . Now the foaming human tidal wave poured noisily into my own house . . . they were climbing the stairs . . . I was
lost!" Having powerfully evoked the fears of its middle-class
readers, *Kladderadatsch* then proceeded to console them. The
awakened Schmidt, who had dashed out into the street in his
nightshirt, suddenly heard military music heralding the approach of soldiers. "To me it was the most beautiful music in the
world. Law and order still prevailed. . . . I could no longer re-
frain from shouting hurrah!" As Schmidt retired to a more peaceful sleep, the readers of *Kladderadatsch* were able to laugh at their
own exaggerated apprehensions.[56]

But while assuaging panic-stricken impulses, the *Kladderadatsch* of the 1890s encouraged long-term anxiety. A recurring
feature entitled "Die Zukunftsstaat" was inspired by *Sozialdemokratische Zukunftsbilder,* an anti-socialist tract published in
1891 by the liberal deputy Eugen Richter. The book, which by
1893 had sold an impressive quarter of a million copies, depicted
a fictional socialist seizure of power, followed immediately by
the confiscation of all private property, the abolition of money,
and the dissolution of the army. Further changes included the
abolition of class differences and the removal of children from
the parental home to communal nurseries. Implying not only the
immorality but the impracticality of such a society, Richter ended
his parable with the breakdown of the system due to drastically
falling rates of production. Always an admirer of Richter, *Kladderadatsch* expanded upon his dystopian fantasy. One issue depicted the sad plight of parents attempting to pick up their children at the communal nursery who invariably receive the wrong
child! Another implied that the uniformity imposed in the name
of egalitarianism would affect not only economic status but personality and ultimately even appearance. "Any observer cannot
fail to notice how similar the members of the younger generation
are to each other," read one supposed "editorial" from the *Vorwärts* of 1920. "Individuality is vanishing; a uniform type emerges
everywhere. Soon we will have to brand every citizen with a number, in order to avoid confusing mistakes. What a triumph for the

human spirit! At last we have succeeded in imposing the law of democratic equality on Nature herself." Such comments reflected the deep-seated fears of liberals that economic levelling might destroy individualism and impose a colorless and repressive conformity. Like a dream, the joke translated vague fears into vivid and fantastic images. And the important question whether socialism might actually mean not a denial but an extension of freedom to those previously enslaved by hunger and economic hardship was successfully evaded.[57]

While *Kladderadatsch* thus reinforced existing class attitudes, *Simplicissimus* aggressively challenged them. Like the naturalist artists and authors of the 1890s, the *Witzblatt* exposed its middle-class readers to the frequently grim realities of the world outside the comfortable drawing room. Far from defending traditional middle-class virtue, *Simplicissimus* often debunked it as a front for selfishness and complacency. An 1896 cartoon showed an elegant dinner party. "Excellency," says one guest to another, "I think that we should drink to the poor, who can't enjoy this good Burgundy." "Oh, nonsense!" replies his companion, "those people should save their money." Rejecting the *Kladderadatsch* image of the lazy worker, *Simplicissimus* contrasted his hard-working life with the gentlemanly idleness of his employers. A cartoon which appeared during the bitter Ruhr coal strike of 1905 showed a ragged group of workers interrupting their employer's leisurely tea party. To the angry inquiry, "What do you bums want?" the workers reply, "Sir, we only wanted to find out what one does all day when one isn't working." And *Simplicissimus'* picture of the misery of the slums was as macabre as any to be found in the naturalist art and literature of the period. A central theme of Heine's "Bilder aus dem Familienleben" was the contrast between ostentatious middle-class wealth and squalid working-class poverty. Heine often seemed positively to revel in grim detail, as in a cartoon depicting a dark tenement in which a mother and several small children stand around a hideously disfigured corpse. "Go with the gentleman," says the mother to a young daughter, who stands in the doorway with a well dressed, middle-aged man, "then we'll have enough money to bury Father." Thus the tendency of the poor to riot and disorder was often shown as a spontaneous, almost involuntary response to the unbearable conditions of their lives. A cartoon of 1908, for example, showed a revolutionary crowd lashed on by a huge symbolic figure of "Poverty" which hovers in the background. "You shoot individuals," the caption admonishes the police, who are shown firing upon the crowd, "but you don't see the Spectre which drives the masses on."[58]

The contrasting views of the socialist movement found in *Kladderadatsch* and *Simplicissimus* reflected the development both of liberal attitudes and of the socialist movement itself. The older magazine's fearful speculation on the *Zukunftsstaat* was based on a serious, literal interpretation of the socialist party's revolutionary rhetoric. In the early twentieth century the party's moderate and reformist policies reflected a considerable modification of its earlier revolutionary program. Thus *Simplicissimus* usually emphasized not the impending revolution but the absurd contrast between rhetoric and reality. An example is a verse of 1908 entitled "The Resolutionaries," mocking a recent party congress.

> "Long live the Classless State," we loudly sing,
> The wicked System will be dead and gone!
> Take warning, Folks, we're changing everything—
> We only have to say it and it's done!
> We'll pass this Resolution, one and all!
> Unanimous! Now watch the System fall!
> At least, on paper.

Far from overthrowing the Wilhelmine authority structure, the German socialist party now imitated both its rhetorical pomposity and its authoritarianism. Like the French socialists who criticized the characteristically "Prussian" organization of the Social Democratic Party, *Simplicissimus,* too, laughed at its rigid discipline in a cartoon showing August Bebel (to whom historian Arthur Rosenberg referred as a "counter-Kaiser") alongside Czar Nicholas above the caption "Two Autocrats." Indeed, the rigidly Marxist rhetoric and the tight, authoritarian structure of the SPD constituted two major barriers to the liberal-socialist cooperation which *Simplicissimus* advocated.[59]

In spite of these deep intellectual reservations, however, the *Simplicissimus* group showed an increasing sympathy for many working-class goals. The Bavarian magazine's greater openness to socialism may be explained at least partly by the political atmosphere of South Germany, where class distinctions and antagonisms were far less rigid than in the more industrialized North. For this reason, liberal-socialist cooperation was easier, more frequent, and more productive in this region. Like other intelligent liberals, moreover, the *Simplicissimus* group saw an alliance with the well organized and powerful socialist movement as the only constructive course for left-wing liberal parties otherwise condemned to political impotence.[60]

Thus by contrast to *Kladderadatsch,* which continued to regard the labor movement with only slightly mitigated distaste, *Simplicissimus* aggressively supported the massive strikes which shook German industry in the early years of the twentieth century. The often brutal and uncompromising response of employers was exemplified by the Zwickau-Crimmitschau lockout of 1903–04, in which employers sought to break a textile workers' union by shutting factory gates for five months. Entrepreneurs throughout Germany contributed huge sums to support the lockout. *Simplicissimus* responded with a grim and uncompromising symbolic representation of the class struggle. In a cartoon entitled "Crimmitschau," Heine depicted a group of obese, cigar-smoking industrialists and policemen standing on a platform supported by the emaciated bodies of workers. "We need more policemen up here," reads the caption, "the people are not sufficiently crushed." A verse by Ludwig Thoma alluded to the similar plight of the Silesian weavers sixty years earlier.

> To cries of hunger, pain, and grief,
> "We're starving—help us please!"
> The Dresden bosses were not deaf,
> They called on the police.

> And that solution never fails,
> To cure all pain and need,
> We die a softer death in jail,
> Than on the cold, bare street.

The confiscation of the "Crimmitschau" issue for "incitement to class conflict," a penalty usually reserved for the socialist press, reflected the authorities' concern for its "subversive" message.[61]

In 1905, labor conflict erupted still more bitterly in the Ruhr coalfields. While *Kladderadatsch* counselled both workers and employers to moderation, a cautious modification of its earlier antilabor stance, *Simplicissimus* sided passionately with the workers and denounced the rapacity of the employers. The inadequacy of miners' health benefits, for example, was grotesquely exposed by a cartoon showing a miner receiving the birthday congratulations of his employer. "Müller, you are now sixty years old," declares the latter. "Miners don't usually pass

"Prussian Electoral Reform." "Come on, Bethmann, we dare you!" A comment on the Conservative Party's rejection of Chancellor Bethmann-Hollweg's program of suffrage reform. (Heine, *Simplicissimus*, Oct. 11, 1909.)

the age of thirty-five, so you'll soon be dead. Bequeath your lungs to me—I want to recover the coal particles in them." As an advocate of miners' rights, *Simplicissimus* incurred the hostility of the coal industry. In 1909 the management of a mining firm in Hamm sued the magazine for libel. The provocation was a cartoon by Gulbransson based on an account in the Dortmund *Arbeiter-Zeitung* of the eviction of the widow and children of a mine-disaster victim from their company-owned housing. The drawing shows a conversation between two miners buried under tons of rubble. "Now the bosses have thrown my wife and eight children out onto the street," complains one. "Don't grumble," replies the other, "they've given us free lodging down here." Giving credence to the company's argument that the widow had been evicted for misconduct, the judge sentenced Gulbransson to six months in prison—a severe penalty which was later commuted to a fine of fifteen hundred marks.[62]

The response of *Simplicissimus* to the Russian Revolution of 1905 added to its international stature as a symbol of political radicalism. For the young Russian art students who had flocked to Schwabing at the turn of the century, *Simplicissimus* had provided an influential and admired example of art as a political weapon. At the outbreak of the Revolution of 1905, a group of these young artists, supported by the eminent author Maxim Gorky, founded a satirical sheet, *Zhupel (Bugaboo)*, closely modeled on *Simplicissimus.* The German artists sympathized passionately with their Russian colleagues, denouncing the czar as a blood-stained monster and rejoicing in the highly temporary success of Russian liberalism. The carnage of the Revolution inspired cartoons more macabre and gory than ever before, a few of which—such as a drawing of the Kremlin awash in blood—were actually reprinted from *Zhupel.* The offensiveness of these cartoons to the Russian ruling class was reflected in 1905 in the widely publicized trial of a Russian nobleman who, while residing in a hotel in Dresden, had ordered the porter to buy him a selection of newspapers. Upon discovering a copy of *Simplicissimus* among these, the infuriated prince had summoned the porter, exclaimed, "How *dare* you send me a copy of *Simplicissimus*—that rag which insults the Russian nobility!" and kicked the unfortunate man in the stomach, injuring him severely. The easily affordable fine of 1,000 marks inflicted upon the nobleman was justified by the presiding judge on the grounds that *Simplicissimus* was indeed a "shameless rag."[63]

"If you're well dressed, the mob beats you up; if you're poorly dressed, the police beat you up. Oh well—in this outfit nothing can happen to me!" (Heine, *Simplicissimus*, Oct. 17, 1910.)

In its unqualified support of the Revolution, *Simplicissimus* once again distanced itself from more moderate liberals who, like the editors of *Kladderadatsch,* feared that the extremism and "immaturity" of the Russian people might doom the Revolution to failure. A cartoon entitled "The National Liberal" showed a well-dressed man expounding on the Revolution at a dinner party. "Of course I basically approve of the libertarian principles of the Revolution. But what I cannot accept is their really vulgar ignorance of proper manners." Even after the defeat of the 1905 Revolution put an end to *Zhupel, Simplicissimus* continued as a major influence on Russian political art throughout the 1917 Revolution and the early years of the Soviet state.[64]

In the year 1905 another issue gained prominence which until the outbreak of World War I would be the primary focus of liberal-socialist cooperation—the reform of the Prussian three-class voting system. Using a property qualification to distinguish three classes of voters, whose votes were unequally weighted, the system virtually assured the predominance of the land-owning aristocracy in the Empire's largest and most powerful state. As an attack on anachronistic feudal privilege and the assertion of an important political right, suffrage reform was an issue on which liberals could easily cooperate with a socialist party now increasingly committed to evolutionary change through the democratic process. Both satirical journals worked to mobilize public opinion against a system whose patent absurdity was pointed out by *Kladderadatsch* in an account of a certain Königsberg street where a notorious brothel owner voted in the first class and a minister in the third. But even the tentative reform efforts of Bülow and his successor Bethmann were doomed to failure by the hard-line resistance of the Junkers, whom *Simplicissimus* showed viciously shoving Bethmann away from a voting urn with their pitchforks.

The frustration of reform efforts led to a polarized political situation in which the liberal and progressive parties occupied an uneasy middle ground. In 1910 the socialist party organized massive demonstrations which frequently escalated into violent clashes between demonstrators and the police. Some of *Simplicissimus'* most eloquent cartoons protested police brutality. Heine's drawing "After the Demonstration," which showed a doll lying in a pool of blood, was modelled almost precisely on a cartoon published by *Zhupel* in 1905. The allusion to the violence of Bloody Sunday was obvious and striking. *Simplicissimus* also recorded

"After the Demonstration." (Heine, *Simplicissimus*, Mar. 28, 1910.)

the humorous moments in this bitter struggle, as in a cartoon showing police vainly waiting in Berlin's Treptow Park for a demonstration which had been rescheduled at the last moment. But often the cartoonists depicted violence and ugliness on both sides. Heine, for instance, showed a smiling naked man walking calmly through a bloody street battle. "If you're well dressed, the mob beats you up; if you're poorly dressed, the police beat you up. Oh well—in this outfit nothing can happen to me!" And when at the Magdeburg Party Congress of 1910 the party's revolutionary wing under Rosa Luxemburg succeeded in passing a resolution defining the demonstrations as only a prelude to a mass general strike, *Simplicissimus* responded with a graphic evocation of the bloodthirsty mob of the French Revolution. "Danton," read the caption, "will always be killed by Robespierre." Although this resolution was never implemented, the spectre of the *Zukunftsstaat* had once again frightened cautious liberals.[65]

In the electoral campaign of the year 1912 the socialists launched their most determined effort so far to win the cooperation of liberals in the struggle for the liberalization of the Prussian state. The slogan "from Bassermann [leader of the National Liberal party] to Bebel" was supported by many thoughtful members of the liberal parties. The historian Friedrich Meinecke, for example, called for "the cooperation of all healthy forces" in the "struggle to adapt the state and society to the immense changes in our economic life, and the huge increases in our population which we have experienced over the past three decades." In an unprecedented show of liberal-socialist solidarity, *Kladderadatsch* urged citizens of all classes ("Hammer or pen, drop your tools," read a cover verse) to join in the struggle against "Junker pride and clerical arrogance." On election day *Simplicissimus* triumphantly predicted a socialist victory by showing a Junker and a priest huddling together under a shower of red ballots. The election was indeed a triumph—the socialists polled one-third of all votes, and socialists and liberal parties together received 61 percent. Certainly these results showed a broad-based support for constitutional reform among both working-class and middle-class voters. But *Simplicissimus'* hopes for liberal-socialist cooperation were soon shattered when the National Liberal party under Bassermann, forgetful of the substantial support which they had received from the socialists in the recent campaign, refused to support Phillip Scheidemann for the vice-presidency of the Reichstag because of the socialist leader's refusal to attend a court reception. Once again *Simplicissimus* bitterly mocked National Liberal spinelessness in a verse entitled "The National Liberal Slut."

> A blood-red scarf upon her hair,
> She hustled voters everywhere,
> She traipsed through bar and music-hall,
> For votes prepared to give her all.

> But she repented in a hurry.
> "Herr Scheidemann, I'm so, so sorry,
> "I cannot be your chambermaid,
> "At Court they'd scold me, I'm afraid.

> "But please don't be surprised, my friend,
> "For I'm a lackey to the end,
> "And years of grovelling, I'm sure,
> "Produces spinal curvature.

> "For our success we're in your debt,
> "But oh! How quickly we forget,
> "We Basser-men are slippery guys,
> "Upon whose word no one relies.

> " 'Watch on the Rhine' we'll sing to you,
> "But we do not stand firm and true.
> "From left to right, from black to red,
> "We're so mixed up we're almost dead."[66]

The ultimate failure of the reform movement, however, was caused not so much by the defection of the liberals as by the total impotence of political parties, even those which commanded immense electoral support, to change a system defended by an irresponsible and powerful monarchy backed by a wealthy and influential aristocracy. Although *Kladderadatsch* reverted with the National Liberal politicians to a moderately anti-socialist stance, *Simplicissimus* continued to praise the workers as the only positive force for social change. In 1913 a drawing of sober, determined workers on the march illustrated this optimistic if somewhat sentimental verse:

> We're as free as the sky,
> We are happy and brave,
> The first foam from the wave
> Of a time that is nigh.

> There's a vision we share,
> That no man can destroy,

And we look back in joy
On our years of despair.[67]

Thus the contrast between *Kladderadatsch* and *Simplicissimus*
suggests a genuine evolution in the image both of the worker and
of the socialist movement itself. By its one-sided hostility to socialism, *Kladderadatsch* continued to restrict its appeal to its traditionally middle-class readership. By its far more sympathetic
image of the movement, *Simplicissimus* sought to reach a broader
constituency which transcended class barriers. The appeal of the
liberal *Witzblatt* to some socialist readers reflects the trend toward liberal-socialist rapprochement, especially on such issues
as electoral reform and antimilitarism, which was manifested by
the election results of 1912. The effectiveness of *Simplicissimus*
as an advocate of cooperation thus illustrates the role of humor
in promoting group solidarity by providing common objects of
ridicule. Nonetheless *Simplicissimus* also offered ample evidence of the continuing class prejudice which ultimately prevented an effective liberal-socialist alliance in both the prewar
and the Weimar periods. Unlike the highly differentiated depic-
tion of the bourgeoisie, the portrayal of the working class was
confined for the most part to one stereotype—half-starved, victimized, and inarticulate. There was a grain of truth in the hostile
opinion expressed by the *Kölnische Zeitung.* "In its radical game,"
stated an editorial, "*Simplicissimus* loves to use the working class.
. . . We seriously doubt that this benefits our lower-income population. The German worker simply does not look the way *Simplicissimus* portrays him. The worker, who strives courageously
for the recognition of his personal worth, is insulted when he is
portrayed as a drunkard or as a ragged street urchin living in
an evil-smelling hovel." Not until 1912 did some cartoon images
begin to resemble the ideal worker of contemporary socialist art—
strong, autonomous, and politically committed. This marked dif-
ferentiation between working-class and middle-class stereotypes
hardly encouraged genuine egalitarianism or even communication. Both the outright hostility of *Kladderadatsch* and the condescending compassion of *Simplicissimus* ultimately reinforced
rather than undermined class divisions.[68]

Bismarck and the Epigoni

Thus the political humor of *Kladderadatsch* and *Simplicissimus*
contained overtones of disappointment, anxiety, and foreboding.

Accurately perceiving the impotence of the monarchy and the ingrained passivity of the bourgeoisie, both groups of satirists viewed the growing power of the working class with deep reservations. Plagued by doubts and fears, the satirists turned easily to the nostalgia which pervaded much of the intellectual life of the period. By contrast to their incompetent successors, the figures of Moltke, Bismarck, even the unpretentious Wilhelm I assumed heroic proportions. The contemporary generation of politicians were often termed *epigoni,* meaning "those born after," or by implication "those born too late," a classical allusion to the myth of the Seven against Thebes. In 1895 Max Weber lamented the fate of his own generation, born too late to share in the noble work of unification. "We were born under the harshest curse with which history could ever burden the consciousness of a generation—the curse of political *epigonentum."* Bismarck's successes, continued the perceptive Weber, had inspired not energy but apathy in the rising generation, to whom "German history seemed to be at an end. The present was the fulfillment of the previous millenia. Who dared to ask whether the future might be different?" Like Weber, the satirists evoked the memory of past triumphs as a reproach to an inadequate generation.[69]

At the center of this nostalgic picture was the personality of Bismarck. *Kladderadatsch* and *Simplicissimus* illustrated the development of the Bismarck image during the period from that of a controversial elder statesman to that of a legendary hero. The older satirists, some of whom had known the old chancellor personally, saw him even after his death as a human (albeit awesomely respected) individual. To the younger generation who had hardly known the real man, he appealed much more as a figure of fantasy, an idealized Nietzschean superman embodying the competence and mastery which younger leaders lacked. To a generation tired of the theatrical trappings of power, Bismarck came to symbolize the unadorned reality.

Upon Bismarck's retirement in 1890, *Kladderadatsch* unambiguously mourned the passing of a great man.

> O, what a mournful sight his parting is,
> For we all know that no one can replace him
> And that his name will evermore be bound
> To that great office which he filled so greatly.
>
> How painfully, how sadly will we miss him,
> Remembering his patient, skillful hand

Which plucked the flower, "Safety" from the thorns
Of threatening and never-ceasing Danger.[70]

Another verse pictured the aged statesman retiring "lonely to
the Sachsenwald."

The stormy days of youth
Remember, when you made your daring plans,
And longed to save our dearest Fatherland,
From shame, from weakness, impotence, despair.
And think how you began that noble work,
With mighty muscle piling stone on stone,
Until at length the edifice was built
Which filled the world with wonder and applause.
And so, when you look back on your great work,
Which patience, strength, and dedication wrought,
Think, "It is still more great and still more wondrous
Than I had ever dreamed in boldest youth."

All hail great Prince! Forevermore, while we,
The German people, live upon the earth,
The memory of your noble deeds will live.[71]

But Bismarck did not, in fact, disappear from the political scene.
Refusing to sink gracefully into retirement, he continued to comment vocally, sometimes very maliciously, on the work of his
successors. "Never has a retired statesman worked with such
ruthless persistence to make his successors' life difficult," commented his biographer Erich Eyck. In order to publicize his opposition, Bismarck used periodicals and newspapers which had
supported him in the past, including *Kladderadatsch.* Often the
cooperation of friendly journalists was rewarded by hospitality
or other conspicuous gestures of personal friendship (such as the
luncheon invitation to Johannes Trojan). Sometimes Bismarck used
the press not only to comment on but to manipulate the political
scene, as in the *Kladderadatsch* affair of 1893–94, in which one
prominent participant, Maximilian Harden, almost certainly acted
under his influence.[72]

Shortly before Bismarck's retirement in 1890, *Kladderadatsch*
made an important contribution to the Bismarck legend by publication of the *Bismarck-Album,* which contained the magazine's
literary and pictorial responses to the chancellor over the years.
The introduction asserted that even the "sharpest attacks" had
been included and further adduced the allegedly impartial col-

lection as evidence that *Kladderadatsch* had not "fallen into a certain political position tending to the right," as critics had claimed. Actually many of the sharpest comments from the *Konfliktzeit* were omitted, and the tone of the volume was generally laudatory. The *Bismarck-Album* was a great success; appearing almost exactly at the time of Bismarck's resignation (mid-March of 1890), it went through seven printings by the end of April.[73]

Throughout the decade of the 1890s *Kladderadatsch* continued loyally Bismarckian. To be sure, the magazine poked gentle fun at too-worshipful biographies, which it parodied in a description of a relic from Bismarck's boyhood, a cigarette stub, which was said to prove his outstandingly precocious interest in natural history! In general, however, *Kladderadatsch* publicized Bismarck's own picture of himself as a grievously persecuted man. It constantly reproached editors and organizations for refusing to pay tribute to the retired chancellor for fear of offending Wilhelm. In 1895, for example, a verse reproaching the Berlin city council for its refusal to honor Bismarck on his eightieth birthday provoked a considerable popular reaction; hundreds of favorable letters and telegrams poured in and Bismarck himself sent a message of appreciation. In 1896 the journal similarly reproached the students of Bonn for calling off a tribute to Bismarck for fear of political repercussions. Thus the retired Bismarck was depicted as a champion of free speech against absolutist oppression—an image which he himself helped to create by a speech to the student body of Jena in which he warned against "purely dynastic politics" and advocated a stronger Reichstag which "warns, controls, and under certain circumstances even leads the government." The irony of Bismarck's highly opportunistic defense of the liberal institutions which he had previously scorned seemed to escape the satirists of *Kladderadatsch* altogether.[74]

After Bismarck's death *Kladderadatsch* continued to mourn the absence of his guiding hand at every moment of crisis. Thus it responded to the breakdown of authority in 1908 with nostalgia.

Once did a loyal Watchman stand,
To guard us and to guide us,
But now for shame, O Fatherland,
The nations all deride us.
The glory that we knew of yore,
O, we shall see it nevermore.

Thus the contrast between the giant Bismarck and his unworthy successors was used to justify a pessimistic and passive reaction to the problems of the present.[75]

Simplicissimus' Bismarck image was from the beginning less affectionate and more awe-inspiring. To be sure, the younger humorists also had their memories. Ludwig Thoma, for example, recalled his indignant reaction to the German people's passive acceptance of the kaiser's arbitrary action: "With astonishment I saw how an entire people accepted the loss of their greatest statesman . . . as an irresistible stroke of fate. I saw how people found homely explanations—a young Kaiser didn't want an old Chancellor—and bore the whims of a dilettante with consent or at least resignation. Not the triumph of Bismarck's enemies but the patience of his former friends robbed me of my faith and sharpened my perception of the servility of the German *bourgeoisie.*" The correct perception of Bismarck as victim of malicious intrigue soon developed into a full-blown heroic image in which the deposed chancellor was seen as a champion of integrity in a nation of sycophants. One prominent creator of this image was Maximilian Harden, who alluded to Bismarck in a fable of a land called Phrasia. "A man appeared, the forenamed anti-Phrasius, who had the curious intention of confronting the Phrasians with the truth, of being blunt in the company of deferential men. . . . And as he learned in the course of time to endure the phraseology and hypocrisy of his countrymen . . . he became the idol of the masses."[76]

In its obituary tribute to Bismarck in 1898, the recently founded magazine's first extensive comment on the chancellor, *Simplicissimus* likewise pictured him as a lonely giant.

Your work was always yours, and yours alone,
You were a giant, lonely and sublime.
Now we must follow you, O mighty one,
The last great Person of our modern time.
But we must be like you, both bold and free.
Or else we'll always in your shadow be.[77]

Memories of a real, intensely human man were here almost submerged in a cult of the heroic personality. Furthermore, *Simplicissimus* even justified Bismarck's unconstitutional actions as a reluctant response to inexorable necessity. A verse recounted a conversation between the recently departed chancellor and the

Devil, in which the former alluded to the political immaturity of the German people in order to justify his high-handed policies:

> "Prince Lucifer," the Chancellor said,
> "What Conscience bade, I did,
> But every night upon my bed,
> In tears my face I hid."

> "And as to the Germans, now I tell you
> That the only freedom I took
> From that half-baked, dreamy, impractical crew
> Was the freedom they'd learned from a book."

Thus the fertile fancy of the *Simplicissimus* group had transformed Bismarck not only into a superman but into a crypto-liberal forced to use authoritarian tactics against his will.[78]

Like *Kladderadatsch, Simplicissimus* continued to evoke the allegedly sad fate of Bismarck as a reproach to the kaiser. In a special issue of 1906 entitled *Bismarck redivivus* (responding to the publication of the chancellor's memoirs), *Simplicissimus* published two cartoons. The first, entitled "1871," showed the child Wilhelm viewing a parade from his window. "The man riding by down there gained the crown for your grandfather." The second, labelled "1890," showed a pathetically bent and frail old man walking alone through the snowy woods of Friedrichsruh. "I could send the old guy to Spandau," read the caption, "but I don't want to make a martyr of him." In 1908, on the tenth anniversary of Bismarck's death, *Simplicissimus* once again reproached not only the kaiser himself but now the whole of the German people for their supposedly heartless ingratitude.

> Ten long years by now have slowly passed
> Since his death. His countrymen stand here,
> Showing him the reverence at last
> Which they never showed beside his bier.[79]

The massive figure of Bismarck provided the standard against which his successors could be measured and found wanting. The perfect embodiment of Wilhelmine theatrical politics was Wilhelm's third chancellor, Bernhard von Bülow (sometimes hailed as a "second Bismarck"), who aped Bismarck's authoritarian style without displaying the least trace of his great predecessor's political ability. *Simplicissimus* deplored both Bülow's political showmanship and the stupidity of the German people, who once again mistook theater for reality.

It's rather easy to get in the papers,
In Germany, and elsewhere? Maybe so.
You only have to cut some crazy capers,
We love the man who puts on a good show.
The German father tells his son, "My lad
"You know, our second Bismarck isn't bad,
"In fact, I'd say,
"He's quite O.K.!"

And when he kicks the Reichstag in the ass,
Or—pardon readers!—in the derriere
Just hear the German people bleat, en masse,
"At last we've really got a man up there!"
And German says to German over beer, "Oh
Let's drink a rousing toast to our great hero!"
But in my cup,
I'm throwing up.

Like all *Simplicissimus*' denunciations of theatrical politics, this
verse expresses a highly ambiguous attitude toward authority.
Castigating the *epigonos* Bülow not for his authoritarian beliefs
themselves but for flaunting the trappings without the substance
of authority, it cries out for an authority figure who can be trusted.[80]

These contributions to the Bismarckian personality cult show
that humor does not invariably unmask falsehood but can rather
serve to perpetuate and embellish it. Not that the image was entirely false—Bismarck was indeed a political genius whose qualities of moderation, shrewdness, and common sense seemed ever
more valuable by contrast to the ineptitude of his successors. But
to enlist the ghost of Bismarck in the antimonarchical cause, to
portray him as a kind of liberal in disguise was to ignore his
crucial role in the creation of the system to which the inept Wilhelm owed his enormous powers. Indeed, one might reasonably
allot more blame to Bismarck for creating the imperial monarchy
than to Wilhelm for discharging the office assigned to him. And
the portrait of Bismarck as paragon of political integrity reflected
a truly remarkable distortion of his thoroughly devious and manipulative political methods. Finally, the sentimental contrast
between two leaders obscured the real issue—the system which
gave so much power to an individual. The *Daily Telegraph* affair,
one might argue, had demonstrated the need not for stronger but
for weaker, in the sense of more limited and accountable, leadership. The satirists' longing for a strong and wise authority fig-

ure, though a natural response to a crisis, also reflected the same political passivity for which they rebuked their countrymen.

The wide influence of the idealized Bismarck image upon the Wilhelmine public was noted with great concern by many contemporary observers. When Bismarck was dismissed, commented the liberal leader Friedrich Naumann, "the feeling for him was not simply transferred to Wilhelm II; instead, he left an empty place in the world view of the educated German, who had lost the habit of effective political action and never regained the political initiative." Naumann speculated fearfully that in some future crisis "we may seek for political energies and perhaps not find them because the educated classes are too politically apathetic to make great personal sacrifices for the state." And a few courageous dissidents such as Ludwig Quidde openly denounced the Bismarckian legend as a corrupting rather than an elevating influence on public life. "The fact that in this new German Empire brutality, euphemistically called 'keenness' [*Schneidigkeit*], has become our most respected political virtue is, to the extent that any one man can be made responsible for the spiritual development of a people, Bismarck's work." The fact that the satirists supported rather than criticized the personality cult reflects the disturbing effects of the Bismarck legend on even the most progressive segment of the middle-class public.[81]

Köpenick Revisited:
The Satirists Look at
War and Militarism

4

Militarism in Society and Politics

WHEN the shoemaker and ex-convict Wilhelm Voigt, disguised in a cast-off captain's uniform, succeeded both in arresting the mayor of Köpenick, who yielded to military authority without even asking for a warrant, and in confiscating the city's treasury, a few contemporary observers saw the tragic side of this seeming farce. "Germany laughed— Europe shuddered," recollected Walther Rathenau. But some Germans shuddered too, including Ludwig Thoma, who wrote from the fortress of Stadelheim, "Militarism has never looked more ridiculous, not even in all ten volumes of *Simplicissimus.* . . . Let the age of Wilhelm II be forever remembered for this fatal joke."[1]

Throughout the Wilhelmine period the satirical journals found in the army and the militarist cult which glorified it an inexhaustible source of inspiration. On this as on other topics the comments of *Simpliccisimus* were far more radical and penetrating than those of *Kladderadatsch,* earning for the newer journal a well deserved reputation as the foremost organ of liberal antimilitarism. In large measure the satirists' perception of militarism was determined by their attitudes toward German foreign policy and toward the ever-threatening prospects of war. A brief sketch of the historical background will serve to set the satirists' comments in perspective.[2]

By laughing not only at the army itself but at the wholehearted admiration of civilians for military behavior and values, the humorists expressed a keen insight into the social function of militarism. "Militarism," explained Alfred Vagts, "is not the opposite of pacifism, its true counterpart is civilianism. . . . Militarism is more, and sometimes less, than the love of war. It covers every system of thinking and valuing and every complex of feelings which rank military institutions and ways above the ways of civilian life, carrying military mentality and modes of action into the civilian sphere." Thus not the size of the army (for France during this period conscripted a larger proportion of her manpower without becoming a highly militaristic state) but its influence over civilian culture earned Germany its reputation as a uniquely militaristic society. The German Empire owed its very existence to a military victory and was formed by a statesman originally appointed to defend the privileges of the army against the claims of civilian politicians. Under the Bismarckian system, the army had indeed become "a state within a state." Apart from its periodic vote on the military budget, the Reichstag had no control over the army, whose size, recruitment policies, and organization were determined wholly by the monarch and his military advisors.[3]

The immunity of the military establishment from civilian control became especially clear during the reign of Wilhelm II. One historian has described the young kaiser as "a sort of perennial Potsdam lieutenant," whose fondness for parades, uniforms, and military pageantry was widely imitated by his subjects. More sinister was his extensive reliance on his military entourage, which advised him not only on purely military questions but on important foreign policy issues as well. Civilian critics were justified in complaining that these advisors encouraged him in his absolutist pretensions, his contempt for parliamentary authority, and his growing, often hysterical fear of social disorder and revolution.[4]

As an essential prop of the Wilhelmine authority structure, the army, like the monarchy itself, appealed to public opinion through elaborate theatrical spectacle. The fondness of Germans for such events was often noted by foreign visitors. "German ladies never tire of watching soldiers," was the exasperated reaction of a Turkish diplomat to an endless parade. Such spectacles dramatized the sense of unity and common national purpose which military service was often said to encourage. Thus the historian Heinrich von Treitschke, a prestigious conservative spokesman, called the army "the real and effective bond of unity" which, transcending the political and class conflicts which divided civilian society, brought home to the simple man "the realization that the state is one and that he is part of the whole."[5]

Certainly such pompous rhetoric contained a grain of truth. For middle-class men particularly, the opportunity which military service provided to work with men from diverse social backgrounds could prove both entertaining and educational. Some of the very satirists who ridiculed the militaristic ideology recalled their own military experience with considerable affection. Sinsheimer wrote of "standing shoulder to shoulder with other young men who had a harder life behind them and ahead of them than people like us. . . . I felt friendship and even love for most of them. . . . Never in my life have I laughed so hard as during that year." Many of the satirists' comments reflected the lighthearted attitude of a generation which, unfamiliar (except at a distance) with the horrors of modern warfare, associated military service with adventure, exhilarating outdoor life, and a break in the staid middle-class routine. Their sympathy for their lower-class comrades, moreover, probably sharpened their anger against the rigid and often brutal Prussian discipline.[6]

But the sentimental picture of the army as the bulwark of national solidarity became more and more patently false during the Wilhelmine period. Nowhere, in fact, were the multifarious and unresolved class tensions of German society more obvious. For the rapid processes of modernization and industrialization had altered the social composition both of the ranks and of the officer corps. The urban, working-class soldier was far less receptive to military discipline than the typically docile peasant recruit of 1871. The antiauthoritarian attitude of this new recruit was encouraged by socialist politicians, who saw the officer corps (in the words of Karl Liebknecht) as "the executioner of culture . . . the quintessence and sum of all tyranny, the brutal servant and the bloody bastion of capitalism." The increasingly brutal discipline of the barracks was one response of the military hierarchy to the threat of insubordination in the ranks.[7]

At the same time, however, the officer corps was also threatened by political diversity within its own previously homogeneous organization. For, as the enlargement and modernization of the army created the demand for a larger officer corps trained in technological skills not usually cultivated by the sons of the aristocracy, the percentage of middle-class officers steadily increased; by 1913, 70 percent of all lieutenants were of bourgeois origin. One response to this threat was an increased emphasis on the Reserve officer corps, which encouraged aristocratic and feudal values among the upper middle class as a whole. During this period a commission in the Reserve became an important prerequisite to success in many civilian professions. "The doctorate is the visiting card—the Reserve commission is the open door!" declares the tailor in Zuckmayer's *Hauptmann von Köpenick,* "those are the basic facts—that's how it is!" But the assimilation of middle-class officers into the feudal world view was never complete; tension between aristocratic and bourgeois officers increased during this period. By encouraging conservatism, moreover, the Reserve system increased the hostility of the middle class toward working-class socialism. Far from bridging class antagonisms, in short, the army tended to sharpen them. The popularity of *Simplicissimus* was one tangible sign of this growing tension.[8]

The influence of the military establishment in Germany was reflected in the aggressive foreign policy which it encouraged. The reign of Wilhelm II initiated a new era in the history of German foreign policy. Repudiating Bismarck's cautious policies, Wilhelm embarked on a campaign for world power supported not only by his military advisors but by the prosperous business interests which sought world markets for their products. Like military policy, foreign policy was completely outside the control of the people and their elected representatives. Nonetheless many of the new policies were designed to flatter German public opinion with grandiose visions of national superiority and civilizing mission. But the rhetoric of *Weltpolitik* was hollow indeed. The domestic function of imperialism, to distract public attention from internal problems, became apparent as Wilhelm sought to bolster his own failing prestige through a flashy and hazardous foreign policy. Behind the aggressive posturing lay indecision, irresponsibility, and ineptitude. Many historical studies of this period note the striking contrast between Germany's remarkable economic growth and her inability to use her newly acquired strength to gain solid diplomatic or territorial advantages. Instead the results of Wilhelmine *Weltpolitik* were almost entirely negative, ultimately leaving Germany in a perilously isolated and friendless position.[9]

For the satirist, who perceives the discrepancy between form and substance, ideal and reality, the Wilhelmine military establishment was thus a perfect target. Like the monarchy which it supported, the army was a pompous facade concealing an increasingly shaky structure. Its theatrical public image could not conceal the unresolved internal conflicts which seriously impaired its effectiveness as a fighting force. Likewise *Weltpolitik* was bad politics and bad theater—the show without the substance of power. Yet the full expression of these critical perceptions was inhibited by the conflict between two imperfectly reconciled systems of values, those of the literary and artistic subculture which encouraged nonconformity, and those of the dominant culture which saw all social criticism as subversion. Apparent in all the satirists' work, these emotional conflicts emerged most conspicuously in their comments on military and foreign affairs.[10]

Soldier and Civilian

The Freudian theory of humor as a safety valve for hostile impulses which cannot be directly acted out may be aptly applied to the antimilitarist satire of *Simplicissimus* and *Kladderadatsch*. Certainly the army itself used its immense power and prestige to silence its civilian critics, whom it branded as subversives or traitors. A *Simplicissimus* cartoon showed a dog trainer in military uniform cracking his whip at a group of "dogs," some of which are nonetheless obsequiously licking his boots. "My first job is to teach these critters not to bark." Yet the inflexible arrogance of the military caste in the face of social change provoked more and more criticism during this period. While often light in tone, the satirists' comments expressed serious dissatisfaction.[11]

Tensions between officers and civilians were released by an ever-popular *pièce de resistance* of the satirical press, the lieutenant joke. "Who was the first lieutenant?" asks one *Simplicissimus* character of another. "Joseph," is the reply, "because he wore a coat of many colors and lorded it over his brothers." Through the figure of the lieutenant, the satirists mocked not so much the Prussian military ideal in itself as its vulgarization in a period of peace and prosperity. Far richer than many of their aristocratic comrades, the middle-class young men now entering the officer corps often sought approval through a flamboyantly luxurious standard of living. The resulting corruption of the traditionally simple and austere Prussian code was of concern even to some officers. Even *Kladderadatsch,* which confined itself to

"Frida's Most Beautiful Christmas Present." "Frida's wonderful parents have fulfilled her dearest wish and consented to her engagement to the lieutenant." (Heine, *Simplicissimus*, Dec. 26, 1896.)

very good-natured joking, alluded frequently to the young officer's dissipated life-style, as, for example, in this comparison between the salaries of a lieutenant and a schoolteacher. "The lieutenant is always in the red. After all, he's not like the *Hilfslehrer*
who is, of course, a vegetarian. He can't be expected to live on
rice, radishes, and pure spring-water—he needs much better food
and is, of course, entirely dependent on his daily dose of champagne." Since middle-class families often risked bankruptcy in
order to support a son in a fashionable regiment, such complaints
of military extravagance probably had wide appeal.[12]

The relationship of the high-born parasite to his hard-working
fellow citizen was perceptively explored in a typical *Simplicissimus* short story entitled "The Brainy Slob." It commented indirectly on the controversial question of educational requirements for the officer corps which could easily be evaded by
aristocratic candidates. The protagonist is a lieutenant of ancient
name and negligible mental capacity who "never attempted to
conceal his ignorance—on the contrary, he was proud of it. 'Education's for the plebs,' was a favorite remark of his. 'A real
gentleman rides and spends money.' At the former activity he
was excellent—at the latter, not quite so good." But when this
carefree young man is required by his commanding officer to write
an essay on "the use of cavalry at the battle of Wörth," desperation and an imminent deadline force him to approach a shabby
middle-class schoolmate whom he has never before conde-
scended to greet on the street. Agreeing to write the paper for an
exorbitant sum, the "slob" temporarily moves into the lieutenant's living quaters, where a valet has been stationed to prevent
him from stealing. Having paid the fee, the lieutenant is subse-
quently horrified to learn that he has "written" an excellent—
nay a definitive—paper, copied word for word from the standard
text on military history. The light tone of this story did not entirely conceal its critical implications. In 1908 the editorial board
of *Simplicissimus* was sued for libel by a regiment, the Deutzer
Curassiers, whose inadequate educational qualifications had been
spoofed in a cartoon showing an officer remarking to his comrade, "My cousin Hans wanted to write some I.O.U.'s, but he's
been with the Deutzer Curassiers for ten years so naturally he's
forgotten how to write his name." Judging the fine levied too le-
nient, an editorial in the *Hamburger Nachrichten* protested that
through such humor the public "receives the impression . . . that
all officers are mentally deficient and that the educated citizen

is thus entitled to look down on the entire corps. And the implications of such public contempt for the officer corps, the backbone of our army . . . do not have to be explained here."[13]

The advancement of incompetent aristocrats in preference to their better-educated bourgeois comrades seriously impaired the efficiency of the army as a fighting force. A cartoon entitled "The Prince on Maneuver" showed an elegant young officer mopping his brow. "Confound it," he mutters, "I've forgotten what we have to do now. Well, what does it matter? Anyway, I'll soon be commanding a brigade." Proof of his culpable ignorance was the aristocrat's scorn for the technological innovation which changed the nature of warfare during this period. "Personally, I have nothing against engineers," remarks one *Simplicissimus* officer graciously. "On the contrary! My cook's brother was a plumber." And such prejudice was not confined to the army. In another cartoon an admiral delivers this opinion: "I ask you, gentlemen, what does our navy want with submarines? You can't see them in a parade!" The military establishment was thus charged with sacrificing efficiency to glamour and competence to snobbery— a charge which some aspects of World War I would amply sustain.[14]

Like the army itself, its civilian admirers were also shown using patriotic rhetoric to justify class prejudice and social ambition. The Reserve officer, so proud of his colorful uniform, was the butt of many jokes. In this imaginary dialogue between a young lawyer and a state examining board, *Kladderadatsch* dramatized the value of military connections to an ambitious professional man.

> *Examiner:* Well, Herr *Referendar,* you couldn't answer the question about the *dolus eventualis.* What have you been doing?
>
> *Candidate:* During my term of military service, I won the Kaiser Wilhelm Memorial medal, and since then I've been an active member of the Navy League.
>
> *Examiner:* Well, that's different. I thought that, in spite of the gaps in your knowledge, we would find the solid core. You've passed the examination.[15]

Reflecting a more sophisticated psychological awareness, *Simplicissimus* perceived the emotional as well as the professional significance of militarism to the German middle class. The reality behind the patriotic ideology of civilian militarism was the most ruthlessly exposed in the chapter from Mann's *Der Untertan* which describes Diederich's term of military service. His draft-dodging efforts foiled by an inconveniently honest physician, Diederich reluctantly enters the army. While professing great enthusiasm, he soon manages to stage an "accident" and to persuade the army doctor, a former member of his student *Corps,* to exempt him from further service. In later life, of course, we see him as a Reserve officer, full of sabre-rattling slogans and sentimental nostalgia for the military life. A consummate actor, Diederich thus uses military dress, manners, and slogans to justify self-seeking and arrogant behavior. But his complete lack of the soldier's positive qualities—honor, courage, and loyalty—reveals the patent falsity of the role. Mann thus saw middle-class militarism as the bullying behavior which compensated for feelings of inner insecurity.[16]

Thus the satirists, especially the *Simplicissimus* group, debunked the theatrical public image of militarism. Furthermore, their comments on many specific issues exposed the militarist ideology not simply as prejudiced and hidebound but as potentially bloody, murderous, and brutal. To the traditional approach of *Kladderadatsch,* which confined its attention to bourgeois issues, may be contrasted the more avant-garde contents of *Simplicissimus,* which responded increasingly to working-class concerns.

A very important issue throughout this period was that of antisemitism in the military. Early in his administration the kaiser had reinforced the traditional prejudices of the officer corps by a speech which emphasized the basis of the soldier's calling in "Christian morality." More even than other bourgeois officers, Jews were mistrusted both for their supposed political unreliability and for their often superior educational background. For these and other reasons, the army was highly reluctant to give even a very promising Jewish *Einjähriger* a Reserve commission. Yet in spite of the prejudice which they encountered, middle-class Jews were driven by the same social and professional ambitions as impelled their Gentile comrades to compete for military rank. Both *Kladderadatsch* and *Simplicissimus* took up the cudgels for these Jewish candidates. The famous cartoon for which Trojan served his two months' *Festungshaft* in 1897, for instance, was entitled "In the Camp of the Heavenly Host" and portrayed Alexander, Frederick the Great, and Napoleon laughing heartily over the kaiser's statement that "those who are not good Christians cannot be good

"In the Camp of the Heavenly Host." Satan comes to tell Frederick the Great about the kaiser's statement that "a man who is not a good Christian cannot be a good soldier." (Brandt, *Kladderadatsch*, Dec. 2, 1897.)

Prussian soldiers and cannot possibly measure up to the requirements of the Prussian army." And in 1911 *Kladderadatsch* suggested the violence of military antisemitism through an imaginary Reichstag debate in which Jews are denounced in the language of gutter antisemitism.

> Hey! Hey! Hey!
> Send them all away,
> Off with all of them,
> To Jerusalem!

To which a more enlightened deputy responds:

> Let's have a people's army which
> Accepts all men, the poor, the rich,
> The middle class, whoe'er they be,
> And let us give authority,
> To men of strength and dedication,
> Of humble or of noble station,
> To those who vote for Left and Right,
> To Papist, Protestant, Semite,
> Now there's an army that could fight![17]

Thus the passionate defense of Jewish officers supported the satirists' general campaign for an army in which competence rather than birth or "character" would determine advancement. The antisemitic slogans, moreover, once again reflected the greed and hypocrisy of the upper classes. The rather frequent marriages between rich Jewish heiresses and impoverished officers provided rich material for jokes. The caption for one cartoon on this theme ironically states that complaints about military antisemitism must be without foundation, since "even in the families of officers, Jews now hold very influential positions!" But such comments also touched on another major theme—the servility of an upper bourgeoisie, whether Jewish or Christian, which courted the favor of the aristocracy instead of resisting it. Once again the Wilhelmine authority structure was shown to depend on the sacrifice of middle-class self-respect to social ambition.[18]

The still accepted practice of dueling was another issue which highlighted the sinister influence of military values on culture. Attempts to enforce laws against such combat were obstinately resisted by the army, which praised the duel as a requirement of a military code of honor more exalted than that of mere civilians. Ironically comparing the lawlessness of officers to that of their sworn enemies, the revolutionaries of the Left, *Kladderadatsch* noted in 1897 that "the agitation against duels has become more widespread and intense than ever before," and recommended the same punishment for duelists as for other murderers, for "only when prison and the scaffold are an ever-present threat will duels stop." The satirists of *Simplicissimus* accurately perceived the social function of the duel as a distinctive custom which set the aristocratic caste apart from its social inferiors. In 1905 the first of a sequence of cartoons showed an elegant group in a nightclub greeting a friend. "Ah, good evening, Herr von Zeschwitz! . . . There's that crazy Zeschwitz, you know—the one who had an affair with Countess Remberg and shot her husband through the head." In the second, the same group responds with disgust to a worker who appears in the door. "There's a worker—get him out! What right has he in a decent club?" Fontane's famous novel *Effi Briest* also used a duel to point up the grotesque incongruity of the feudal system of values in a modern industrial society. To the satirists, as to Fontane's heroine, the duel revealed not the honor but the unenlightened brutality of the military caste.[19]

While in basic agreement on issues which pitted middle class against aristocracy, *Kladderadatsch* and *Simplicissimus* responded quite differently to the military abuses publicized by the socialist movement. Of all political parties, the Social Democrats were the most radically opposed to militarism, viewing the army as an instrument of the ruling class which forced the common soldier to fight wars which benefited only his capitalist oppressors or to shoot down his own comrades in times of civil disorder. The practice which most clearly exposed such class oppression was, of course, the brutal mistreatment of soldiers. In 1904, when the revolutionary leader Rosa Luxemburg responded to a legal charge of inciting disobedience in the ranks by describing hundreds of cases of serious abuse, many people who were opposed to her political views nonetheless admired her courageous stand on this well known and shocking situation.[20]

The responses of *Simplicissimus* and *Kladderadatsch* to this issue illustrated their contrasting priorities. While *Kladderadatsch* downplayed the problem, *Simplicissimus* emphasized it in stories and cartoons which displayed the contributors' talent for the portrayal of violence and brutality. The cartoonists protested not only the punishments in themselves but also the military rules and regulations which justified and often excused them. One very stark cartoon showed two sergeants standing over the

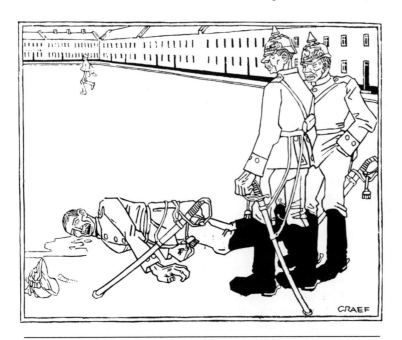

"Barracks Brutality." "It's a good thing he didn't resist the punishment—otherwise he would have gotten two years in the stockade." (Graef, *Simplicissimus*, Sept. 8, 1910.)

obviously unconscious, perhaps dead, body of a soldier and remarking, "It's a good thing he didn't resist the punishment—otherwise he would have gotten two years in the stockade." *Simplicissimus'* many portrayals of barracks abuse were comparable in style and viewpoint to those of the socialist *Witzblatt, Der Wahre Jakob,* which protested against abuse in this parody of a soldier's song, "Oh what a joy to be a soldier!"

> What if he socks you in the gut
> With fists and dagger-handle too?
> What if he kicks you in the butt
> And in the kidneys—what care you?
> And what if, with a sabre-cut
> He punctures your intestines through?
> We'll sing together joyously,
> "The soldier's life's the life for me!"

But the comparison of *Der Wahre Jakob* and *Simplicissimus* also suggests the difference between middle- and working-class perceptions of the military. The dandified young lieutenant whose glamorous social life was so colorfully depicted in the liberal magazine hardly appeared in the socialist sheet, where military arrogance was personified by the brutal sergeant or captain, as in an often-recurring feature entitled "The Speeches of Captain von Krachwitz."[21]

As the years passed *Simplicissimus'* comments on militarism took on an even sharper and more radical tone. The ultimate attack on the rhetoric of patriotism was the picture of officers as an international caste, working together to preserve its political ascendancy in all European societies. In 1914 a cartoon entitled "The Bloody International" showed generals of many nationalities deploring the significant electoral victories won by the socialist parties of their nations: "*Herr Kamerad,* we understand your problem. Our deepest condolences on the results of your elections, which mean no good to us, either." War itself was presented as the last resort of this threatened class against socialist rule. A cartoon of 1910 entitled "The Conservative Solution" showed a skeleton in armor setting a huge torch to a castle swarming with socialists. "If Germany must be red, then let it be red with the flames of war." Such prescient comments reflected the increased receptivity of some liberals to socialist ideas during the immediate prewar years.[22]

Finally, two well known incidents illustrate the nature of militarism as theater and reality. The first, which has already been mentioned, was that of the disguised "Captain from Köpenick." Both *Simplicissimus* and *Kladderadatsch* presented Wilhelm Voigt in a positive light as the humble man whose homespun wit had put the entire establishment to shame. The incident provided an inexhaustible fund of jokes about the Prussian reverence for uniforms and the other external trappings of authority. While *Kladderadatsch* laughed at a *Bürgermeister* who could not tell a false captain from a real one, *Simplicissimus* showed Voigt receiving the Nobel Peace Prize for making Prussian militarism look ridiculous.[23]

But the farce of Köpenick was the prelude to the tragedy of Zabern. In 1913 the garrison of that small Alsatian town, openly encouraged by its young commander, retaliated against demonstrations of civilian discontent by wholly illegal beatings, arrests, and threats of violence. Reichstag debates provoked by these incidents brought all the civilian-military tensions which had built up over the years to the surface. Liberals and even some conservatives joined socialists in clamoring for increased parliamentary control over the army. The incident received international coverage, reinforcing stereotypes of German aggressiveness. For instance, *Punch* parodied the instructions given to the Zabern garrison:

Enough! I leave our honor in your keeping.
What are our bright swords for, except to slay?
Preserve their lustre—let me see them leaping
Out of the scabbard twenty times a day!
Unless we smite the craven churls like crockery
To prove our right of place within the sun,
Our martial prestige has become a mockery
And Deutschland's day is done![24]

The responses of *Kladderadatsch* and *Simplicissimus* to the incident reflected their evolution during these years toward opposite political poles. *Kladderadatsch* expressed its increasing conservatism by avoiding any aggressive criticism of the army, urging only that the few offending officers be punished (a pious but vain hope). By contrast, *Simplicissimus* responded with a nightmarishly transformed image of that traditional figure of fun, the lieutenant. No longer a mere harmless snob, he appeared as a clawed and fanged monster, as an enormous porcupine with bayonets for quills, or as a trap-shooter picking off human quarry. The significance of these terrible visions may be judged by comparing them to earlier caricatures of the lieutenant which had shown him dancing, flirting, riding on parade, but hardly ever doing what he was trained to do, killing people. Perceiving militarism not simply as colorful show but as murderous reality, the humorist of 1913 became a prophet.[25]

The popularity of such humor reflected mounting civilian-military tension during the Wilhelmine period. The Bavarian *Simplicissimus* spoke for many non-Prussian Germans who found the Prussian military code both alien and oppressive. Hermann Sinsheimer likewise recalled the ridicule to which he had been subjected during his term of military service in Munich. "To stand on guard at night certainly wasn't much fun. One was always teased or even insulted by the passers-by. The Munich of that period didn't take the army very seriously. This was known as the *Simplicissimus-Stimmung* and if any of the fortune-tellers who abounded in the city had told me that I was destined to become editor of that infamous periodical, I would not have been able to

"The Alsatian Bogeyman." A comment on the Zabern affair. (Gulbransson, *Simplicissimus*, Nov. 24, 1913.)

laugh at such a bad joke." In the heated parliamentary debate over the Zabern incident, the liberal politician Friedrich Naumann emphasized that the dislike of Prussian arrogance was not merely an Alsatian phenomenon. "If lieutenants had behaved the same way in Württemburg, Baden, or Bavaria as they did in Zabern, they'd see what would happen." And Walther Rathenau recalled the public reaction to Zabern: "Not since the French diamond necklace scandal has there been such biting sarcasm."[26]

Both the critics and the defenders of the military establishment recognized the importance of *Simplicissimus* in articulating and mobilizing such discontent. Karl Liebknecht observed that "the totality of capitalist culture contains many self-destructive elements. Not the least important are those which attack militarism. The undermining effect, for example, of *Simplicissimus,* should not be underestimated." Certainly the disapproving, even paranoid attitude of the military brass indicated that they regarded the magazine as a severe threat both to the public image and to the internal cohesion of the army. "It was really ridiculous," wrote Thoma in his memoirs, "when a war minister, shaking with indignation, defended the lieutenants whose impertinence or arrogance had been mocked by *Simplicissimus.* These were taken as attacks on the army itself, and only harsh, overbearing words could describe the gravity of the offense." Although *Simplicissimus* was banned from German casinos, individual officers often bought their own copies, which provided the more progressive of them with verbal ammunition against their reactionary comrades. "I saw your picture in *Simplicissimus* the other day," remarks the officer hero of Hartleben's popular play *Rosenmontag.* "Yes that disgusting rag," replies his obnoxious comrade. "Frightful—but what *can* one do?" Apparently much disturbed by the popularity of the magazine among the younger officers, War Minister von Heeringen issued an order in 1910 requiring all officers to sign a pledge not to read *Simplicissimus.* The liberal press commented upon this high-handed edict with a mixture of amusement and indignation. "The military administration is interfering in the private reading habits of adult men," expostulated the *Hamburger Fremdenblatt.* "This opens up many other questions—will the Reserve officer too be treated in future as a servile creature, to whom one can dictate what newspapers he can read? This would be as serious an interference with individual freedom as we've ever seen." The prohibition, continued this editorial, was "more than a simple blunder—it was the expression of weakness and anxiety. . . . The Prussian military administration is treating the Bavarian *Witzblatt* . . . as a hostile power, against which it is directing a cavalry attack."[27]

As important as the negative Freudian function of humor was its more positive Koestlerian role as a catalyst for new ideas. The contrast between *Kladderadatsch* and *Simplicissimus* suggests a considerable evolution in the understanding of militarism in all its social and political implications. While *Kladderadatsch* commented only on the most conspicuous problems of the army, *Simplicissimus'* expanded vision extended beyond the army itself to the entire culture shaped by its authoritarian values. Many of its criticisms of the officer corps—their arrogance, their limited grasp of technology, their contempt for civilian politicians, their callous attitude toward enlisted men—were borne out by the experience of World War I. But military leaders such as von Heeringen, who condemned *Simplicissimus* as "the bacillus which destroys all our ideals," grossly overreacted to the magazine's essentially moderate, even constructive criticism. Unlike the socialist leaders, *Simplicissimus* advocated neither the reduction nor the radical restructuring of the army. Indeed, the satirists protested against aristocratic exclusiveness chiefly on behalf of an ambitious middle class whose skills, if fully used, would strengthen and not weaken the army. And, in spite of its occasional prophetic nightmares, *Simplicissimus* still portrayed a stable and peaceful world to which the violence of modern warfare was remote indeed. Note the flippant tone of the verse in which Thoma mocked a war minister who had alluded to the officer's duty to sacrifice his life in battle as a justification of military privilege.

> This noble youth someday may fall
> On bloody field, to save us all.
> The future corpse we'll not profane
> So give him parties and champagne.
> "Do treat him well," von Einem said,
> "Tomorrow, he may well be dead."
> So with this tale of war and death,
> He claims the victor's laurel wreath
> For *future* deeds of derring-do!
> Lieutenant, my heart bleeds for you!

A generation to which death on the battlefield seemed such a remote and improbable idea was ill prepared for the horrors of twentieth-century warfare.[28]

Sitting on the Powder-Keg

A perceptive *Simplicissimus* cartoon of 1906, entitled "The European Thunderstorm," showed a knight in armor sitting on a powder barrel in the midst of a raging thunderstorm. "Get off that barrel," warns the "angel of peace." "Don't you know that iron attracts lightning?" This pictorial message stressed both the ever-more threatening international situation and Germany's own hopelessly vulnerable position. Unlike the family journals, which seldom disturbed the cozy lives of their readers by mentioning war, the satirists returned to the uncomfortable topic again and again. Yet as international tensions increased, so also did the conflict, always perceptible in the satirist's work, between their own critical intelligence and the patriotic impulse toward unquestioning national solidarity. Especially on issues involving Germany's international security and prestige, any criticism, no matter how reasonable, was often perceived as subversive, even treacherous. Thus the satirical journals provide insight into the intellectual conflict and self-doubt which prompted even the most enlightened spirits to submerge critical judgment in the war hysteria of 1914.[29]

In no area was the theatrical atmosphere of Wilhelmine politics more striking than in that of foreign policy and diplomacy. Perhaps the best known of all attacks on the kaiser was the *Simplicissimus* "Palestine" issue of 1898, the substantial public and official reaction to which has already been described. The chiefly commercial purpose of the kaiser's trip to Palestine, on which Wilhelm acted in effect as "travelling salesman" for German business interests, put the monarch's posturing in a particularly ridiculous light. Moreover, the modern "crusader's" irresponsible offer to take the three hundred million Moslems of the world under his protection seriously alarmed the French and British, who perceived a threat to their interests in this vital area.[30]

The "Palestine" issue once again highlighted the glaring discrepancy between aggressive rhetoric and vain, irresponsible action. Heine's cover cartoon showed the ghosts of Geoffroi de

"Palestine." "Don't giggle, Barbarossa. Our crusades were pretty point-less, too." (Heine, *Simplicissimus*, Nov. 1898.)

Bouillon and Friedrich Barbarossa snickering together. "Don't giggle, Barbarossa," remarks the former, "our crusades were pretty ridiculous, too." But more offensive was Wedekind's verse (signed "Hieronymus Jobs"), which portrayed King David rising out of his grave and welcoming his fellow monarch to the Holy Land.

> Oh, welcome to His Majesty, the Kaiser.
> Who brings with him his Better Half, the Queen,
> And many a parson, lackey and advisor,
> And more policemen than we've ever seen!
> With joy we wait at the Historic Shrines,
> In hopes of hearing some immortal lines.
> About your visit we the more enthuse,
> Because you'll get our picture in the news
> . . . .
> So once again we welcome you, My Lord,
> And many thanks for saving our good name.
> For if your far-flung travels had ignored
> The Holy Land, we would have died of shame.
> A million Christians raise a loud "Hurrah!"
> And what a favored spot is Golgotha,
> Which heard the words of Christ, and now is due
> To hear some more well chosen words from you.
>
> Though men are lazy, not too fond of action,
> They have the greatest need to be admired,
> To show off, to be Number One Attraction,
> Like you, who strut so gorgeously attired—
> In sailor suit or ermine robes arrayed,
> Or in rococo suit of stiff brocade,
> As sportsman, huntsman, always on display,
> Oh photogenic prince! Accept this lay.[31]

The strong official reaction to this issue was probably chiefly due to its irritating resemblance to the comments of the foreign press. In a cartoon mocking Wilhelm's fondness for travel, *Punch* portrayed him as "Cook's Crusader." By showing him walking on water, entering Jerusalem on a donkey, and ascending (in a balloon!) to heaven, *Le Rire* spoofed Wilhelm's pretensions to divinity even more directly than had *Simplicissimus*. Similarity of content, however, did not imply similarity of motives. Unlike the foreign humorists, *Simplicissimus* regarded Wilhelm's role as international buffoon not with self-satisfied pleasure but with an-

"Colonial Powers." German, British, French, and Belgian colonial administrations are compared. (Heine, *Simplicissimus*, May 3, 1904.)

ger and shame. Many years later Ludwig Thoma reflected maturely that the trip had been "a great political mistake, one of many tactless and disastrous actions. . . . Later generations will judge these mistakes very harshly, even seeing them as factors which, along with many other decadent cultural trends, led to war." *Simplicissimus* voiced the anger of many perceptive people who were fully aware of Wilhelm's highly erratic personality but could do nothing to control him.[32]

The government's unwise and futile imperial ventures into Africa and Asia called forth the satirists' sharpest barbs. Both journals condemned the incompetence and brutality of the African colonial administration, though as always with different style and emphasis. In both *Simplicissimus* and *Kladderadatsch* we find spoofs of Prussian authoritarianism transplanted to the jungle—giraffes marching the goose-step, or muzzled crocodiles. To *Kladderadatsch*, however, African imperialism was chiefly an unfortunate mistake; reacting to the colonial scandals of 1906, it protested that the colonies, tracts of barren "stones and sand," would always be a "thankless burden." *Simplicissimus* by contrast saw the African venture not as an aberration but as an integral part of German foreign policy. A comment on the bloody extermination of the insurgent Herero tribe revealed a particularly vivid insight into the domestic function of imperialism as a device for preserving stability by distracting public attention from internal to foreign affairs. The cartoon showed hordes of black spearmen swarming into a German factory. "It's time the German government crushed the Hereros," read the caption, "or the black beasts will come to Germany and abolish slavery here." An overseas defeat for the government, so this cartoon implied, might prove a domestic defeat as well.[33]

A still more passionate antiimperialist protest was called forth by the German intervention in the Boxer War of 1900. In a more than usually ill-advised speech, Wilhelm had sent off the German expeditionary force with the admonition to imitate their "ancestor," Atilla the Hun. Whereas *Kladderadatsch* merely warned the German troops "not to break the Chinese porcelain," *Simplicissimus* responded to the "Hunnen-Rede" with a nightmarish cartoon entitled "The Dream of the Empress of China," showing a knight in white armor pouring out a cornucopia of blood over the globe. "The European pours out the benefits of civilization over the whole earth," reads the caption. Such bitter mockery of the clichés of imperialism implied not only distrust of official rhetoric but the more positive attitudes toward nonwestern peo-

"The Moroccan War Fury." "All these tiresome negotiations have put the beast to sleep!" (Heine, *Simplicissimus*, Sept. 7, 1911.)

ples which were also exemplified by *Simplicissimus'* obvious admiration for oriental artistic styles.[34]

On other international issues the satirical journals likewise deflated aggressive slogans and called for moderation and sanity. To the Moroccan crises of 1905 and 1911, both impulsive and ill-advised bids for German prestige, both journals took a somewhat belittling attitude. In 1911, *Kladderadatsch* mocked the endless and inconclusive negotiations. "Kiderlen-Wächter and Cambon are speaking to each other every day. . . . Their negotiations are very secret, not a word of them leaks out, only the entire assembled press finds out about them, but no one else! . . . Our correspondent, who is admirably informed, offers this analysis of the situation—either it will change or it will remain the same." *Kladderadatsch* also congratulated Kiderlen on negotiating a settlement and refusing to yield to the demands of extremists. *Simplicissimus* belittled chauvinistic slogans by implying that the issues were rather trivial. "Why are the Germans and the French fighting so hard over this desert?" one Arab is shown asking another. "It's not as if we were rich!" "Well, if we were rich, England would already have got us!" is the reply. Moreover both journals, especially *Simplicissimus,* painted a bitterly negative picture of extremists such as the Pan-Germans who stirred up mass emotions over these trumped-up war scares. A reaction to the Morocco crisis of 1911 was a drawing of two bespectacled reporters attempting to awaken the Moroccan War Fury—a hideous female figure whose yellow-green skin drips with blood—with pricks of a quill pen. Such cartoons reflected genuine opposition to such irresponsible sabre-rattling. "We are now harvesting the fruits of the Kaiser's operetta-style government," wrote Thoma in 1911. "The hostility of France and England, and their disgraceful way of treating us, all express their long-standing aversion to the *Heldentenor* of Europe, who has always behaved tactlessly and often ridiculously." And later in his memoirs Thoma claimed that "the issues [of *Simplicissimus*] from 1898 to 1914 are full of warnings against war and revulsion against all who encouraged it."[35]

In fact, however, the spirit of reason often gave way to the more compelling emotions of hostility and fear. *Kladderadatsch* constantly warned the Fatherland against the threat of "encirclement" by a coalition of hostile powers.

> The days of peace may quickly pass away
> Prepare yourself for bloody war today!

The brave man fights with calm and quiet mind
Knowing that his true allies stand behind.
But without allies we can stand alone,
Whether our friends be treacherous or true,
And we can be victorious on our own.[36]

Like *Kladderadatsch, Simplicissimus* often warned Germany against a too-trustful attitude toward foreign powers. Among its most controversial comments on Germany diplomacy was a cartoon entitled *Gesandtenerziehung* ("the training of an ambassador"), which rebuked a German ambassador to the United States for his allegedly cringing response to the Caribbean crisis of 1903. Earlier in the year Wilhelm's incautious expression of interest in this area had seriously alarmed American public opinion. *Harper's Weekly* for example had responded with mingled anxiety and amusement.

Kaiser, Kaiser, burning bright
You have given us a fright!
With your belt and straps and sashes,
And your upward-turned mustaches.
Kaiser, Kaiser, Man of War,
What a funny joke you are!

Retreating suddenly from this aggressive posture, Wilhelm sought frantically to appease American public opinion by an extravagant show of friendship. Heine's ferocious cartoon, which purported to show the training of ambassadors for such conciliatory missions, condemned this change of policy as timid and dishonorable. When Heine and "responsible editor" Julius Linnekogel were called up before a Munich court on a charge of having published "grossly offensive material," their lawyer supported his contention that the cartoon had served a constructive purpose by calling several "expert witnesses," among them Georg Hirth, editor of *Jugend*. The drawing, argued Hirth, was not unpatriotic—on the contrary, it was "infused with a stubborn patriotism. It admonishes the German people. 'Don't let your representatives appease a foreign power in such a humiliating fashion! . . .' Th. Th. Heine only wants to warn us not to be misled by our love of peace into a flirtation with a foreign power." *Simplicissimus* thus correctly perceived Wilhelm as floundering between excessive arrogance (as pointed out in the *Palestine* issue) and excessive cringing. No more than Wilhelm himself, however, did the satirists seem to conceive of an appropriately moderate and constructive German foreign policy. On the contrary, their own attitudes vacillated almost as sharply between hostility and conciliation as did those of the government itself.[37]

Such conflicting impulses were evident in the images of foreign countries presented in both journals. Both, especially *Simplicissimus,* deplored the noisy chauvinism of the era. "I can't really stand Prussian patriotism," wrote Thoma to Langen. "Let's forget about all those silver spoons stolen in 1807, and all those grandmothers raped by Napoleon's soldiers. Let's concentrate on the present!" While *Kladderadatsch* still dwelt on the hostilities of 1871, *Simplicissimus* expressed Langen's real affinity for French culture by printing many works of French authors and even (as in 1906, on the anniversary of the Battle of Jena) by extolling the ideas of the French Revolution and their triumph over German backwardness. To Langen's plan to sell *Simplicissimus* in Paris, Thoma initially responded with misgivings. "Your plan is dangerous because our entire opposition will gang up on us," he wrote to Langen in 1900. Such critics, he explained, would see a French edition not as "high-spirited" satire but as a "treacherous, low-down insult to the Fatherland." By 1908, however, Thoma was prepared aggressively to defend the sale of *Simplicissimus* in France against superpatriots who charged that the satirists were "fouling their own nest" by exposing internal German disunity to the "hereditary enemy. "Whatever they may say and write," affirmed Thoma in a letter to the Viennese *Arbeiter-Zeitung,* "we will never agree to view France as a 'hereditary enemy' from whom we must hide our opinions. France is more closely related to us artistically than any East Elbian backwater. And we are concerned with artistic values here."[38]

Images of other European nationalities, however, encouraged hostility rather than tolerance. For both journals the chief villain on the international stage was the greedy and scheming John Bull. The anti-British campaign peaked at the time of the Boer War, which the satirists portrayed as the struggle of heroic peasants against power-mad imperialists. *Kladderadatsch* idealized "the little Boer nation,"

> Who, risking all that they possessed for freedom
> In desperate and earth-defying struggle
> Took up the Holy War for a good cause
> And so chastised the armies of the British
> That they will not forget the Boers soon.

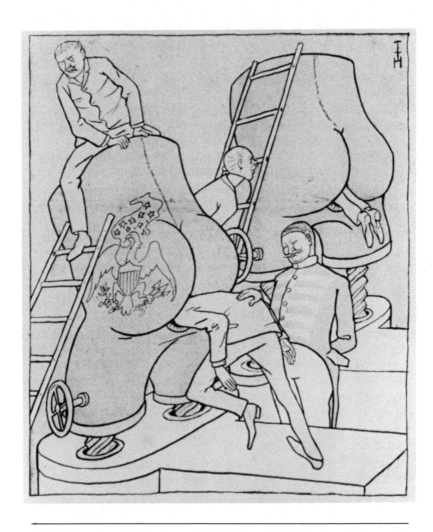

"The Education of an Ambassador." (Heine, *Simplicissimus*, May 1904.)

Simplicissimus expressed an even more passionate Anglophobia. The British use of concentration camps, which outraged public opinion toward the end of the war, was protested in a cartoon showing an obese figure of Edward VII trampling tiny inhabitants of a camp into a bloody pulp. "This blood is splashing me from head to toe," remarks Edward. "My crown is getting filthy."[39]

Although some perceptive journalists decried the sentimentality of such pro-Boer rhetoric (the popular idealization of the Boers, remarked Theodor Barth, "was about as accurate as Cooper's characterization of the noble Indian"), the vast majority contributed to the torrent of Anglophobic propaganda which (as Albert Langen himself had feared) became a significant factor in the deterioration of Anglo-German relations. The confiscation of the issue on the Boer War—instigated, the editorial board suspected, by the protests of some English visitors to Munich—was greeted by Thoma as a triumph. "I hate the English, and if I could shoot one of them, I'd be delighted," he wrote to Langen's wife, Dagny, who had expressed reservations about his Anglophobic propaganda. "Who cares about decency and good taste? I want to *hurt* them." Even after the South African war the satirists' stereotype of the English character was thoroughly hostile. *Simplicissimus,* for example, portrayed two buck-toothed, tweed-clad English tourists looking down their noses at their German hosts. "I like it in Germany," remarks one, "you don't have to be *nice* to people!" Such comments clearly reveal the mingled resentment and envy felt by a new nation for its more established rival. Britain's importance as the home of precisely those parliamentary institutions which these German liberals admired was hardly ever mentioned.[40]

Germany's neighbors to the east and south were portrayed with far less ambivalence and far more contempt and hostility. Both the *Kladderadatsch* and the *Simplicissimus* groups showed Russia primarily as the land of autocracy, superstition, and political reaction. Protest against the czarist police state provided material for the many scenes of torture, violence, and mass murder which proliferated in the pages of *Simplicissimus.* Though aware of the moribund state of the Austrian monarchy, neither journal expressed any sympathy for its Slavic nationalities, not even *Simplicissimus*, which had championed oppressed minorities, such as Poles and Alsatians, within the Reich. *Kladderadatsch* pictured the Serbs as mere tools of the Russians, and ridiculed Czech nationalism. To *Simplicissimus* the Balkan peoples provided material for funny, deeply insulting jokes which portrayed them as primitive, bug-ridden, and generally subhuman. The Serbs, asserted one cartoon, always fight to the death because they can never find a white flag clean enough to be convincing. Images of rodents and insects expressed a profound disgust for the Slavs, who were portrayed as lice in the sick eagle's feathers, or as a swarm of devouring rats. Such comments not only encouraged German-Slavic antagonism but expressed a prophetic fear that the disintegration of the Austrian ally might destroy Germany as well.[41]

These images of other cultures bear out Freud's generalization that society permits a far more direct expression of aggression against foreign peoples than against one's own. To be sure, the contrast between the two journals' views of France suggests an attempt by the younger generation to overcome old hatreds. But, especially after the death of Langen in 1909, even such tentative cosmopolitan impulses were overwhelmed by the ever more strident nationalism of Thoma. Although in part a concession to public opinion—"*Simplicissimus* still suffers from the fact that the first few volumes were regarded as antinational," he wrote to Langen in 1900—this nationalistic stance also expressed Thoma's deepest convictions. "The cosmopolitans have played out their role," he continued; "now we see how right Treitschke was forty years ago, when he saw nationalism as the guiding principle of our future development. The view that we should treat the human race as if it were in one big melting pot belongs to our political childhood." The satire of *Kladderadatsch* and *Simplicissimus* illustrated not only the emotional priority given to nationalism over political principles (such as liberalism) or aesthetic preferences (such as admiration for French art and literature) but also its distorting effect on the critical faculty. For while vividly aware of the hostility of other powers, the satirists failed in many cases to point out how Germany's own policies might have provoked or aggravated such hostility. Thus was the self-fulfilling fear of "encirclement" reinforced.[42]

Over the endless allusions to international tension and hostility hung the terrifying vision of war. Although both journals warned of the imminent explosion of the international powder keg, *Simplicissimus'* far more vivid and compelling imagery reflected a greatly heightened anxiety. While *Kladderadatsch* portrayed war only occasionally in reaction to such obviously bloody events as the Balkan conflicts, *Simplicissimus* explored violence in all its forms—duel, torture, battlefield, pogrom. Its reactions to the Russo-Japanese war (a cartoon of 1904, for instance, showed a battlefield piled high with horribly mutilated corpses) prophetically portrayed the effects of modern weapons. Like the early Expressionists, whose devastating visions were presented in dream imagery in which "the most monstrous fears become envisioned reality," the cartoonists often depicted violence in symbolic form. The armies of the endlessly warring Balkan states appeared as tiny figures swimming in an immense sea of blood, and the Italian invasion of Tripoli inspired apocalyptic imagery—a skeletal horse carrying allegorical figures of war and cholera tramples over a heap of corpses. Sometimes the nightmare became even more explicit, as in a two-page spread entitled "The War of the Future." Under a deep-red sunset two military bands play on either side of a vast battlefield piled high with corpses. "When our modern weapons have killed everyone, friend and foe," reads the caption, "then the military bands will take up the struggle and the war will end as a musical competition." The combined horror and absurdity of this cartoon, which appeared in 1906, suggest the importance of satire in general, and of *Simplicissimus* in particular, in the formation of the Expressionist style and consciousness.[43]

Thus their warnings against war, their mockery of noisy chauvinism, and their criticism of the militarist ideology all expressed the satirists' hope for a peaceful resolution of European conflicts. Yet even here there were contradictions and inconsistencies, well expressed in Ludwig Thoma's response to the Morocco crisis of 1911. "A few years ago I would have been more anxious about such sudden threats of war," he wrote to his friend Haussmann; "now I've gotten angrier at the stupid gestures with which *la France militaire* provokes the Kaiser and us. . . . Of course I tell myself in calmer moments that we Germans must bear some of the responsibility for the French misunderstanding of Germany's peaceful intentions . . . I realize that my Bavarian tendency to 'have things out' is pretty stupid," he concluded, "and I'll be happy to observe the changing seasons . . . in peaceful comfort." Clearly, however, a crisis could destroy this precarious equilibrium between hostility and caution, reason and aggression.[44]

Thus the exhilaration of August 1914 may be partly explained by the sense of relief at the resolution of long-standing intellectual and emotional conflicts. During the month of July both *Witzblätter* published more jokes on the extraordinary heat than on the international crisis. On August 9, the first issue after the out-

"War and Cholera." "Civilization comes to Tripoli." (Heine, *Simplicissimus*, Dec. 11, 1911.)

break of war, *Kladderadatsch* published a melodramatic cartoon of a bearskin-clad Wagnerian figure calling on his countrymen to defend their native land. "Beware, German brothers, the Huns are coming." The transformation of *Kladderadatsch* into an organ of war propaganda occurred fairly easily, only adding to the hysterical intensity of the hostility to the *Entente* powers which it had expressed since the 1890s.[45]

For *Simplicissimus* the transition from an aggressively critical to an affirmatively patriotic stance was far more difficult and abrupt. According to Hermann Sinsheimer (later editor-in-chief in the 1920s), Ludwig Thoma called a meeting to propose that *Simplicissimus* cease publication. In a defensive war "from which . . . no German could stand aside" Thoma asserted that "there was no place for a satirical sheet which opposed the ruling powers of Germany." But Thomas Theodor Heine persuaded him otherwise, arguing that "it was very wrong to believe that *Simplicissimus* was obsolete . . . maybe its great age was just beginning . . . the Fatherland needed a periodical of such international prestige to support the war effort." Sinsheimer cynically commented that patriotism and economic self-interest coincided very fortunately for the *Simplicissimus* staff, which would otherwise have faced unemployment and the loss of substantial incomes.[46]

In any event, the change was swift and complete. Within a week *Simplicissimus* was publishing odes to "our hero, Hindenburg"—a strange hero for these long-time foes of Prussian militarism! Thereafter the magazine devoted most of its energy to vivid, grotesque, and violent caricatures of the enemy, a task to which the artistic talents of the satirists were eminently suited. To glorify the German war effort, all the Germanic and neomedieval imagery which the prewar *Simplicissimus* had hilariously parodied was now used with seriousness and pathos. The mood of *Simplicissimus* resembled that of most of the war literature which flooded from the presses in the last months of 1914. "In the center of the 'German apocalypse' of 1914," states one recent article, "is the interpretation of war as the judgment of God on Germany's enemies. The enemies of the German Empire were portrayed through classic apocalyptic symbols as embodiments of Absolute Evil, and identified with Satan and the Antichrist." The fervor if not the imagery of *Simplicissimus* was thoroughly religious.[47]

Many years later Ludwig Thoma reflected on the events of August 1914. "All of us had supported peace," he asserted. "With

"In the Name of Culture!" "Marianne" pleads with the British to hold back the Russian beast. A comment on the outbreak of hostilities. (Gulbransson, *Simplicissimus*, Aug. 3, 1914.)

no cautious reservations we had denounced the personal rule and all its harmful manifestations. . . . But when the war was there nothing mattered but our own country." Far from a sudden transformation, however, *Simplicissimus'* conversion was consistent with many opinions which it had expressed since the turn of the century. Like his countrymen, the satirist had a high stake in the preservation of the society which he criticized. Like them, he rejoiced in the war fever which seemed for the moment to have solved class and political conflicts and to have created an instant unity.[48]

The study of satirical literature sheds light on the complex and ambiguous situation not only of the humorist but more generally of the dissenter in Wilhelmine society. The role of outsider and critic was even less comfortable in Germany than in more liberal societies. Like his countrymen, the humorist revealed in his enthusiastic reaction to the *Burgfrieden* of 1914 a deep-seated revulsion against political controversy, a longing for a unity which would transcend party strife. From some of their comments, one could even interpret the fervid wartime patriotism of the *Simplicissimus* staff members as the expiation of their guilt over their prewar role as social critics. Though one cannot condemn them for supporting their nation's war effort, one can criticize them— and the culture whose values they had internalized—for equating patriotism with unquestioning conformity. For the war into which they so eagerly plunged was, as they themselves in a calmer moment had imagined it, brutal, bloody, and senseless. If more intelligent and enlightened Europeans had retained their critical judgment instead of joining so wholeheartedly in the war hysteria, some of the carnage might have been avoided.

Sex and Satire:
Simplicissimus Looks
at Family Life

5

The Social Context

AT the turn of the twentieth century, social critics leveled sharp attacks on the institution of the family and its traditions. Feminists challenged the family's legal basis, socialists its economic structure, psychologists its sexual norms, artists and writers its ideals of respectability and good taste. "It was an era of hope and action," wrote one contemporary observer, Holbrook Jackson, of the decade of the 1890s. "Dissatisfied with long ages of precedent and of action based upon precedent, many set about testing life for themselves. The new man wished to be himself, the new woman to lead her own life. The snapping of apron strings caused consternation in many decent households as young men and maidens were suddenly inspired to develop their own souls and personalities."[1]

Jackson's impression that "never was there a time when the young were so young or the old so old" is borne out by the contrast between the attitudes of the traditional *Kladderadatsch* and the avant-garde *Simplicissimus* toward the subject of family and sexual mores. In the area of foreign policy and politics the two magazines differed less in basic point of view than in the style and intensity of their criticism. But in the area of cultural criticism *Simplicissimus* (along with its counterpart, *Jugend*) represented a new trend in German popular humor. Until the 1890s German satirical periodicals could be classified into two groups— "political" magazines such as *Kladderadatsch* which concentrated almost exclusively on the public issues, and "family" mag-

azines such as the *Fliegende Blatter* which offered a very harmless type of social satire. The definition of family life as
"nonpolitical," which placed it almost above criticism, was in
itself a political judgment of major importance. Although grad-
ually giving more space to social comment, *Kladderadatsch* remained as firm as its British counterpart *Punch* in its commitment to accepted standards of decency and literary taste. Thus
the decision of *Simplicissimus* to include the German family
among its chief targets was in itself a major departure from tradition. By viewing the family as a political institution, *Simplicissimus* sought the roots of political behavior in social and cultural conditioning. The integration of social, cultural, and political
criticism produced a many-faceted and penetrating view of German society.[2]

Simplicissimus challenged the conventional family with two
types of humor, the sardonic picture of bourgeois home life (of
which the best examples were contained in Heine's "Bilder aus
dem Familienleben") and the comments on changing sexual mores
contained in the risqué story, anecdote, or cartoon. Although
Simplicissimus often made use of the standard slapstick characters—nagging wife, henpecked husband, *enfant terrible*—the
result was less a domestic farce than a comedy of manners, for
the careful portrayal of the dress, manners, and environments of
the people identified them not merely as universal human types
but as inhabitants of a specific time and place whose problems
were not simply those of the human condition but often had an
explicitly topical significance.[3]

On this as on other issues, humor served a dual function, as a
release for repressed wishes and as a catalyst for new ideas. Tradition was still well established. The wry picture of the cat-and-
dog middle-aged couple reflected the stability of even the most
dismal unions, while the pervasive jokes on adultery gratified a
powerful forbidden impulse among a class where many marriages were not made for love. "Among the institutions which
humor is wont to attack," wrote Freud, "none is more completely
protected by moral precepts, and yet so inviting of attack, as the
institution of marriage. Most of the cynical jokes are directed
against it. For no demand is more personal than that made upon
sexual freedom and nowhere has civilization attempted to exercise a more stringent suppression than in the realm of sexuality."
Simplicissimus exemplified the cynical spirit which Freud described and provided a safety valve for impulses which had no

other socially acceptable expression. And yet the very popularity of such humor attested to the increasingly open and frank discussion of previously taboo subjects. The decade of the 1890s, in fact, was a time of pervasive change, not only in sex roles and stereotypes (as advocated by the feminist movement) but in the structure of the family, where the gradual trend away from traditional authoritarianism and toward a more informal and egalitarian atmosphere was widely evident. The frequent bitterness of *Simplicissimus'* attack on the conventional family reflected not only the anger but the rising expectations of a generation which demanded the transformation of rigid institutions to conform to new social conditions. These demands met with entrenched resistance from conservative groups such as the clergy, who saw social change as a threat to their continued political dominance. In the 1890s, therefore, the family was widely discussed by both Right and Left not only as a private but as a political institution of central importance.[4]

The German conservative tradition had always stressed the parallel between the state and the family, which inculcated the citizen's essential virtues—loyalty, obedience, and industry. In a book entitled *Die Familie,* published in 1855 but still popular in the 1880s (by 1882 it had gone through nine editions) the sociologist W.H. Riehl described the family's function as the preservation of social stability through the transmission of hallowed traditions from one generation to the next, a duty which women, because of their passive and nurturing qualities, were ideally suited to perform. Another well known conservative, the historian Heinrich von Treitschke, claimed that the unity of the state depended upon that of the family. "The moral existence of every country is so deeply rooted in the stability of healthy family life," he asserted, "that we can cite instances in which nothing else stood firm in a shattered national life." As the microcosm of the state, the family was based on the principles of authority and inequality to which the demand for egalitarian marriage was an affront. Therefore Treitschke urged women to give up their claims to equal rights and instead to accept the "esteem" of their husbands and the security of the home.[5]

While the political right wing defended the family, the left wing resolutely attacked it. The lapse of the anti-socialist laws in 1890 had allowed the wide circulation of August Bebel's *Die Frau und der Sozialismus* (first published in 1879 and reprinted throughout the 1890s). "The women and the worker," Bebel began, "have always had something in common—they have been oppressed."

Like the conservatives, the socialists also viewed the family as the microcosm of the state, but of a state which had condemned the majority of its population to slavery and degradation. Moreover, Bebel analyzed the oppression not only of the proletarian woman but of her middle-class sister, the victim of the capitalist system which forced her into a mercenary and loveless but indissoluble marriage. Only the fall of capitalism and the establishment of the socialist future state—where Bebel predicted that marriage laws would be abolished, the sexes would be equal, and children would be communally reared—would end the oppression of women. *Simplicissimus'* substantial agreement with Bebel on many issues reflected the impact of the book, which sold widely among middle-class as well as working-class readers.[6]

Since the founding of the Reich the attempted socialist subversion of the family had been viewed with considerable alarm by substantial segments of the public. In 1874 right-wing parties had attempted to add a paragraph to the proposed Press Law providing severe penalties for publications which "undermined the values of bourgeois society, especially the family and universal military service." This proposal, rejected by the Reichstag, was only the first of a long series of similar attempts at censorship. After 1890 both the lapse of the anti-socialist laws and the development of artistic modernism prompted anxious conservatives to redouble their efforts to preserve traditional values. In 1892 clerical and right-wing groups proposed the so-called Lex Heinze, which would have forbidden the display not only of pornographic works of art but of those which "without being pornographic, affronted feelings of decency." In 1894, only a year after this measure was temporarily shelved, another measure, the "Umsturzvorlage" of 1894, again sought to punish not only incitements to riot or class conflict but also "all insults to religion, the monarchy, marriage, family and private property." Like the Lex Heinze, this bill was strongly opposed not only by socialists but by liberals, who feared its inhibiting effect on freedom of expression, and it was voted down in the Reichstag. In 1897, however, the Lex Heinze in revised form was once again placed before the Reichstag, this time supported not only by the conservative parties but by powerful citizens' pressure groups called *Sittlichkeitsvereine* (morality leagues). This bill caused the greatest controversy of all and was finally defeated only by the combined efforts of the left-wing parties in collaboration with the artistic and literary community.[7]

The many confiscations of allegedly pornographic issues of

Simplicissimus during this period reflected the diverse attitudes within the community toward the limits of permissible sexual frankness. The clergy and their lay sympathisers kept up constant pressure upon the police to remove offensive issues from shop windows or to forbid their sale. When the offending editors were brought to trial, however, they were usually either acquitted or given very trivial sentences, such as the fine imposed in 1904 for the allegedly indecent cartoon "Gesandtenerziehung" ("The Education of an Ambassador"). The judge justified his verdict in this case by alluding to the discrepancy between the sensibilities of the artistically sophisticated segment of the public which defended *Simplicissimus* and those of the "man in the street." "With all respect for the opinions of these gentlemen," he concluded, "they only represent a very limited segment of the public. . . . They express only the opinion of a very small group of supporters of modern art and literature. The favorable reaction of this small group to [publications which] offend and outrage the public cannot be taken into account in measuring the defendants' guilt." But since *Simplicissimus*' risqué items, particularly the cartoons of Reznicek, were exceedingly popular, one is moved to doubt this picture of widespread outrage and disgust. Not only the editors themselves but the merchants who displayed allegedly indecent material were vulnerable to prosecution. In 1905 a Cologne bookstore owner was denounced to the police for displaying a Reznicek cartoon depicting an adulterous couple discovered by the offended husband.[8]

Though not in itself a novel phenomenon (for *épater le bourgeois* had been the motto of many artists throughout the nineteenth century) the artistic critique of the family was given new urgency by the social conditions of the 1890s, which revealed the discrepancy between traditional ideals and new realities in a lurid light. In Germany rapid urbanization, much of which occurred as late as the 1880s and 1890s, had disrupted established communities and exposed a shocked population to the evils of urban poverty, rootlessness, and crime. Among the greatest of these problems was the rapid increase in prostitution. While the total number of active prostitutes in Germany (always an inexact figure since most did not register with the police) was estimated in 1900 at between 100,000 and 200,000, by 1914 it had risen to 330,000. "Whereas today it is as rare to meet a prostitute on the streets of a big city as it is to meet a wagon in the road," recollected Stefan Zweig in 1941, "then the sidewalks were so sprinkled with women for sale that it was more difficult to avoid than to find them." One reaction to this situation was the panic expressed in repressive measures such as the Lex Heinze. But more thoughtful observers saw prostitution not as an aberration but as an inevitable product of a rigid system which provided few healthy outlets for the human sexual urge. In the words of Zweig, it constituted a "dark underground vault over which rose the gorgeous structure of middle class society with its faultless radiant facade." Thus artists and writers of the 1890s demanded an end to such sordid concealment and a franker acceptance of human sexuality. In its seventh issue, *Simplicissimus* already felt the need to defend itself against criticism by disavowing any interest in pornography, the exploitation of sexual subject matter purely for its shock value. "But it is not immoral," the statement continued, "to expose with bitter laughter the moral corruption into which our decadent civilization is sinking. It is *not* immoral for the artist to illuminate those depths of our social life in which outmoded prejudices, crumbling principles, the cult of the golden calf, and the crippling impact of poverty turn healthy passion into a decadent caricature. It is not immoral to proclaim to an emasculated generation the eternal, holy right to true passion."[9]

In its challenge to traditional moral standards, *Simplicissimus* often found itself in agreement with the German feminist movement, for which the decade of the 1890s was a period of major growth. Although it involved only a rather small number of people, the movement cogently expressed a wide range of social, cultural, and intellectual dissent. Unlike the British and American movements, which during this period concentrated chiefly on political rights such as suffrage, the German feminists emphasized social issues such as prostitution, the rights of mothers, and the protection of illegitimate children. Their frank, sometimes daring exposé of previously taboo subjects debunked the conventional picture of the home as a place of peace, harmony, and sheltered contentment. The popularity of Ibsen's plays among the women of this period was but one sign of a growing discontent. "Into the sleepy sitting-rooms of the middle class," wrote the feminist Laura Marholm, "he shed a harsh and painful light, which revealed the greasy and faded state of 'respectable' family life with disgusting clarity. Disgust, nausea, and a nervous drive to escape, to find herself, to live in this short life in which so much was already lost—these were the feelings which he awakened in women."[10]

The feminist movement by no means rejected the family in it-self—indeed, it placed a very high value on motherhood, which many feminists, such as the influential Swedish author Ellen Key, regarded as the highest fulfillment of women's peculiar gifts. But it denounced the existing form of the family as an oppressive institution which justified the subjection of women by a hypo-critical appeal to religious and moral principle. The sexual pru-dery of the family, they claimed, perpetuated the oppression of women. In the name of chastity women were bound to husbands they did not love (while husbands in fact, if not in theory, were permitted much more sexual freedom), and in the name of social propriety their behavior was hedged about with restrictive con-ventions "bound by a thousand invisible threads more securely than by chains."[11]

Simplicissimus relentlessly attacked the sentimental cult of domesticity and showed the often sordid reality under the re-spectable facade. At the same time, however, its call for the lib-eration of the individual from outmoded restraints was not with-out ambivalence, for in the private as in the public sphere, change could produce anxiety as well as exhilaration. Feminists often voiced their misgivings about the emotional dislocation pro-duced by an all-too-precipitate breakdown of traditional values. Ellen Key wrote eloquently that "the restlessness, the insecurity, the feeling of emptiness, the suffering that the modern young woman so often experiences is caused chiefly by the disintegra-tion of religious belief. . . . To the external homelessness, an in-ternal homelessness is added. And men, too, suffer in the same way, perhaps more, in our culture which is unstable precisely because it has no religious basis." While appealing to its readers discontent with traditional mores, *Simplicissimus* also reflected their anxieties through a sometimes very hostile picture of the sexually emancipated woman and of the sophisticated world in which she moved. Thus in both its positive and its negative com-ments on changing sex roles, *Simplicissimus* provided a percep-tive picture of a society in transition.[12]

Pictures of Family Life

The attitudes of *Simplicissimus* toward conventional family life were exemplified in two typical cartoons. In the first a beautiful young woman, elegantly dressed, sits beside her husband in a carriage after a ball. "Oh my God," she groans, "now we return to our tranquil domestic bliss!" In the second, two highly decorative devils lead a stout and weary looking man into a bright orange Hell. "What?" he exclaims, "no kids? No piano practice? I must be in Heaven?" The mildly cynical tone implied that family life was to be accepted, if at all, with wry or bitter resignation. A really happy family was seldom shown or described.[13]

Some of this cynicism, to be sure, was prompted by a timeless grief at the passing of youth, beauty, and romance. *Simplicissimus* contained many jokes on this theme, among the best of which was a cartoon series entitled "Love's Spring and Summer" showing two scenes. In the first a slender young man stands in a lady's garden beside a clothesline on which hang several small and dainty undergarments. In the second the same man, now portly and middle aged, stands beneath the same clothesline on which hang garments now about three times as big! Even this harmless and universal joke ridiculed the saccharine clichés of the time, deriving its punch from the juxtaposition of sentimental title and very unsentimental imagery. Such indecent facts as the size of undergarments would never have been treated in conventional fiction or in traditional comic papers such as *Punch*.[14]

Simplicissimus' debunking of popular sentimentality served a definite and serious purpose. The cult of romantic love seemed to some not only mawkish but harmfully misleading. Rosa Mayreder, a prominent Austrian feminist, complained that the sugary fiction of the women's magazines gave their young female readers a picture of love so "false and deceitful" as seriously to impair their marital adjustment. The disappointment of young people fed on second-rate literature was lampooned in many stories and cartoons. In one picture a plump, pouting young woman lounging in an arm-chair with her lap dog whines, "Hubby, you don't love me anymore—you haven't called me your sweet little sugarplum all day." Though this cartoon could equally well have appeared in *Kladderadatsch* or *Punch,* there were others which could not have. One, entitled "The Interrupted Honeymoon," shows a young girl weeping disconsolately on the shoulder of her fat, disapproving mother while her husband looks on rather helplessly. "Oh mother," she sobs, "let me come home to you. Why, I thought men were some kind of higher being." No mere humorous exaggeration, this cartoon portrayed the same real-life conditions as did a contemporary writer, Stefan Zweig, in his autobiography. "Good breeding for a young girl of that time was identical with

"A Visit to the Master of the House." Overstuffed furniture and over-stuffed people. (Heine, *Simplicissimus*, April 3, 1897.)

ignorance of life. . . . I am still amused by a grotesque story of an aunt of mine who, on the night of her marriage, stormed the door of her parents' house at one o'clock in the morning. She never again wished to see the horrible creature to whom she had been married. He was a madman and a beast, for he had seriously attempted to undress her. It was only with great difficulty that she had been able to escape from this obviously perverted desire." Thus *Simplicissimus*' protest against sentimentality echoed the serious plea made by feminists such as Ellen Key and authors such as Frank Wedekind for the sexual education of young girls so that they could enter marriage with realistic expectations.[15]

But the tendency of this generation to question traditional sexual stereotypes emerged in jokes on this same theme whose impact depended on the reversal of the expected sexual roles. For in a culture where sex was seldom discussed openly, sexual ignorance and the apprehensions which it caused were by no means confined to females. To be sure, respectable society had arrived at what Zweig termed a "remarkable compromise" whereby premarital experience, forbidden to everyone in theory, was permitted to young men in practice as long as discretion was preserved. But in the story of the betrothal of the worthy Professor Bindinger, Thoma portrayed a male who had been so unwise as to take accepted moral standards seriously. Having spent a chaste youth following the example of Tacitus's ancient Germans, the Professor (as he pompously confides to the reader) finds himself on the eve of his marriage in a state of lamentable ignorance. "I expected that my bride would have received some motherly counsel which might enable her to recognize my complete ignorance . . . and this might have gravely reduced, if not altogether extinguished, the natural reverence of a wife for her husband." Alarmed by this regrettable prospect, Bindinger vainly seeks the advice, first of a friend who is reputed (unfortunately without justification) to have spent a wild and immoral youth, and next of an eminent biologist whose narrow specialization in animal reproduction has left him no time to investigate the irrelevant subject of human mating. Bindinger is finally saved from his dilemma by that popular household reference work, *Meyers Konversationslexikon.* "It was a wonderful coincidence. To be sure, I didn't find everything I was looking for, and was forced to the conclusion that the most important knowledge was often taken for granted. Nevertheless I was able to master a number of technical expressions, which would surely put me in a position to

"The Little Optimist." "Isn't a marriage like yours called a wild [common-law] marriage, Mama?" (Heine, *Simplicissimus*, April 21, 1896.)

demonstrate to my wife a thorough theoretical mastery of the subject. . . . On the following evening when I was alone with Marie for the first time, I was able to conceal my natural anxiety. . . . By the way, during the next few days I gave the German Fatherland a son." This story laughed at traditional morality as the product of an inhibited and overintellectualized culture which had estranged both men and women from their most natural functions.[16]

The romantic young couple did not live happily ever after—they soon became the middle-aged pair whose stolid life-style provided most of the material for Heine's most famous cartoon series, "Bilder aus dem Familienleben" ("Pictures of Family Life"). Heine, the cartoonist of overstuffed furniture and overstuffed people, pictured this couple against a typically fashionable and hideous background of fringed lampshades, potted palms, heavy curtains, and bloated upholstery. These settings themselves expressed a major impulse in the modern art of this period—revulsion against nouveau-riche tastelessness—reflected also in the simple, graceful, and functionally honest *Jugendstil* of which Heine, a furniture designer as well as a caricaturist, was a major proponent.[17]

As usual *Simplicissimus* perceived the political dimension of private behavior. Did not the spirit of empty ostentation and pompous traditionalism pervade the political as well as the domestic sphere? In a doggerel account of German history entitled "Development," Thoma described the ornate home as the perfect backdrop for the complacent and sentimental cult of nationalism:

> The German home was then transformed
> Into a stage for high-flown drama
> Where Dad as Attila performed
> And as his warlike consort, Mama!

> And how we loved the striking pose,
> The mass-produced, heroic style!
> How we admired the pompous rows,
> Of statues stretching mile on mile![18]

The aesthetic insensitivity of the bourgeoisie was to Heine only one sign of their general coarseness. Heine's cartoon "The Little Optimist" showed a middle-aged couple engaged in a violent fight, using fists, feet, and even a broom. The baby, hit by an enormous broken vase, lies howling on the floor, but the older children, clearly accustomed to such fights, view the proceedings with considerable pleasure. Such jokes—and there were many such—implied that beneath the decorous facade of middle-class life lay a less than respectable reality. Heine's figures were executed with a ruthless sense of the grotesque, and the corpulent bodies and respectable clothes added to the effect. This picture of middle-class life was incomparably more ugly than anything to be found, for example, in the contemporary *Punch,* which showed domestic violence only in the sordid slum, never in the respectable drawing room.[19]

Although the *Simplicissimus* family was not held together by love, it was united by powerful social forces. The most important was material greed. The eighties and nineties were opulent years when wealth was displayed on a scale seldom matched before or since. *Simplicissimus* wryly depicted the effects of this new wealth—snobbery, ostentation, idleness. One Heine cartoon showed a family lounging on the veranda of a suburban villa, the mother yawning over a novel, the father smoking a fat cigar, the butler bringing yet another meal. "Daddy," asks the frilly little boy, "what are you going to do when you grow up?" Still less admirable than the nouveau riche himself was the climber, whose willingness to do almost anything for money provoked much cynical, even cruel humor. "But please madam," says a lawyer to a fashionable young woman, "now we've arranged it all and suddenly you won't hear of divorce." "My God," she replies, "why, he's inherited half a million!" Another cartoon showed a doctor examining a deformed child in a typical overstuffed living room. "I'm terribly sorry, madam, but I must tell you that the abnormal shape of your son's head is sure proof of mental retardation." "Thank God he'll be very rich someday," is the cool response; "then no one will ever notice." The effect of new wealth on morals and manners was a common theme in the humor of this period. *Punch,* too, used the comic figure of Sir Gorgius Midas to mock the wealthy parvenu.[20]

Along with greed went social ambition, for wealth alone could not guarantee acceptance. The son of the nouveau, disdainful of his humble origins, strutted through the pages of *Simplicissimus* in the uniform of the student dueling fraternity. Through fraternity membership he acquired a prestigious job and the manners of a gentleman. For the daughter of the family there was the even more alluring prospect of an advantageous marriage.[21]

The marriage market was the subject of an enormous number

of jokes, some light, some cynical and even gruesome. "The Chinese are certainly barbarous," a man informs a woman at a party. "Captain Larsen tells me that they sell their girls openly in the market-place!" "Why, isn't that awful!" cries the woman. "How long will it take them to learn to sell their girls in private, as we do?" "Don't refuse me," croaks a decrepit but rich old man to a young girl. "I have a life insurance policy and terminal cancer of the liver." Jokes on this theme served the broader purpose of exposing the discrepancy between pious principle and cynical practice. The most sacred principle of the Victorian home—female purity—was debunked by anecdotes showing parents encouraging girls to pursue men by any means possible. Prudery increased a girl's market value. "Prudery is a very useful thing, my girl," remarks one father. "Of course, men don't believe in it themselves, but they expect you to." But purity could be sacrificed to ambition, as in one ribald verse describing the response of a lower-middle-class family to their daughter's premarital affair:

> When her father saw her hair dishevelled
> He began to scold, in tone judicial.
> But her mother simply sighed, and murmured,
> "If your beau were only an official!"[22]

Again, the political implications of private morality were never far from the humorists' minds. A cartoon entitled "The Return of the Prodigal Daughter" showed a very pregnant girl bursting in on her obviously horrified parents. "Dear parents," she announces, "I request an indemnity." The allusion to the well-known "Indemnity Bill," passed by the Reichstag in 1866 to give retroactive approval to Bismarck's illegal conduct of the "constitutional crisis," was apparently considered politically sensitive, for the Munich police forbade the sale of the issue. "I've complained to the government," wrote Thoma, "not that I hope for results, but we just have to show the police that we won't take this kind of thing lying down." One suspects that the "Prodigal Daughter's" request for retroactive forgiveness was less successful than Bismarck's because her sin (unlike the chancellor's, which resulted in the victory of 1866) would not bring the desired results. Had her affair led to a desirable marriage, all might yet have been pardoned.[23]

Simplicissimus thus echoed the opinion of the socialist August Bebel, who saw bourgeois marriage under its pious facade as a kind of legalized prostitution. "At present," he complained, "the marriage market is carried on with a shamelessness which makes the hackneyed phrases about 'holy matrimony' seem an empty mockery." The economic powerlessness which forced middle-class women into mercenary marriages was protested in many works of contemporary literature, such as Shaw's *Pygmalion.* "I sold flowers," says Eliza Doolittle, "I didn't sell myself. Now you've made a lady of me, I can't sell anything else. I wish you'd left me where you found me."[24]

In marriage, as outside it, the humorists protested the oppression of women. Heine mocked contemporary ideas of the female role in a grotesque cartoon entitled "Education for Marriage." In a beer-garden a concerned observer is shown trying to stop a little girl from drinking a huge mug of beer. "Oh, I know," responds her father nonchalantly, "it will arrest her mental development. Well, give her some more. After all, we want her to be a good wife and mother."[25]

Simplicissimus saw patriarchy not only as a private but as a social and political problem. The family as microcosm of the state was the theme of a remarkable story by Ernst Freissler entitled "The Family," which appeared in 1913. The protagonist, Alois Pospischil, is a lowly government bureaucrat whose behavior on the job is a model of obedience and servility, expressing at all times his awareness of the "unbridgeable distance between his own nothingness and the exalted power of his superiors." As he walks home, however, Pospischil undergoes a complete change of personality and by the time he reaches his front door has become a ruthless tyrant, recreating exactly the repressive atmosphere of his office. "The nearer he came to the apartment building where he lived, the more authoritative, dignified, and masterful his bearing became," Freissler wrote. "As he rang the bell at his front door . . . the deep wrinkles of a tyrant's frown appeared around his eyes and mouth. His wife, a pallid, downtrodden creature, opened the door. He ignored her greeting—for did *his* superiors ever greet *him*?—threw her his hat and stick and only then asked irritably, "Well, what's for dinner?" When his wife and children, under extreme provocation, finally rebel, Pospischil in turn suddenly goes berserk in his office and nearly strangles his boss to death, "shouting the most frightful curses which soon turned into unspeakable blasphemies against Throne and Altar."[26]

The same theme was treated in the introductory chapter of the greatest satirical novel of this period, Heinrich Mann's *Der Un-tertan,* parts of which first appeared in *Simplicissimus.* Mann's portrait of the protagonist Diederich Hessling, a symbolic figure for the typical German, showed the effect of the patriarchical home on the future citizen's attitudes. Fearing and respecting his tyrannical father, despising and exploiting his submissive mother, Diederich learns from childhood both to cringe and to bully. Entirely lacking in autonomy and self-control, he depends on his father's harsh discipline. "When he had pilfered or lied he hung. . . around his father's desk until Herr Hessling noticed him and took down the cane from the wall," Mann wrote. "Any undiscovered misdeed shook Diederich's faith and trust in his father." Using his very punishments as a sign of superior privilege, Diederich in turn bullies his father's working-class employees. "As he walked by the factory after a whipping," Mann continued, "his tear-stained face sometimes made the workers laugh. But Diederich only stuck out his tongue and stamped. For he knew who he was. 'I got a beating, but from my father. You would all be proud and lucky to be whipped by him. But of course you're too low down and insignificant to deserve it.' " In school as at home, the child Diederich shows the same dependence on discipline. "To participate in power, cold power, even though suffering, was his pride. . . . On the teacher's birthday, the pupils decorated his desk and chair with garlands. Diederich even decorated the cane." As the child regarded family and school, the adult regarded the German monarchical state, which conferred on the properly obedient citizen a sense of superior status and security against outsiders. Such insights into the function of the patriarchal home as microcosm and mainstay of the autocratic state foreshadowed more systematic theories of the authoritarian personality. *Simplicissimus'* portrait of the German family, far from a mere light comedy of manners, was an integral part of its protest against the oppressive Wilhelmine system.[27]

A further comment on sexual politics was the contrast, deliberately drawn, between the rich and the poor family. The conservative nineteenth-century press had extolled middle-class Christian charity, to which the poor, it was implied, should respond with respectful gratitude. Not so *Simplicissimus,* which constantly lambasted the complacency of the affluent, as in one cartoon which shows a prosperous family reciting the traditional German grace, "Komm, Herr Jesu, sei Du Unser Gast" (Come, Lord Jesus, be our guest). In the next picture Jesus actually appears at the door. "Sorry," the hausfrau says, "we've already eaten." The most bitter of Heine's "Bilder aus dem Familienleben," depicting the slum family, were executed in the most ruthless naturalist style. Heine's workers, totally unlike the idealized heroes of socialist art, are stunted, deformed figures shown against a bleak background of tenements and garbage pails. In one cartoon a little girl watches her mother working on a building site and wonders whether she will ever have any family life; in another a whole family gathers around a bloated corpse which they cannot afford to bury; in yet another, one of the grimmest, two ragged children huddle together in the corner of a bare room beneath the dangling feet of their mother, who has hanged herself. Such social realism probably seemed much more shocking in newly industrialized Germany than in contemporary England, where the sights, sounds, and smells of urban poverty had been familiar since the 1820s. *Simplicissimus* spoke to the awakened social conscience of a generation increasingly aware of the socialist threat to middle-class prosperity.[28]

Although these cynical comments on the bourgeois family provided fewer legal grounds for confiscation than did openly pornographic or politically subversive material, they undoubtedly produced a strong public reaction. Even the most sympathetic readers regarded Heine's series "Bilder aus dem Familienleben" not as good-natured spoofing but as sharp, even black humor. Maximilian Harden praised the "Bilder" for having "exposed a new aspect of the eternal Philistine spirit," while another contemporary critic, Hermann Esswein, gave this evaluation: "The *Bilder aus dem Familienleben* may very well survive artistically. They are inspired at the deepest level by the loathing of the sensitive artist for the petit-bourgeois world, the coarseness and narrowness of the Philistine—and thus they express a very modern philosophy." The impression of still another critic, that "people are far more outraged than amused by Heine's satire," is borne out by the reactions of the conservative press, which took even more offense at the magazine's social than at its political satire. A passage from the *Rheinische Kurier,* approvingly quoted in the Bavarian Landtag, denounced *Simplicissimus'* effect on the moral fibre of the nation. "A flood of artistic and moral poison flows from this magazine. It is characterized by a tone of astonishing and uniform cynicism, which shrinks from nothing, attacks everything, poisons everything."[29]

The tone of such extreme reactions was not confident but defensive, expressing anxiety at the threatening change in values. Indeed the popularity of *Simplicissimus* attested to the growing tension between the still-powerful authoritarian family and the individuals who increasingly questioned its authority. Not only the feminist movement but also the youth movement, which during this period attracted thousands of middle-class young people, gave active expression to this skeptical and rebellious spirit. And even for those who did not join these movements, *Simplicissimus* provided a more passive and harmless outlet for unarticulated doubt, skepticism, and anger. The humorists' picture of German social life may be compared to that of contemporary novelists. Theodore Fontane's *Frau Jenny Treibel*, for instance, was written in the same satirical spirit. But *Simplicissimus* went much further. By contrasting the worlds of rich and poor it exposed not only the frivolity but the political irresponsibility of the affluent society.[30]

Love and the New Woman

Simplicissimus' images of women in all their varying roles—young girls, wives, mothers, career women, and prostitutes—reflected a perplexity characteristic of the *fin-de-siècle.* Whether light or grim, affectionate or sardonic, humorous comments on female behavior emphasized surprise, change, discontinuity, and the revolt against tradition. Nineteenth-century man had idealized woman as a sweet and submissive being whose sheltered life permitted her a far higher standard of moral purity than could be reached by the male. This ideal, though by no means unchallenged earlier in the century, was much more openly and vigorously attacked in the 1890s than before. "Never before have the ordinary conceptions of femininity, of the imaginary 'ideal woman,' been so imbecile as in the nineteenth century," wrote the Austrian feminist Rosa Mayreder. Another German feminist rebutted a well known book on sexual differences with the argument that the conventional "feminine" personality reflected not innate characteristics but the pressures of male-dominated society. "Not only has society stamped out women's more 'uncomfortable' qualities, but it has also artificially bred those qualities which contribute to the comfort and pleasure of her lord and master. . . . And now, people believe . . . that the plant grows by nature in the way it was forced to grow and use these supposedly 'feminine' characteristics as a hindrance to women's participation in public life."[31]

The breakdown of the Victorian stereotype reopened the question of sexual differences. Far from the Victorian china doll, women were often described as more dominated by instincts, thus more natural, more primitive, and less moral than men. Nietzsche had anticipated such an anti-Victorian reaction in his hymns to "the great cat woman," to her "nature which is more natural than a man's, her genuine jungle-like wily flexibility, the incomprehensible wide sweep of her desires and virtues." Ellen Key described women as "more intimately bound up with nature, more vegetable-like," while classical Freudian theory saw them (in the words of Philip Rieff) as living "dangerously close to the archaic. Hence the ascription to them of [such] deficiencies [as] greater vanity, less sense of justice and weaker social interests." In the literature of the period the heroine often assumed an active, even formidable role, and the battle of the sexes became a popular theme.[32]

The humor of *Simplicissimus* reflected this cultural transition by portraying two coexisting but totally different female types. On the one hand was the housewife (as we see her in Heine's "Bilder," already described)—fat, dowdy, and conventional. On the other hand was the emancipated or "new" woman—glamorous, sexy, but mysterious and not to be trusted. *Simplicissimus* portrayed the new woman in all her various guises.

Although the opening of new job opportunities during this period gave middle-class women a new sense of independence and self-respect, they still encountered many obstacles. The first female medical students were admitted to German universities in 1901, and by 1914 there were 4,126 women in medical training. *Simplicissimus* expressed its sympathy for the problems of professional women struggling to survive in a man's world in a little anecdote mocking old-fashioned prejudice concerning the first woman physician hired by a hospital. The old nurse on the ward, we are told, at first befriends her but, as the days pass, begins to look worried. "Tell me, Fräulein," she finally asks, "isn't the doctor ever going to come?" Another story told of a man who attempts to pick up a young schoolteacher and is rebuffed by her independence and good sense. But most stories about single women emphasized their vulnerability. In one entitled "The Sewing Machine" an upper-class man meets a working-class girl who tells him that her one desire is to possess a sewing machine with which to support herself. After seducing her, he offers her the money for the machine, which she proudly refuses. But when he meets her a few months later she has become a prostitute—a poor woman cannot afford virtue. The grimmest of these stories tells of an ugly single girl who hangs herself because she does not appeal to men. Such stories expressed the period's doubt about the ability of women to pursue a career other than marriage. Even some feminists believed that a woman's place was, ideally, in the home.[33]

But in the 1890s she spent less and less time there. The expansion of recreation and entertainment in this prosperous society afforded women many opportunities to escape the authority of father or husband. Social life, at mid-century centered in the home, shifted in the eighties and nineties to the ballroom, the cafe, and the street. The social freedom conferred by these new surroundings was wryly characterized by the contemporary British humorist Hilaire Belloc:

The Husbands and the Wives
Of this select society
Lead independent lives
Of infinite variety.

One *Simplicissimus* cartoon showed a woman in an elegant restaurant, surrounded by friends. "Gentleman, whenever I have such a fabulous meal, I do thank the Lord that my good husband doesn't have to pay." The carefree life of resorts encouraged independence. "Do you go to the beach every summer while your husband takes the cure in Karlsbad?" asks a man of an alluring 1890s bathing beauty. "Oh yes!" she laughs, "we always escape from each other in the summer." The new sports—skiing, skating, hiking—provided wonderful cartoon material. *Simplicissimus* laughed both at the cycling craze itself and at stuffed shirts who considered the pastime unladylike. A young clergyman was shown transfixed with horror at the sight of his knicker-clad mother on the new-fangled machine. "Oh Mother, dear Mother!" he groans, "have you lost your belief in God?" The cartoonists' intuitive perception of the bicycle as a threat to conservative values was justified, for by providing women with a cheap means of transportation, it greatly increased their mobility.[34]

But *Simplicissimus* ventured beyond such gaiety onto much more dangerous ground when it explored the effect of the new freedom on women's sexual behavior. Again attacking a sentimental stereotype, it implied that the old idea of female innocence could not last in the new environment. The very idea of a sexually knowledgeable young girl was still so incongruous as to be funny in itself. Modern art and literature were often held responsible for sullying girlish purity, as in one anecdote in which the eighteen-year-old daughter of a respectable family shocks her parents with the following succinct literary analysis of some recent novels: "In olden times they either got married and had children, or they didn't get married and didn't have children. Nowadays, they either get married and don't have children or they don't get married and have children anyway." But *Simplicissimus* went further, implying that the new freedom permitted not only knowledge but, in some cases, experience. Jokes debunking the sacred ideal of virginity were, by the standards of the time, very risqué indeed. "Quit play-acting," says a young bridegroom to a bride too experienced to feign innocence successfully. In another cartoon it is the bride who is cynical. "Just pretend you've married a widow," she quips. Jokes such as this, shocking in their own time, recorded an early stage of the change in sexual standards which influenced the social life of the 1920s.[35]

The satirists' reaction to this change in female sexual behavior was highly ambivalent, combining approval and misgivings. Their revulsion against euphemism and romantic cliché led some of the *Simplicissimus* group—especially Thoma, whose humor was of the broad Bavarian type—to advocate an earthy, even animal approach to sexuality. Thoma's verse "In May," which appeared as caption to a drawing of a group of dogs, used mock-romantic imagery to convey a highly unromantic message.

> In the spring, when hearts are gay,
> Every dog his bitch pursues,
> Pines for her both night and day,
> Quite laid low—
> Bow-wow! Bow-wow!—
> By those Springtime lovesick blues.

In a less delicate version of the classical "gather ye roses while ye may" argument, Thoma urged females—canine and human—to take advantage of their best years:

> When your youth is fled, my dear,
> And you're old and ugly, too,
> You'll be willing, never fear,
> But then who—
> A-hoo! A-hoo!—
> Who will want a dog like you?

Men, like dogs, all feel the mood,
Spring brings thoughts of sweet romance,
So, my girl, don't be a prude—
Go on, do—
A-hoo! A-hoo!—
For it may be your last chance.[36]

It was perhaps this final admonition which offended Thoma's
friend Karl Rothmaier, to whose reproaches the author replied in
a letter of May 20, 1902. "I am not in the least troubled by moral
scruples," argued Thoma, "for two reasons. First I believe that
one should be allowed to say anything as long as it is well and
artistically said. And I believe especially that sex, as one of our
most natural and most human activities, is one of the best subjects for art and literature. . . . Secondly, I am a free adult, and
I write for free adults. I will leave it to the impotent hacks—of
whom, heaven knows, Germany has enough—to write for the
family or for silly teenage girls. I have nothing to do with these
sweet young things and have no concern with their education,
which I gladly leave to their parents. I myself refuse to debase
my own work to the level of ladies' magazines. . . . And finally,
if my friends think I'm disgusting because they suspect that I like
sex, then they are right in one sense and very wrong in another.
Right because I do like sex, and wrong because natural functions
are not disgusting." Quoting Martin Luther's opinion, "One should
restrain it no more than any other animal function," Thoma urged
both sexes to straightforward and uncomplicated sexual enjoy-
ment.[37]

But such simplistic evocations of animal spontaneity ignored
the social and psychological complexity of human sexuality. A
sketch by Arthur Schnitzler entitled "Die überspannte Person"
("The Hysterical Woman") was typical of the many anecdotes,
stories, and cartoons which recounted the often painful consequences of unconventional sexual behavior. Announcing to her
carefree lover that she is pregnant, the married heroine of
Schnitzler's one-act skit plunges him into acute anxiety by as-
suring him that, out of true devotion, she has refused sexual relations with her husband since the beginning of their affair. Unable to take responsibility for the pregnancy and unwilling to
consider abortion—"since you do have a husband, that would be
pretty stupid"—the pragmatic lover finally urges his tiresomely
faithful mistress to spare him inconvenience by initiating "a little
second honeymoon" with her husband. To her genuinely shocked

and hurt reaction he responds cynically, "Oh, these hysterical women—you give them good advice and they spit in your face. Heaven preserve me from women in love!" Thus the defiance of conventional morality could bring not unfettered animal pleasure but pain, disillusionment, and dishonesty. The cynical tone of this piece so offended the Munich police that they prohibited the sale of the issue.[38]

More often, however, the truly amoral partner in such unconventional relationships was the woman, usually portrayed as a scheming, heartless femme fatale, at best frivolous, at worst cold and heartless. A cartoon series depicting sophisticated social life was entitled "Gemütsmenschen," or "people of feeling," a heavily ironic title calling attention to a cynicism sometimes verging on the macabre. In one cartoon of this series an elegant woman casually suggests to her lover that they take flowers to her husband in the hospital; in another, entitled "Monte Carlo," a woman and her gigolo walk past her husband's body, which is hanging from a tree. This challenge to the Victorian stereotype of sexless female purity could sometimes be taken to extremes, as in a story by Ernst von Wolzogen in which the heroine, a seemingly sweet and refined woman, explains her decision to marry a convicted murderer. "The sighing, the flirting, the good manners, and the elegant frivolities—I was bored with all that! . . . I longed for the only new sensation. . . . You know, I don't think that's so perverse. The most natural female desire of all is for the wild man." And what would happen when modern society released the female of the species from the traditional restraints on her behavior? Though humorists attacked patriarchy, the very idea of matriarchy often gave rise to Strindbergian fantasies. One cartoon by Heine, undoubtedly inspired by Strindberg's *The Father,* shows an imposing woman standing over a strait-jacketed man. "Your husband is suffering from a very severe delusion, Madam," the doctor tells her, "he thinks he is sane!" The popularity of such hostile responses, published alongside the more positive ones mentioned earlier, reflects the extreme ambivalence of this period's reaction to the changing position of women.[39]

The new sexual frankness of the 1890s extended to many subjects previously considered unmentionable, such as unwed motherhood and prostitution. On these as on other issues *Simplicissimus* rejected conventional moralizing and called for honesty and compassion. The feminist movement had publicized the plight of the unwed mother and her child, neglected by a society embarrassed by their existence. "My son is getting married now," a fashionable *Simplicissimus* matron says to a shabby girl with a baby, "so stop writing to him. You'll get four marks a month for the child. Oh, and remember—have him baptized." Many cartoons protested the sexual exploitation of servant girls, who when dismissed often had no alternative but prostitution. "My God, Herr Baron," protests an elderly housekeeper to an elegant gentleman, "first you seduce my daughter and then you throw us both out on the street!" "That's not my problem," he replies, "you should have brought her up better." The satirists' sympathy for the unwed mother reflected the influence of a feminist organization, the Mutterschütz League, which was founded in 1904 to campaign for the extension of welfare programs to single mothers and for the establishment of homes for them and their children. The League's refusal to condemn the unmarried mother provoked much opposition from "respectable" people. "Horrifying, how immorality is always being encouraged," comments an elegant *Simplicissimus* lady on a home for unwed mothers. And Heine defied the conventional stereotype of the depraved and irresponsible unwed mother in this cartoon entitled "Mutterglück" ("Maternal Bliss"), in which a pretty smiling girl in the midst of a flock of children remarks, "I only need a husband—then we'd be a family."[40]

Simplicissimus' approach to the ubiquitous problem of prostitution likewise took sides in a contemporary debate between reformers who advocated stiff penalties for prostitution and others who, regarding the prostitute as victim rather than criminal, urged the abolition of legal control. *Simplicissimus* supported the latter view by presenting a picture of prostitution which debunked both traditional moralizing and romantic idealization. In a special issue depicting a notorious Viennese brothel, an editorial contrasted the poet's glamorous image of "the hetaera" who "obeys only the sweet laws of love" with the sordid and shocking reality. A cartoon series by Heine criticized state regulation by exposing the ineffectiveness of inspection procedures. "Come out of there, Camilla," the madam commands a girl hiding under a toilet lid, "the doctor who came to do the inspection is gone now!" The actual complicity of the police was exposed in a macabre portrayal of the madam and an officer looking down at a girl's hideously mutilated corpse. "Don't worry, Madame Riehl, that's not abuse—I swear by my oath of office." Not laws but the improvement of social conditions would end the horror of prostitution. Like many socialist writers, the humorists of *Simplicis-simus* saw the prostitute as the victim of capitalist exploitation, and bitterly mocked solid citizens more shocked by prostitution itself than by its root causes. Of one campaign for public decency, led by the empress, an editorial expressed the complaint that "none of the pious clergymen ever told her that twenty steps from her palace girls work through the night in miserable garrets and finally turn to prostitution out of sheer, bitter poverty." On a more frivolous level, the *Simplicissimus* prostitute faced a new and unprecedented problem—unemployment! "Strike! Not us!" remarks one streetwalker to another. "Those fine ladies give us too much competition!"[41]

From the year of its founding, *Simplicissimus'* sexual frankness had outraged conservatives. Ludwig Thoma recounted in his memoirs how he had seen the first issue of the magazine in the waving fist of a choleric neighbor who, offended by Wedekind's short story "The Princess Russalka," demanded legal action. Certainly the frequent confiscations on the grounds of obscenity suggest that the magazine's sexual content was fully as controversial as its political message. In fact, Karl Arnold recollected that the staff often purposely published racy and politically controversial jokes in the same issue so that, in the event of confiscation, no one could tell which had given offense. *Simplicissimus'* sexual jokes aroused much indignation in the right-wing press. "Its whole approach to the sexual joke—an ancient and very understandable form of humor—offers us much that is disgusting, repulsive and low," fulminated an editorial in the *Kölnische Zeitung.* "All this expresses not the sense of humor but merely a craving for crass sensation. It pulls these things out of the darkest corners of human depravity into the light of day with the ostensible purpose of satirizing our social conditions. . . . Often these are things of which those of us who have not frequented the lowest nightclubs of all the world's cities can have no understanding. Thus they bring a new tone into our German humor, which is the more objectionable because so many people had already erred in that direction."[42]

The most extensive and reasoned defense of *Simplicissimus* against such criticism was prepared by Thoma for his trial in 1905 for a verse which allegedly insulted the Protestant clergy. Ridiculing a recent clerical conference on "morality" in Cologne, Thoma had reproached the pastors' hypocrisy by a most irreverent allusion to their own traditionally large families:

As in the marriage bed they lie,
They do God's will and multiply,
So godly are our pastors' habits,
They reproduce themselves like rabbits.

What do they know of lust untamed?
Can so much passion be enflamed,
By wives who pray to God Almighty,
All wrapped in robe and flannel nightie?

Provoked by this "grave insult" to the pastorate (not to mention their wives!) the *Oberkirchenrat* instituted a formal lawsuit against Thoma and "responsible editor" Linnekogel, which was brought to trial in Stuttgart, where *Simplicissimus* was printed. Not content simply to refute the specific charges, Thoma and his legal counsel expounded eloquently on the general implications of the case before a courtroom packed with sympathetic observers. Advocating a tolerance based on moral relativism, lawyer Max Bernstein attacked the rigidity of the pastors, who had expressed "an opinion which is completely inconsistent with the findings of modern science, which sees individuals as the product of a specific environment: the conviction that whoever does not share my views is an evil human being." Furthermore, contended another lawyer, Thoma's close friend Conrad Haussmann, the proposed limits on sexual subject matter would prevent the writer from fulfilling his true mission, "to express his deepest insights into the psychological problems of human beings, to explore their most complex emotional conflicts." Most telling of all was Thoma's own defense. The pastors, he charged, were not really worried by obscenity in itself; the art and literature of the Biedermeier period had been just as risqué as that of the 1890s. The true purpose of their pious crusade was to regain control over a population which, by rejecting their religious ideology, had undermined their political power base. His hatred of religious bigotry led the liberal Thoma into an uneasy alliance with socialism. Praising the virtues of the "industrious, struggling" workers of his own time, he contrasted them with the pious and apathetic Germans of past generations who "laughed at the debauchery of the upper classes, or looked on in terrified silence. . . . These reverend gentlemen would have no objection to an immoral population distracted by sensuality from their (political) rights, they are only outraged by the attempts of the hard-working people to shake off their tyranny." Alert to the political implications of sexual morality, Thoma saw the struggle against clerical prudery as part of a larger campaign against political as well as religious oppression.[43]

Parent and Child

To the satirical critique of the family another dimension was added by the picture of the child. Like other Victorian clichés, the idealized conception of pure and innocent childhood yielded at the turn of the century to new and more complex theories. *Simplicissimus'* unsentimental picture of the child indirectly reflected this important cultural change.[44]

Simplicissimus showed that family life varied widely at different levels of society and that one of the most important variations was simply in the number of children. The poor and the lower middle class were shown with large broods of children, often five or six. These large families were obviously unwanted. One of the "Bilder aus dem Familienleben" shows a shabby but respectable sitting room in a lower middle-class home where a father, in worn coat and trousers, plays with his six children. "The stork can't come this year," one child says to another. "Daddy needs a new suit." A socially prestigious group well known for its large families was the Protestant clergy, whose priggish sexual attitudes *Simplicissimus* lost no opportunity of mocking. A cartoon entitled "Increase and Multiply" showed a Protestant pastor on his Sunday walk, surrounded by a swarm of homely children. "But Herr Pastor," asks a woman of the congregation, "why did you leave your other children at home?" "Ah, Frau Bohn, if people saw all my children together, they'd think we pastors did nothing else." But with this exception, families above a certain social level were seldom shown with more than three children, and often with only one or two. A cartoon mocking both middle-class militarism and the child-centered family showed one curly-headed child in miniature uniform, goose-stepping through piles of opulent birthday presents, while his obviously rich parents look on fatuously.[45]

These cartoons illustrated the general decline in family size which began in the 1880s and 1890s predominantly among the rich and educated. To the spread of family limitation, as to other changes in sexual behavior, the humorists reacted ambivalently. On the one hand there was exuberant scorn for stodgy conservatism. Thus a verse of 1914 lampooned clergy and right-wing politicians who saw the falling birth rate as a threat to the nation:

And who, in this great land of ours
Still venerates the Higher Powers,
The Church, the Throne, the Family?
Oh, what an age! Oh, woe is me!

Who does his duty to the nation?
By adding to the population?
My friends, we see the consequence
Of creeping modern decadence.

Another speaker gloomily remarked on female obstinacy:

The Modern Woman—haughty hag
Thinks yearly childbirth is a drag.
And German men have lost their starch.
They don't say "Into bed! Now march!"

On the other hand there were misgivings, reflected in the humorists' own view of the upper-class young woman's supposed aversion to childbearing. "Oh, well, I suppose everyone has to have the little brats sometime," drawls one unpleasantly fashionable young mother to a stranger who admires her baby. Many contemporary writers of all shades of political opinion criticized the rich mother's negligence. For example, Ellen Key's *The Century of the Child,* a popular Swedish book on child-rearing which was translated into German in 1907, urged mothers to care for their children themselves instead of entrusting them to a nurse.[46]

In nineteenth-century literature the child's purity had confounded the adult's hard worldliness. *Simplicissimus* attacked this stereotype by showing him as simply a small-scale copy of his disagreeable elders. A cartoon ironically entitled "Sentimental Education" shows a middle-class family at the gate of their palatial villa, calmly watching their dog ferociously attacking a small, ragged trespasser. "Shame on you, Caesar," lisps the ruffled little girl, "aren't you ashamed to bite such a *filthy* pair of pants!" In this and other examples the child was not more innocent but only more honest than his elders, directly expressing the prejudices concealed behind the polite adult facade. Directly contrasted to the rich child was the poor child. "Go tell your parents that they should be ashamed to send such a little boy as you out to buy liquor at this hour of the night," a benevolent suburbanite says to a slum urchin carrying a bottle of *schnaps.* "It ain't for my parents," comes the cheeky reply, "it's for me!" To portray the slum child, a hard-bitten little adult, was to expose the emptiness of conventional sentimentality.[47]

"Sentimental Education." "Shame on you, Caesar, aren't you ashamed to bite such a *filthy* pair of pants?" (Heine, *Simplicissimus*, June 1897.)

The increasing sexual sophistication of small children was, of course, an excellent subject for jokes. Despite adult efforts to keep them in innocence, children, the humorists implied, now knew the facts. Viktor Mann, himself a child when *Simplicissimus* was founded, described his gleeful reaction to a joke that must have seemed to him very daring. "I laughed and blushed over the little story of the governess who, when bidding farewell to little Mary, announced that she was getting married and might receive a visit from the stork. To which little Mary replied, 'The *stork*? Boy, have you ever got a lot to learn!' And I thought it very swell of *Simplicissimus* that it showed twelve-year-olds exposing the silly stories of adults." Such jokes rejoiced at the decline of Victorian prudery and indirectly advocated a franker approach to sex education. It is significant that the discovery which destroyed the myth of childish innocence, that of infantile sexuality, belonged to this period.[48]

Conclusion: Sensation and Satiety

Freud saw the sense of humor as a compound of rebellion and inhibition, wishful fantasy and anxiety. In their comments on family life the humorists of *Simplicissimus* exhibited all of these varying moods. Humor functioned not only negatively as a safety valve, releasing resentment against still-powerful institutional controls, but positively (in the Koestlerian sense) as the catalyst for new ideas. The success of *Simplicissimus* among middle-class readers suggests a growing public acceptance of such ideas—jokes which would have deeply offended mid-century sensibilities were now openly displayed (to the horror of some conservatives) in many a respectable drawing room. A Catholic newspaper denounced a liberal deputy, further identified as "the father of a family," who had said that *Simplicissimus* and *Jugend* were available in his home alongside other works of modern literature, and he had never noticed that the ladies objected to it. "Now this is outrageous! . . . Is this proper reading matter for ladies?" *Simplicissimus'* perceptions of sexual mores, changing male and female roles, and the political implications of family life paralleled those of the innovative social thinkers of the period. Like their comments on the similarly sensitive topics of politics and militarism, the humorists' jokes on familial and sexual mores cushioned the often highly disturbing impact of social change by enabling readers to defuse anxiety through laughter.[49]

But the humorists' very ambivalent attitude toward this process of social change was far from the unquestioning and dangerous radicalism which their critics attributed to them. For along with late Victorian radical chic went the sense that something was wrong. The children who questioned parental authority were portrayed sometimes as junior heroes but more often as precocious monsters. The alluring "emancipated" woman in her bathing suit, cycling knickers, or ruffled petticoat was sometimes depicted as strong and independent, sometimes merely as frivolous and cynical. Though supportive of some feminist causes, moreover, the humorists regarded genuinely radical feminist activities, such as the British suffrage movement, with undisguised disapproval. And the "new" sexual morality was pictured sometimes as more free and genuine than the old, sometimes as simply more casual. The entries to a short story contest provoked the comment that "among every fifty stories forty, on the average, are about love, and this love is never depicted in a pure and beautiful way but always from the point of view of the gourmand, the satiated man of the world, the bored courtesan. . . . It is never a pure, fresh, exhilarating love." Later the editors, now exasperated beyond all endurance, offered "a prize of 300 marks for a story that does *not* concern sexual love." The lifting of Victorian literary taboos had resulted not in real honesty but in sensationalism and ultimately in boredom with the whole topic. Thus *Simplicissimus* looked into the future not with simple optimism but with skepticism, even with foreboding.[50]

The Assault
of Laughter:
The Satirists versus
the Establishment

6

The Classroom Tyrant

THE humorists' comments on the German educational system contributed to a widespread, often heated national debate which continued throughout the Wilhelmine period. Few issues reflected the conflict between tradition and modernization so clearly as that of school reform. In the school controversy the kaiser, in whose genuinely split personality the reactionary tendencies usually triumphed over the modern ones, emerged in the unusual role of a reformer. Recalling the dryness of his own classical education, he supported the substantial segment of professional and public opinion which advocated a curriculum more relevant to the culture and interests of German pupils. "Whoever has sat on the school-bench himself," he proclaimed in 1890, "and has looked behind the scenes knows what is lacking. Above all, we lack the national basis. We want to bring up young Germans, not young Greeks or Romans." The patriotic emphasis of the school reform movement heightened its appeal to the German public. Another aspect of the school system criticized by reformers was the stress on competition and academic achievement which deprived students of free time for exercise and healthful recreation. Criticism of the educational system was a common theme among Wilhelmine authors of all political persuasions, from the liberal Heinrich Mann (*Professor Unrat*) to the right-wing Julius Langbehn (*Rembrandt als Erzieher*). The humorists commented perceptively both upon those aspects of the education which changed and upon those which remained the same.[1]

The picture of the schoolmaster, the personification of academic authority, was highly ambivalent, reflecting both adult sympathy and childish rebellion. As a middle-class professional the schoolmaster was often portrayed as the impotent victim of official callousness and irresponsibility. *Kladderadatsch* protested the scandalously low teachers' salaries often and vigorously. "The shortage of elementary-school teachers has caused the government profound embarrassment," reported the magazine in 1900. "The official newspapers are searching desperately for the answer, but they don't get the point. We dare to state quite openly that it is the shocking lack of true idealism which has caused the teacher shortage—the outrageous desire . . . of our contemporaries to have a meal once, or even twice a day." *Kladderadatsch* ingeniously suggested that the recruitment of candidates without stomachs might solve the problem.²

In 1914 a *Simplicissimus* cartoon entitled "Der Lehreraudienz" ("The Teachers' Audience") nearly involved the staff in yet another suit for *Majestätsbeleidigung*. In the cartoon, a comment on a recent meeting between the king of Bavaria and a teachers' delegation, the decrepit monarch declares, "Gentlemen, if you're so badly off, why don't you beg your bread? After all, that's what the Capuchin monks do." Thus the cartoonists protested the real poverty of teachers by comparing it to the purely mythical poverty of their favorite targets, the clergy. Three days after the issue appeared, a member of the royal cabinet called the attention of the Ministry of Justice to the "outrageous caricature of his Majesty the King." The cartoon, this memorandum stated, had caused much official displeasure. "His Excellency the Minister of Education and Religion, who is leaving today on an offical trip, got in touch with the Chief of Police to discuss what should be done about this deeply deplorable and completely untrue attack on His Highness." But by this time Bavarian officials were wary of lawsuits, which the *Simplicissimus* staff could so successfully turn to their own advantage. Thus the memorandum further noted that a suit against the editors, however welcome to the undoubtedly "monarchist sentiments of the majority of the people," would require the possibly embarrassing testimony of the three teachers who attended the audience. The same argument was used in the response of the Ministry of Justice. "It did not seem suitable that the proceedings at the audience, a purely internal matter, should be brought to the attention of the public," argued a spokesman for the ministry. "But this could not have been avoided." At any rate the king's advisors advised him against a lawsuit, perhaps because they feared that public opinion might support not only *Simplicissimus* but the underpaid teachers themselves. The incident attests to the evolution of *Simplicissimus* from its beginnings as an obscure avant-garde periodical into an organ of oppositional opinion powerful enough to be feared even by reigning monarchs.[3]

But far more often the satirists identified themselves with the student and portrayed the schoolmaster as the personification of rigid and arbitrary authority. A beloved stock figure of *Kladderadatsch,* the eternal schoolboy Karlchen Miessnick, who could never pass *Quarta* and was thus condemned to repeat it forever, expressed the common adult fantasy of eternal, carefree, irresponsible childhood. In response to the endless and complex discussion of school reform Karlchen made the sensible suggestion that all schools be closed until a solution was found, "which naturally, in view of the complexity of these questions, will take a very long time." The reformers' suggestion that more sports and other extracurricular activities be incorporated into the curriculum also met with his approval. When the Latin essay, traditionally the most important and difficult school assignment, was abolished, *Kladderadatsch* exhorted Karlchen and his schoolmates to "dance on the desks."

> The terrible spectre that haunted you daily
> Is vanished, is banished; so sing aloud gaily,
> Farewell to the old Latin Essay! It's gone!

The muscular, outdoor spirit of some of the reformers was gently spoofed:

> Out with Old Man Cicero!
> Latin? No—we've had enough!
> Tan and healthy let us grow,
> Sturdy, muscular and tough.
> Let us romp o'er hill and dale,
> Carolling this joyous song,
> We were learned, weak and pale,
> How much better to be strong![4]

But while criticizing the traditional curriculum, *Kladderadatsch* challenged the traditional authority structure hardly at all. Even the smart-alec schoolboy Karlchen Miessnick was condemned for his sins to eternal school drudgery, thus reminding the reader of the social penalties for irresponsible behavior.

In *Simplicissimus,* however, the emphasis shifted from the

Two comments on the school system, one showing decrepit schoolmasters and undersized, nearsighted schoolboys; the other commenting on elementary education in East Prussia. (Heine, *Simplicissimus*, March 13, 1911.)

curriculum to the teacher himself. To be sure, the Latin curriculum was ridiculed as pointless busywork. "You don't recognize that rare but famous metre, the *Procleusmaticus?*" an outraged schoolmaster scolds a pupil. "And you expect to graduate in a few weeks and enter practical life?" But some of the most scathing satirical pictures of school life portrayed teachers of that supposedly patriotic and relevant field, German literature. Like Mann's novel *Professor Unrat*, Ludwig Thoma's series of fictionalized childhood reminiscences, which appeared in *Simplicissimus*, portrayed the schoolmaster as a sordid, petty tyrant. "Professor Bindinger couldn't stand me, nor I him. He was so dirty. He always ate soft-boiled eggs for breakfast—you could see that because his beard was always full of egg-yolk. He sprayed you with saliva when he spoke to you, and his eyes were as green as a cat's. All teachers were dumb, but he was dumber than any of them. When he lectured on the ancient Germans, he stroked his beard and spoke in a bass voice. But I don't believe that the ancient Germans had such a potbelly and such worn-out boots!" Unlike Karlchen Miessnick, who confined himself to passive resistance, the child Thoma felt and expressed scorn and ridicule, and reacted to his teacher's scolding—"You will never be a useful member of society, miserable child!"—not with rueful resignation but with pride, as a special tribute to his superior qualities of intelligence and independence.[5]

Simplicissimus, moreover, noted an aspect of school discipline seldom mentioned by *Kladderadatsch,* the prudery which was a symptom of overintellectualization. One of many comments on this issue was a verse by Thoma which told of a schoolboy who had been discovered by his professor in a disreputable tavern (the incident closely resembled the plot of *Professor Unrat*). For the heinous crime of reading some of the allegedly "disreputable" magazines displayed in the tavern, the boy was expelled from the gymnasium.

> And our Rector shed some righteous tears,
> At the magazines, which openly
> Mentioned matters which, in younger years,
> He had only pondered secretly.

> So our Hans was thereupon expelled
> From the school's exalted atmosphere,
> Wretched boy! He now will be compelled
> To take up a business career.[6]

Here again, school authority was so thoroughly discredited that expulsion became a liberating escape into a saner world. But as Frank Wedekind (an erstwhile *Simplicissimus* contributor) had shown in his play *Frühlingserwachen,* the combined prudishness and harshness of school discipline could have far more destructive consequences. Like Wedekind, *Simplicissimus* commented on the epidemic of schoolboy suicides—for example, in a cartoon which showed two grotesque and decrepit schoolmasters discussing the deplorable phenomenon against the background of a graveyard. "These schoolboy suicides fill me with concern, Herr Kollege. Unfortunately we have not been able to come up with a punishment severe enough to restrain the brats from such foolishness." The caption illustrates the humorous technique which, in Freud's words, "consists in advancing something apparently absurd and nonsensical which, however, discloses sense that serves to illustrate and represent some other absurdity and nonsense." In the logical absurdity of punishing a child for suicide is revealed the moral absurdity of the schoolmasters' narrowly punitive approach to their pupils' problems.[7]

Thus in the conflict between teacher and pupil was mirrored the larger social conflict between age and youth, decrepitude and vitality, conformity and dissent. The most conspicuous manifestation of anti-school feeling during this period was the German youth movement. "I'll wipe out this youth movement thing," croaks one typically aged *Simplicissimus* schoolmaster to another. "I'll keep everyone in detention who smells of fresh air." As usual, the *Simplicissimus* caricature oversimplified and exaggerated. Reforms such as the reduction of student workloads, the introduction of more practical and modern subject matter, and the encouragement of physical education received support not only outside but inside the academic community.[8]

The student who survived the gymnasium usually attended the university, by far the most prestigious of academic institutions. Images of the university student in *Kladderadatsch* and *Simplicissimus* were only superficially similar. The stock *Kladderadatsch* figure of "Biermörder" displayed the outward attributes of the student—the distinctive fraternity cap, the dueling scar, and the beer belly. In personality he was Karlchen Miessnick's older brother, defying the system only by a cheerful and harmless laziness. By contrast the *Simplicissimus* student's laziness and drunkenness took on a more sinister connotation as symptoms of underlying arrogance and irresponsibility. One is at first surprised to notice the lack of continuity between the images of the undersized, nearsighted, overworked schoolboy and the fat, lazy university student. This disparity may in part reflect the rate of attrition in the gymnasium, from which three out of four students departed without receiving the *Abitur.* In sympathy with the dropout, the satirists may have been inclined to view the graduate unsympathetically as the thick-skinned survivor of a system which punished his more sensitive peers.[9]

Like *Kladderadatsch, Simplicissimus* confined its attention almost exclusively to the *Korpsstudent,* or member of one of the prestigious dueling fraternities which set the tone of student life. By far the deepest and most scathing picture of such a society is a chapter from Heinrich Mann's *Der Untertan,* characterized by Eugen Roth as "the crassest literary caricature of fraternity life that has ever been written in Germany." Here we once again meet Diederich, this time as an enthusiastic junior member of the prestigious Korps Neuteutonia. The coarse drinking and dueling rituals of the fraternity have become the center of his life. "He was submerged in his corporation, which thought and acted for him. And he was a man, and could respect himself and was a great personage because he belonged to it." The *Korps* schooled its aspiring middle-class members in the conservative, militaristic, and feudal ideology of the aristocracy. "The Neuteutonen all agreed . . . that Jewish liberalism was the first step toward socialism and that German Christians should all rally behind Chaplain [Adolf] Stoecker" (a conservative and antisemitic clergyman active in politics in the 1880s). The militaristic values reflected in the dueling ritual also emerged in the boastful references of one member to his allegedly aristocratic "Cousin von Klappke" (who turns out to be not a Guards officer but a mere common soldier) and in the solemn mock-military funeral held in honor of another member, whose heart attack in the midst of a drinking bout is hailed as a "death on the field of honor." Thus *Simplicissimus* observed not only the colorful customs of student life but their political effect—the erosion of the liberal traditions of the university. "Why don't you sing that old song, 'Here's to the free word, hurrah!' " a cartoon father asks his son. "Oh, father," replies the latter, "now that we have royal princes in the *Korps,* we've given up such tactless rhymes." In a more serious vein Max Weber complained of the patent absurdity of a military custom such as dueling when practiced by civilians, and saw such servile imitation of the aristocracy as yet another sign of middle-class political immaturity.[10]

The image of the university professor in the satirical journals reflected the same ambivalent attitudes as did that of the school-master. On the one hand the professor was a petty tyrant (although mocked more for senility than for ferocity). On the other hand, like the schoolmaster he was also a victim of heavy-handed official interference and prejudice. The academic freedom of university faculty, seldom impaired during the relatively stable Bismarckian period, was now frequently challenged by a less secure government obsessed by fears of social unrest. The celebrated case of Leo Arons, a *Privatdozent* at the University of Berlin who was also active in the Social Democratic party, was only one of many confrontations between governmental authority and a traditionally self-governing academic community. Despite the concerted support of the Berlin faculty, Arons was deprived of the *venia legendi* (license to teach in higher education) in 1900; the former Prussian minister of culture, Bosse, had declared that "membership in the Social Democratic party cannot be reconciled with the duties of a Prussian official." Heine commented on this case with a grim cartoon from his series "Aus dunkelster Deutschland" ("In Darkest Germany"), showing white-haired professors goose-stepping in a barracks courtyard. "I'll teach you professors," barks a Prussian drill sergeant. "Pretty soon you won't be able to tell me from a Minister of Culture." This cartoon illustrates the grotesque and unflattering tendency of even relatively sympathetic comments on professors and teachers, who were always portrayed as old, doddering, personally and politically impotent. Such an image arose from an intuitive perception of the role of education in reinforcing middle class political passivity by encouraging what Thomas Mann termed a "privileged contemplative life" (*machtegeschützte Innerlichkeit*) far removed from social and political reality.[11]

Perhaps their lack of respect for the academic establishment accounts for the scant attention paid by the satirists to the major educational problem of this era, the admission of disadvantaged groups to schools and universities. *Kladderadatsch* paid slightly more attention to this issue than did *Simplicissimus*. In 1899 *Kladderadatsch* congratulated the first woman to earn a university degree at the University of Berlin. (At this time women could not be regularly admitted to most German universities and had to gain special permission to attend lectures.)

A hundred happy girls, I'm sure
Become "Frau Doktor" every day,

Of "Fräulein Doktors" there are fewer,
They must be very bright, I'd say!

But usually both journals confined themselves to tired old jokes on the frivolity of women's education and the plainness of blue-stockings. One feminist cause of the period was the admission of women to teaching posts in girls' secondary schools. *Kladdera-datsch* envisaged a special *Lehrerinnenprüfung* (certification examination for female teachers) in the field of history, asking questions about such important facts as "the color of the Princes' eyes." Thoma's short story "Gretchen Vollbeck," in which an un-distinguished male student (presumably his own younger self) confronts a female prodigy who can conjugate Latin verbs by the hour made fun not so much of the boy's wounded ego as of the girl's highly unattractive, even freakish intellectual ability. Some *Simplicissimus* jokes portrayed the hostile reaction of the "nor-mal" woman to her few university-educated sisters. "I'm afraid that women who get their doctorates here on earth will be com-pelled to darn stockings in Hell forever," one elegant young woman is shown remarking to another at a tea party. While making fun of old-fashioned prejudice, *Simplicissimus* thus still perpetuated the conventional image of the educated woman as a strange, slightly humorous phenomenon. Certainly the feminists' impas-sioned campaign to open up educational opportunities to women received little positive support.[12]

Satirical attacks on the still prestigious and respected teaching profession, especially in periodicals known to appeal to young readers, could not fail to provoke public response. Through the appealing character of Professor Schmidt, Theodor Fontane in his novel *Frau Jenny Treibel* remarked favorably on the role of the satirical journals in deflating pompous pedagogical authority. If the old-fashioned schoolmaster were to come to life in a modern classroom, Schmidt remarked, "he would appear three days later in *Kladderadatsch,* and the boys themselves would have written the verse." The far more hostile humor of *Simplicissimus* called forth some predictably negative responses. Fulminating against a drawing by Heine which showed "a group of German teachers with the well known ugly features and clumsy posture," an ed-itorial in the *Berliner Neueste Nachrichten* declared, "We cannot believe that the German teaching profession will accept this out-rageous insult passively!" The hostility of the academic estab-lishment to the new satirical style emerged in the rejection by the administration of Kiel University of a student petition for the addition of *Simplicissimus* to the periodical collection in the university reading room. The socialist newspaper *Vorwärts* described the assembly called to discuss the issue, where "a lively debate took place. Professor von Schubert described the magazine as pornography . . . from which the student body must be protected." A professor of jurisprudence added that although "thank God, he had never read *Simplicissimus*," he was able to form an "objective" judgment on the dangers of "such literature." A student who thereupon offered to distribute ten free copies of *Simplicissimus* a week to professors who had not read it was disciplined and later expelled when he made an account of the meeting available to the editors of *Vorwärts*. Like the students of Kiel, Viktor Mann's fraternity brothers were enthusiastic readers of *Simplicissimus* and responded to Heinrich Mann's highly unflattering picture of the fraternity not with hostility but with utter delight; references to "my cousin von Klappke" became a standard inside joke. The popularity of *Simplicissimus* among students, as among other elite groups such as officers and government officials, suggests increasing criticism of the authority structure not only from outside but from within.[13]

On this as on other issues, the contrast between *Kladderadatsch* and *Simplicissimus* illustrates a considerable evolution in both the content and the style of satirical journalism. While *Kladderadatsch* emphasized public issues such as curriculum reform and teachers' salaries, *Simplicissimus* stressed the psychological complexities of teacher-student relations. No longer content with stock figures such as "Biermörder," *Simplicissimus* explored the social and political dimensions of student life through the far better developed figure of Diederich Hessling. To the learned verbal satire of the Karlchen Miessnick pieces, bristling with classical allusions and Latin puns, may be contrasted *Simplicissimus'* graphic caricatures of the schoolmaster, which through their grotesque and distorted lines evoked strong emotion. Such images, though like all caricatures exaggerated, commented upon the considerable erosion of respect for the educational establishment and even for education itself. Such doubts were shared by many serious contemporary writers, among them the philosopher Friedrich Paulsen, who observed that "material ostentation and arrogance, limited, narrow-minded class snobbery, a noisy, rhetorical, thick-headed jingoism which calls itself patriotism," were prevalent "not only among lower-class people but especially among the educated, that is, among those who according to the theory should be the disciples of Plato and Sophocles.''[14]

The Purity Preachers

An institution which clearly exemplified the combined rigidity and spiritual stagnation of the Wilhelmine authority structure was the Christian church. Bismarck's *Kulturkampf* had stimulated intense antagonism between the Protestant church, secure and privileged, and the Catholic church, united by persecution. Despite the phasing out of the *Kulturkampf* in the 1880s, moreover, Catholics continued to suffer from economic and social discrimination in many parts of the Empire. Yet in the early years of the twentieth century Catholic politicians, responding to an influential pamphlet entitled *Heraus aus dem Turm* (*Let's Get Out of the Tower*) attempted increasingly to overcome their isolation and make common cause with like-minded Protestant leaders, usually of the conservative parties. The result was powerful right-wing alliance against progressive trends in politics, society, and culture. Alarmed by the growing secularization of modern society, both churches subordinated confessional rivalries to their common struggle, which, barren of new and creative ideas, took on an almost wholly negative and defensive tone. The political organ of the Catholic clergy was the Center party, which, as an indispensable ally of the conservatives, exercised an influence disproportionate to its actual numbers, particularly during the period of the so-called Blue-Black alliance (the dominant coalition in the Reichstag from 1909 to 1912). As self-proclaimed champions of enlightened modernity, the humorists opposed the churches' fervid religiosity with an equally passionate anticlericalism. The contrast between *Kladderadatsch,* still obsessed by the memory of the *Kulturkampf,* and *Simplicissimus,* which addressed a far wider range of church-state issues, will illustrate the evolution of a modern secular system of values.[15]

Kladderadatsch advocated the modernization of the school system and saw the church as one of the chief obstacles to that goal. The magazine's attack on the Zedlitz-Trützschler School Bill of 1891 was part of a liberal campaign which had important political results. The bill, designed to give the churches more extensive control over the school system, was seen by *Kladderadatsch* as a threat to academic freedom and to educational quality, and further as a move on the part of Chancellor Caprivi to effect a coalition between the Conservative and Center parties. *Kladder-adatsch* warned of a Center conspiracy and in effect called for a renewal of the *Kulturkampf.*

> Behind the scenes—they're there again
> They're busy plotting, more and more.
> I hear a cry—"let darkness reign!"
> So bold is now the black-robed corps.
> O knowledge—source of life and gladness
> Dark powers threaten your great light
> The "new course" leads us into sadness
> And plunges us in deepest night.[16]

The comments of *Kladderadatsch* on the School Bill showed the effectiveness of satire as a polemical tool. In order to show its readers the consequences of religiously oriented schooling, *Kladderadatsch* simply imagined a history lesson and the different views of the Inquisition which a Catholic and a Protestant would impart. "The Inquisition—a holy institution—was intended to warm up souls whose faith had become tepid," states the Catholic teacher. "The possessions of the heretics were distributed by the Church, which took care that their descendants should not be contaminated by the temptations of Mammon. Let us hope that, as the religious spirit is strengthened, this very useful instrument of the Holy Church may once again be revived." Thus, in order to combat the influence of the church, *Kladder-adatsch* portrayed the School Bill as a Catholic conspiracy to crush intellectual freedom, and conjured up lurid visions of the state and the Inquisition.[17]

The *Kladderadatsch* image of the Catholic clergy—reactionary, furtive, and lascivious—drew upon the standard imagery of nineteenth-century anticlericalism. Opposing the repeal on the ban on the Jesuit order, one of the few laws remaining from the 1870s, the humorists even raised the sinister and improbable specter of cooperation between those two treacherous and conspiratorial groups, the Jesuits and the socialists. In response to a socialist statement that the Jesuit law was unenforceable, *Kladderadatsch* accused the order of secret cooperation in the building of the "Future State" and pictured them as ravening wolves:

> For German souls they pant, no doubt,
> Like wolves in sheepskin coats,

And if we let them in, watch out!
They'll have us by the throats!

In the face of such dangers *Kladderadatsch* was overcome with nostalgia for the leader of the *Kulturkampf.* Even the most trivial incident could revive that glorious memory. For instance, when a Center deputy paid tribute to the recently deceased chancellor, the magazine fumed indignantly, "If he hadn't been entirely dead, he [Bismarck] would certainly have taken the wreath which they offered as a token of respect and hit them in their lying faces!" But such hostile fantasies misinterpreted the actual policies of Bismarck, who himself had finally realized that persecution had tended to strengthen rather than weaken the church. The call for a return to the measures of the 1870s was a counterproductive approach to the present based on a distortion of the past.[18]

By contrast, *Simplicissimus'* attack on the clergy was self-consciously modern and innovative. While, like *Kladderadatsch,* denouncing the Catholic clergy as a power-hungry faction, *Simplicissimus* extended its critique to Protestants as well as Catholics and to the social and cultural as well as the political sphere. Both its more radical message and its Bavarian origin made *Simplicissimus* a far more conspicuous object of clerical persecution than *Kladderadatsch.* Since 1887, Bavarian local politics had been dominated by a struggle between a liberal ministry and an increasingly powerful Center party, which by 1889 had attained a majority in the Landtag. In 1903 the influence of this faction had brought about the replacement of this ministry by a firmly Catholic one under the leadership of the conservative former minister of culture, von Podewils. The heightened militancy of the *Simplicissimus* "Zentrums-Nummer" of 1904 expressed the indignation of embattled Bavarian liberals at the increasingly repressive cultural policies imposed by this pro-Catholic regime.[19]

The "Zentrums-Nummer," which retaliated against the many attempts of clerical deputies to suppress the allegedly obscene and blasphemous *Simplicissimus,* was largely the work of the most determined of anticlerical propagandists, Ludwig Thoma. Entirely devoted to the Catholic clergy, the issue contained a mildly lascivious Reznicek cartoon of a Jesuit confessor casuistically counselling a beautiful society lady. "To be sure, your Highness has sinned against God's commands. But, after all, perhaps your Highness's concern for the morality of the lower classes led you to forget your own—and the Church regards such problems very

leniently." But above all, it was a mock sermon by Thoma entitled "The Lenten Sermon [*Fastenpredigt*] of Saint Abraham of
Santa Clara" which brought down the wrath of the Bavarian censors upon *Simplicissimus*. Excoriating clerical censorship, Thoma
observed that an institution which had controlled the European
conscience for centuries should not need the police to enforce
its authority. "When the individual comes into the world, you
[the clergy] are there, when he goes to school, his mind, malle-
able as wax, is formed by *you*, when he gets married, *you* must
tie the knot, and when he dies, you are by the bed. And do you
mean to say that through all these thousand years of mastery you
have not managed to convey your message? You need the police
to help you? Oh yes, gentlemen, you've tried *that* before! For you
and with you the princes beheaded, tortured, hanged, impaled,
until the earth swam in blood! And you yourselves kindled the
merry flames, and made sure that your Church *killed* infinitely
more martyrs than *died* for it during the first centuries of the
Christian era. Was this bloody work not sufficient? Have your
executioners still not convinced us?" Moreover, Thoma continued, the economic and cultural backwardness of such church-
dominated areas as rural Bavaria revealed the effects of clerical
education. "Here live people who are farther removed from the
culture of Europe than the Negro tribes of Africa; they know
nothing that you do not teach them, they read not one book, not
one pamphlet that you forbid. . . . And have you taught them
Christian morality? We know that they murder their neighbors
for a trifle. We know that they drink, gamble, squander their
money, mistreat their parents, abandon their children. And has
any of you ever taught these animal creatures anything about *true*
morality? No, gentlemen!" Here again are evocations of the Inquisition, but unlike the *Kladderadatsch* group Thoma emphasized the social and cultural, rather than the purely political effects of clerical domination. Indeed the hostility of the Catholic
hierarchy to modern, secular education may have been reflected
in the significantly lower-than-average educational levels among
German Catholics.[20]

On January 9, 1904, the Munich prosecutor ordered the Stuttgart police to confiscate the "Zentrums-Nummer" from the local
firm of Strecker and Schröder, where the magazine was printed.
"The completed numbers were placed under lock and key," reported the *Münchener Neueste Nachrichten*, "and any further
printing was forbidden." Thoma wrote immediately to his legal

advisor and close friend Conrad Haussmann. "How the [Munich] magistrates came into possession of the issue is extremely puzzling," he remarked, "but it's possible that the indiscretion of a postal official and an informer brought it about. As 'responsible editor,' Julius Linnekogel was summoned on Monday because of an 'offense against religion.' I'm no expert on the law, but this whole proceeding seems an unbelievable abridgement of freedom of the press." The next day, the *Münchener Neueste Nachrichten* echoed Thoma's suspicion that an informer (presumably of clerical sympathies) had given the information which prompted the confiscation. "We know that the black troops use any methods, even those that are scorned by all right-thinking people, such as betrayal and denunciation," it editorialized bitterly. "But there is something else that we don't understand—the control which these deplorable people exercise over our law-enforcement agencies." The *Fastenpredigt*, continued this editorial, attacked not the church itself but only its "unworthy servants." "In the whole article there is absolutely nothing which could be interpreted as blasphemous or as insulting to religion. But it seems that any attack against those who consider themselves the arbiters of all religion and morality will be punished as an attack on religion itself." Thus the confiscation raised an issue of the utmost political importance—the control of the Center party over the flourishing artistic and cultural life of Munich. The case received national attention. "All the Catholic papers report triumphantly that since the stern guardians of morality, who are now a majority in the Landtag, moved into the joyous city of Munich, the window displays of the bookstores and art stores have conformed to the pseudo-moral taste of these gentlemen. . . . From this restriction on display to the actual pressure on working artists and writers was only a short step, which in the *Simplicissimus* affair has already been undertaken," commented the *Frankfurter Zeitung.* "But under no circumstances is it acceptable that the morals and taste of the Center should provide the guidelines for the Munich censors. . . . It will be the responsibility of the government to make clear to the authorities that the demands of the clergy do not govern censorship. If this does not happen, then Bavaria's reputation as a center of artistic life will be forever destroyed." The editorial further speculated that, having failed in the attempt to pass national legislation such as the proposed Lex Heinze, right-wing and clerical groups now intended to push for the enactment of such laws on the local level.[21]

The confiscation immediately touched off a debate in the Bavarian Abgeordnetenkammer. Center deputies denied that their party had in any way connived at the confiscation. But while proclaiming their innocence, they vehemently denounced *Simplicissimus* and advocated legal restriction on its sale and display. One speaker repeated a rumor that Langen himself had arranged the incident in order to advertise his infamous publication. A parliamentary crisis was precipitated by the attempt of a socialist deputy to read the offending *Fastenpredigt* aloud; when the president of the chamber, a prominent member of the Center party, refused to permit the reading, the liberal vice-president resigned his office in protest. In Stuttgart the discovery that the local police force, and not a clerical "informer," had forwarded the incriminating issue to the Munich police was greeted with indignation by the liberal and socialist press, which protested such unnecessary cooperation with the church-dominated Bavarian government.[22]

Meanwhile Thoma and Haussmann prepared their defense, delighted at the predominantly favorable public attention which the case had already attracted. "The parliamentary discussion is naturally very opportune," wrote Haussmann on January 15, "and a public trial by jury would be even better for us." But the judge assigned to the case, anxious to avoid placing the defendants before a possibly sympathetic jury, invoked a convenient provision in the Bavarian legal code whereby, if the persons responsible for an infringement of the Press Law were declared innocent on the "subjective" grounds of mental incompetence, the publication itself could still be destroyed on the "objective" ground that it was offensive. This judge, a Center party member whose fitness Thoma and his attorneys had unsuccessfully challenged, acquitted the defendants on the patently ridiculous "subjective" ground but left the confiscation of the issue in force. "All this means is that they don't want to bring me before a jury," wrote Thoma indignantly. "They don't want twelve unprejudiced men of the people, among whom there are no Center deputies, to judge whether an attack on the dominant party in Bavaria is an attack on religion. . . . Perhaps I should be grateful that I have been acquitted? . . . I'm sorry that I can't appreciate this kind of mercy." On April 20, 1904, Haussmann as representative of the absent Thoma appeared along with other members of the *Simplicissimus* staff at a second hearing which was to decide the fate of the still-confiscated issue. "It was really fun," wrote Haussmann to his client. "In the second bench sat Her Majesty, Mrs. Albert Langen, crowned with her golden hair and surrounded by her bodyguard from *Simplicissimus*—Langen elegant, Geheeb dignified, Gulbransson looking around for cartoon-subjects with the gaze of a sea-lion." Haussmann read aloud the offending *Fastenpredigt.* "Everyone was impressed with it!" Having completed his planned defense, he then pointed out that further suppression of the issue was utterly futile. "Gentlemen, for an hour this argument has been absolutely pointless. The *Fastenpredigt* which I have read aloud will appear tomorrow in the courtroom reports of all the newspapers. . . . The defense recommends in the best interests of this Court that it avoid the universal ridicule with which it will be covered—and not only by satirical journals—if it tries to suppress what has already been made public." The issue was released, the *Simplicissimus* staff celebrated in the "Odeon" bar, and the *Frankfurter Zeitung* exulted, "There are still judges in Bavaria!" "Number 42 can now be sold—all 150,000 copies!" chortled Haussmann, whose anticipation of an "enjoyable" trial had been amply fulfilled. Reading the continued clerical fulminations, Langen "beamed with joy. . . . If our enemies, who were trying to find the most malicious possible words to say against us, could have seen how we read their articles aloud and laughed," recollected Thoma in his memoirs, "then they might have given up . . . but the gentlemen of the Center were so sensitive that they would never have been able to visualize their effect on us."[23]

Thus clerical opposition did nothing to moderate the tone of the struggle, which, as Thoma observed, grew "rougher and rougher." In April 1905 he was once again brought to trial, this time on a charge of insulting not the Catholic but the Protestant pastorate. By this time the editors had obviously learned to exploit the full publicity value of such events. So great was the throng of spectators that the trial, which could not be held in the courthouse itself, was moved to a spacious art gallery, the Lindenmuseum. Again Haussmann argued for the defense, this time aided by Max Bernstein, who in addition to his legal practice also engaged in literary and theatrical criticism. The offending verse, "To the Purity Preachers of Cologne," has already been quoted in another context. Based on sociological and psychological data, the arguments for the defense advocated the recognition of sexuality as an important artistic and literary theme. Haussmann attacked the position of the "purity preachers" on the broadest ethical, patriotic, and aesthetic grounds. Not only was the iden-

"To the Purity Preachers of Cologne." The cartoon and accompanying verse were considered an "insult to the Protestant pastorate" and led to a lawsuit in 1905. (Gulbransson, *Simplicissimus*, Nov. 1904.)

tification of morality with traditional sexual prudery contrary to the "ethical views of all modern people," but the moralists' ceaseless harping on moral decadence held Germany up to the scorn of other nations (an offense of which *Simplicissimus* itself had often been accused by these same groups). Furthermore the charge of "incitement to immorality" was "an overestimation of literature which in the interests of literature itself should be combatted." These arguments reflected a serious and self-conscious search for a secular system of social ethics to replace the allegedly outmoded principles of the church. Lest the numerous and predominantly sympathetic audience grow bored with such a high intellectual tone, the defense lawyers enlivened the proceedings with titillating allusions to the highly prurient imaginations of these self-appointed guardians of public morality. "His comments on marital sex relations indicate that Herr Bohn [the "insulted" pastor] has some very strange attitudes," Haussmann commented. "I must say that there are passages in his speeches and pamphlets which prevented me from giving this brief to my secretary to type, because in my opinion they offended against decency." But unlike the humorists of *Kladderadatsch,* who had confined themselves to oblique insinuations, the *Simplicissimus* group openly challenged the use of religious authority to enforce sexual repression. "The Founder of the Christian church expressly forbade such self-righteous judgments," argued Thoma, "the first time, when he defended the adulteress against the attacks of the Jewish officials with the words, 'Let him among you who is without sin cast the first stone,' and the second time when he pardoned the repentant sinner, who had 'loved much!' " The cover of the issue, which displayed a somewhat sentimentally drawn Savior turning away from a group of plump and worldly priests, held up the example of Christ himself as a reproach to his unworthy modern servants.[24]

On June 26, 1905, the judge handed down a verdict of guilty, sentencing Linnekogel to a fine of 200 marks and Thoma to a six-week prison sentence, and further requiring that all copies of the offending verse and cartoon, including the matrices from which they were printed, be destroyed. The judge justified the sentences by condemning the personally insulting tone of the attacks on the Protestant pastors. "Like any other form of verbal self-expression, satire is subject to the general rules governing the respect for persons and consideration for one's fellow men. If the accused believes that he can go further in insulting and ridiculing his opponent in the form of a satirical poem than in any other form of literary self-expression, then he is most seriously in error." This judicial opinion thus indirectly acknowledged the function of satire as a disguised and "harmless" form of protest. The prison sentence, formally justified by "the seriousness of the insult" and "the number of those insulted," may in fact have been imposed for the reasons urged by the prosecuting attorney. "A fine is not enough," argued the latter, "because it affects, not the accused themselves, but only the treasury of *Simplicissimus.* I therefore demand a prison sentence for Dr. Thoma of two months and for Linnekogel of four weeks." Having failed in an attempt to appeal his sentence, Thoma served it philosophically, spending part of his unwelcome leisure time reading and unmercifully reviewing an edition of Kaiser Wilhelm's speeches.[25]

The contrast between the anticlerical humor of *Kladderadatsch* and that of *Simplicissimus* reflects both change and continuity. The older satirists' opposition to the sinister political designs of the Catholic clergy in no way affected their basic support of traditional moral values. The younger group presented a far broader critique of the role of both churches in society. While *Kladderadatsch* implicated priests and socialists in the same subversive conspiracy, *Simplicissimus* emphasized the opposition between the two groups and championed the workers against clerical oppression. Among Thoma's most serious accusations against the clergy was that they used their much-publicized antiobscenity campaign to avoid serious discussion of the really pressing problems of an urbanizing society. "By resounding speeches they avoided the hard task of alleviating the conditions which encouraged immorality. These were created by poverty, exploitation, the housing shortage, etc., much more than by the display of nudes in bookstore windows." The enormous and largely favorable reaction to the courtroom battles periodically waged by the magazine against its clerical opponents contributed to *Simplicissimus'* growing prestige. However, the tone of both journals—alternately snickering and venomous—often exuded the same intolerance of which they accused the clergy. Although both magazines protested many cases of discrimination—against Jews, Poles, Alsatians, socialists—neither ever mentioned the pervasive prejudice in Protestant Germany against Catholics. The picture of the priest or clergyman was likewise a completely negative stereotype which ignored progressive developments in theology and church policy. Thus the satirical journals both reflected the still deeply divisive effect of the *Kulturkampf* on German society.[26]

The Jew: Pariah or Parvenu?

Satirists whose mocking gaze fell upon all classes and groups could hardly overlook the Jews. Indeed, the editors of *Kladderadatsch,* which numbered several Jews among its founders, and of *Simplicissimus,* which had several prominent Jewish staff members, could have been expected to take a particular interest in the social status of Jews. Although antisemitic parties received only minor electoral support during this period, antisemitic ideology influenced much political thought and popular culture, even gaining increased respectability in the works of much-venerated scholars such as Heinrich von Treitschke. In the face of pervasive prejudice, German Jews were not passive. Two organizations, the Abwehrverein (founded 1890) and the Zentralverein deutscher

Staatsbürger jüdischen Glaubens (founded 1893) vigorously protested racial prejudice and kept issues such as the army's dis-
criminatory promotion policies before the public eye. But Jews
were often disposed to endure rather than to protest racial slurs.
Proud of their highly conspicuous achievements in such fields
as art, journalism, and the professions, they were often oblivious
to the resentment which their rapid rise had provoked.[27]

Given the high visibility of Jews in German society, one is at
first surprised to find relatively few references to them in the
Wilhelmine *Kladderadatsch* and *Simplicissimus.* The tone and
content of such jokes as did appear will suggest the reasons for
this surprising neglect of the issue. The contrast between *Kladderadatsch* and *Simplicissimus,* moreover, will indicate an important transformation in the image of the Jew which reflected
changes in his status and social position.

From its first issue in 1848, *Kladderadatsch* had gloried in the
Jewish dialect, anecdotes, and allusions which (along with the
Berlin idiom) largely defined its journalistic personality. At first
such jokes emphasized the Jews' separate and distinctive traditions. For instance, a piece from 1850, entitled "Talmudic Wisdom of the Great Jewish Scholar," attributed to "Baruch Itzig Meyer
Levi Mausche Kapaun," compared the abortive 1848 revolution
to Jacob's frustrated courtship of Rachel, and used traditional
Jewish names, religious imagery, and dialect. In the 1870s and
1880s the image of the Talmudic scholar was replaced by a new
stereotype, that of the financier Baron Itzig von Itzigstein, the
supposedly "typical" stockmarket speculator of the *Gründerzeit.*
In 1885 when *Kladderadatsch* came under the control of a Gentile editor-in-chief, Johannes Trojan, the Jewish jokes and allusions grew markedly less frequent as the magazine strove for a
more conservative and genteel image.[28]

Despite this personality change, the Wilhelmine *Kladderadatsch* paid frequent attention to Jewish issues. Focusing chiefly
upon antisemitism in both its political and its cultural manifestations, it held up the antisemites' theories to ridicule as paranoid and hysterical fantasies. In 1893, for example, it spoofed a
pamphlet entitled *Judenflinten,* published by the notorious antisemitic leader Hermann Ahlwardt, who had charged that the
Jewish arms firm of Loewe, treacherously in league with the
French, had delivered defective rifles to the German army. The
Kladderadatsch piece, entitled "Judenkanonen," alleged that the
Gruson works in Magdeburg, recently acquired by Krupp, had

patented a revolving turret, which by means of a spring "in-stalled by the right person at the right time" could be caused to spin "so that the enemy can simply pass by the dizzy defenders unheeded." A Jewish conspiracy? "The fact that Gruson is a Jew-ish name," alleged *Kladderadatsch,* "needs just as little proof as Krupp's descent from a rabbi." The frequent complaints of an-tisemites that Berlin was being overrun by Jews (a reaction to the influx of Eastern European Jews, often conspicuous through dress and customs) was mocked in a verse entitled "The Antisemite's Spring Song." The antisemitic singer lamented:

> To me the fair Springtime will bring no delight
> But only more worry, I'm sure.
> For the parks, and the woodlands and every place
> Will be full of that bowlegged, crooked-nose race.

To feel threatened and overwhelmed by a group constituting a small percentage of the population is certainly to suffer from an obsession.[29]

The myth of fabulous Jewish wealth was likewise exploded in a piece entitled "Ahlwardt's Dream" in which the demagogue, having become mayor of Berlin, orders all Jews to deliver up their wealth or be roasted alive in the square "with Spanish onions." Expecting bags of gold, he receives only sacks of old clothes. And *Kladderadatsch* likewise mocked antisemitic literary criticism by praising "the discovery that the 'Lorelei' is a Jewess. Her real name is Lore Levy. She comes from the Frankfurt ghetto and lures Ger-man youths . . . she buys golden combs with the money she steals from them. . . . It's really time to ban such 'German folk songs' from our schools!"[30]

Such telling parodies of antisemitic propaganda stressed both the status of the Jew as a still-persecuted outsider and his claim to just and equal treatment. As the antisemitic parties declined into insignificance after 1900, the number of references to the "Jewish question" in *Kladderadatsch* also decreased. But the de-cline of the antisemitic parties had not signalled the end of an-tisemitism, which still infected many aspects of culture and so-ciety.[31]

Despite the persistence of prejudice, the 1890s had been a good decade for German Jews, many of whom had gained conspicuous success in business, the arts, and the professions. In *Simplicissi-mus,* a product of that era, the Jew appeared no longer as a victim but as an assimilated social climber, competing with his Gentile counterpart for status and success. Yet despite his attempts at assimilation, the Jew was never portrayed as simply another ambitious bourgeois, but always as a crude and recognizable racial type. This unflattering image may in part reflect the prejudice of some (by no means all) Gentile staff members. A dispute between Langen and Thoma over a proposed tribute to Heinrich Heine revealed their different attitudes toward Jews in general. To Langen's presumably admiring comments on the great Jewish poet and satirist, Thoma replied by condemning not only Heine himself, whom he accused of frivolity and political radicalism, but the so-called "Jewish" press of his own time. "To be sure, the antisemitic papers write a lot of stupid stuff about Heine . . . but whose fault is it that the dispute never ends? It is the fault of the Jewish press which . . . gives the man a significance which he doesn't deserve." The idea that the Jew himself, rather than the antisemite, was to blame for the hostility of his Gentile countrymen was often echoed in the humor of *Simplicissimus.* And Jewish staff members such as Thomas Theodor Heine and Jakob Wassermann, far from protesting such an attitude, were inclined to share it (as we see from their opinions expressed in *Simplicissimus* and elsewhere). Thus the appearance of a distinctive Jewish stereotype in a magazine so seemingly advanced and liberal as *Simplicissimus* attested to the disturbingly ambivalent attitude of even the most progressive segments of society (Jews and Gentiles alike) toward Jewish assimilation.[32]

The *Simplicissimus* Jew was almost always rich, successful, and ambitious—an image which, entirely ignoring the many poor and lower-middle-class Jews, reinforced fears of Jewish economic dominance. Some cartoons, to be sure, revealed the rich Jew as the victim of cynical Gentile prejudice and exploitation. For instance, a Bruno Paul cartoon entitled "Aristocratic World-View" showed a typically vapid and effete young nobleman leading a dark, hook-nosed, and hunchbacked girl to the altar, while her equally unappealing father looks on approvingly. "Honor, love, and hunger determine the course of history," reflects Paul's aristocrat complacently; "for honor we have the duel, for love the chorus girl, and for hunger, thank God, a rich bride." The treatment of Jewish-Gentile marriages (one issue was devoted entirely to the "Verjudung" of Junker family trees) implied criticism of both the Junker's greed and the Jew's social ambition. Often, however, the Jew was shown simply as the exploiter of his Gentile countrymen. Another cartoon, entitled "Christmas at Wert-

heim's" (a large Jewish-owned department store, frequently resented by small businessmen), showed a prosperous and obviously
Jewish family sitting comfortably around a traditional German
Christmas tree. "Why shouldn't we celebrate His birth?" asks the
father of this clan. "He brings us all the lovely Christmas trade."
And the newly ennobled Jew, sedulously aping aristocratic manners and values, was a great figure of fun. A cartoon character,
"Baron Goldstein," reacts to the birth of a daughter with a combination of newly acquired feudal and traditionally Jewish attitudes. "God the Just," he exclaims, raising his eyes to Heaven,
"must I be the first and last of my dynasty?" The life of Gerson
Bleichröder (recently recounted by Fritz Stern) provided a real-
life example of just such a Jewish patriarch turned aristocrat.[33]

Another aspect of the so-called "Jewish" personality was explored in the image of the Jew as artist or patron of the arts. Here
again the satirists commented on the process of assimilation by
picturing the Jew as an alien imitating artistic traditions which
he did not understand. The career of an Eastern European Jew,
one of those whom Treitschke described as "a troop of ambitious,
trouser-selling youths," was depicted in a cartoon strip entitled
"Metamorphosis." "Moishe Pisch sold old clothes in Tarnopol"
the caption begins. "When he moved to Posen he became Moritz
Wasserstrahl and sold Paris fashions. Now he's changed his name
to Maurice Lafontaine, he lives in Berlin, and he has founded a
new artistic school. Again he sells second-hand Paris fashions."
The cartoons themselves stressed the unchanging Jewish physical type beneath the progressively more elaborate clothing. Thus
Simplicissimus echoed the fears of antisemites such as Treitschke
that pushy immigrants might create "an age of German-Jewish
bastardized culture." Antisemites commonly denied that the Jews
could possess true artistic genius, belittling their achievements
as imitative and unoriginal. Treitschke alluded to the "well-known
fact that the only art in which the modern Jew shows real genius
is the art of the theatre. Imitative faculty, without any inward
originating power, has always been a strong point of Jewish literature." This same stereotype was reinforced by a *Simplicissimus* cartoon of the prominent theatrical director Max Reinhardt
staging the Oberammergau Passion Play. "Come on in, Ladies and
Gentlemen! Come on in, enjoy the fun! Modern production . . .
the life of Our Lord, from cradle to grave! It's new, it's exciting!"
This image of Reinhardt the ringmaster desecrating the Passion
Play would seem to appeal to both racial and religious hostility.
And yet Jewish writers themselves often accused their co-reli-

gionists of much the same faults. Wassermann, for instance, deplored the Jew's alleged showiness as a symptom of his perennial insecurity. "In him everything is gesture, nervousness, affectation."[34]

Such mockery of Jewish assimilation strongly implied that it was impossible. Banker, soldier, artist, or old-clothes peddler, the Jew was always the familiar caricature figure—short, fat, kinky-haired, hook-nosed, thick-lipped. The coupling of characteristic psychological with physical traits implied that "Jewishness" was a genetic trait which could never be entirely eradicated by culture. The acceptance of such a crude caricature by the ethnically diverse *Simplicissimus* staff reflects the well-nigh universal belief in "racial" theories among Europeans of this period. Much the same caricature type is found in *Punch*. As Peter Gay remarked, "Nothing demonstrates more poignantly, how solidly Jews were anchored in Western culture than their acceptance of the dubious notion of 'racial' characteristics. . . . They affirmed their distinctiveness like everybody else." It is in the nature of caricature to be insulting, and by the standards of this period, this stereotype, so distasteful to the contemporary reader, may have been considered no more instrinsically offensive than those of the paunchy businessman or dim-witted Junker.[35]

To be sure, *Simplicissimus* did protest the more open forms of prejudice (such as discrimination in the army and the Reserve officer corps). Unlike *Kladderadatsch,* however, which concentrated chiefly upon German manifestations of antisemitism, *Simplicissimus* perceived it as chiefly a foreign problem. By far the most striking evocation of racial violence was a response to the wave of pogroms which struck Russian Jews in the aftermath of the 1905 Revolution. A grim and stark picture entitled "The Russian Court Hunts Jewish Game" showed soldiers piling corpses into a huge mass grave. Such a cartoon, however, might well have served not to frighten but to reassure the German Jew by presenting antisemitic violence as a manifestation of Russian backwardness and czarist reaction, implying that such atrocities could never occur in an "advanced" society such as Germany.[36]

In his comments on the antisemitism of the Wilhelmine period, Peter Gay assigned to *Simplicissimus* a major role in perpetuating antisemitic stereotypes, but added that he knew of no Jewish objections to such humor—a speculation which is borne out by the admittedly incomplete archival evidence. Indeed, the magazine's critics tended to view it as pro- rather than antisemitic, a product of the allegedly subversive and destructive Jewish sense of humor. "Of course, Jews play a prominent role in both of these publications," remarked the *Augsburger Postzeitung* of both *Jugend* and *Simplicissimus.* The same editorial viewed the appearance of Georg Hirth, editor of *Jugend,* as a witness in support of Heine at his trial of 1904 as one more example of Jewish racial solidarity transcending commercial rivalries.[37]

If indeed (as one can assume) the Jewish humor of *Simplicissimus* was popular among both Gentiles and Jews, this fact reveals many of the psychological and cultural tensions caused by the process of assimilation. In the first place, "Jewish" jokes told by Jews often reflect the internalization of the values of the oppressor—a tendency common to all oppressed groups. In the second place, the assimilated German Jew might see the behavior of his less "cultivated" co-religionists, especially the many recent immigrants from Eastern Europe, as awkward and embarrassing. To laugh at the too conspicuously "Jewish" Jew was to exert pressure on him to conform more closely to the German culture which most German Jews genuinely admired. In the third place, the allusion to "racial" characteristics was not in itself considered insulting—many a Jew considered it possible to be a "typical" Jew and good German at the same time.[38]

Thus we return to the question of why the satirical journals made so few allusions to Jews, their problems, and their social status. The neglect of the issue was probably due in large measure to the sense of false security shared by most German Jews during the Wilhelmine period. If, as many thought, antisemitism was "a mere atavism that a great civilization like the German was likely to outgrow," it was perhaps not worthy of much attention. And even the hostile portrait of the social-climbing Jew implied a certain optimism about the results of assimilation. For were not social ambition, ostentatious taste, pseudoaristocratic posturing, and political sycophancy shown as characteristic not only of the Jew but of the entire German bourgeoisie to which he belonged? The Jew was indeed a German, and as such was probably more interested in reading about issues of concern to all his fellow citizens than about the specifically "Jewish" problems which (or so he fondly thought) were on their way to solution.[39]

The Arts

Unlike the issues of educational reform and religion—on which, despite their differences of style and emphasis, the two journals essentially agreed—issues of artistic style and taste provoked a more fundamental disagreement. To be sure, both *Kladderadatsch* and *Simplicissimus* protested the heavy-handed official and clerical censorship of artistic and literary expression. Both mocked the pretentious conventional taste of the period. But the burgeoning modernist movement called forth widely divergent reactions—from *Kladderadatsch* revulsion, from *Simplicissimus* supportive enthusiasm. Previous chapters have discussed the contrasting artistic styles represented by the magazines themselves, as well as many of their responses to laws, such as blasphemy or obscenity statutes, affecting the arts. Thus the only remaining task is to show how the humorists' attitudes toward artistic styles and trends reflected the aesthetic value systems which underlay their work as a whole.[40]

Many of the satirists' comments on the arts focused upon clerical or governmental attempts to dictate standards of decency and taste. The kaiser's speeches, at once dilettantish and heavy-handed, characterized modernism as "gutter art" (*Rinnsteinkunst*). "If art, as so frequently happens now, does nothing more than to paint misery more ugly than it is," he pompously declared at the opening of the Berlin Siegesallee in 1901, "it sins against the German people." Church support for censorship was expressed by the proposed Lex Heinze of 1899. Artists and intellectuals, including the satirists of *Simplicissimus* and *Kladderadatsch,* united to oppose this dangerously vague legislation which, if passed, would have severely impaired the vital and variegated development of German art.[41]

Both journals covered this inept and illiberal measure with ridicule by carrying the well known principle that prurience is in the eye of the beholder to its logical conclusion. *Kladderadatsch* devoted an entire issue to the announcement of a new magazine entitled the "Fig-Leaf Journal," whose masthead announced, "With this number, we inaugurate the era of the *Lex Heinze.* In the spirit of true morality we will try to suppress everything which could possibly inflame wild passion in anyone, from infant to grandfather." A section entitled "News from Our Capital City" included such items as the following: "On the Belle-Allianceplatz, a female dog pursued by a male dog excited attention. The police have closed off the square." And a "Book Review" section announced the appearance of two books in editions for young ladies—Goethe's *Faust,* in which Faust now meets Gretchen through a newspaper advertisement, and the *Memoirs of Casanova,* in which the "hero visits a wide variety of girls' hostels, convents,

and boarding schools and is sent away with virtuous advice."
Through the indirect device of humor *Kladderadatsch* insinuated
that the clerical view of the arts reflected not purity and virtue
but a nasty-minded sexual obsession. Ludwig Thoma exposed this
pathology more explicitly in his many attacks on clerical prudery—for instance, in this verse ridiculing the suggestion that the
Venus de Milo, a familiar ornament of middle-class drawing rooms,
be banned for its alleged obscenity.

> In Milo's Venus, goddess fair and tender,
> He looks for nothing but the signs of gender.
> Her beauty utterly escapes his view,
> So to the cloister, little jerk, with you.
> Turn to the Bible for some dirty stories
> To turn you on, and leave us to the glories,
> Of our great sculpture, painting, poetry.
> We are not fools, or eunuchs—no, not we![42]

Like *Kladderadatsch, Simplicissimus* ironically noted the an-
tipathy of the advocates of censorship to the very hallowed cultural traditions for which they expressed such admiration. "But
if this article can be confiscated for immorality, then all of Goethe's
work is immoral," a cartoon showed an editor protesting. "Sure,"
replies the prosecutor, "do you really think that Goethe should
have been allowed to write his *Faust?*" The ultimate failure of
its official and clerical supporters to enact the Lex Heinze attested in part to the effectiveness of ridicule as a political weapon.
The vociferous support for *Simplicissimus* in its legal confrontations with church or state authority showed the opposition of
large segments of the public to such censorship laws.[43]

Both journals likewise perceived the relationship between the
kaiser's pseudohistorical artistic taste and his reactionary political ideology. *Kladderadatsch* frequently sniped irreverently at
the works of Josef Lauff, author of the pretentious historical dra-
mas commissioned by the court. *Simplicissimus* likewise spoofed
the kaiser's favorite neobaroque architectural style, compared by
cultural historian Egon Friedell to "the art of the upholsterer, the
confectioner, the studio decorator." This resemblance was remarked in a *Simplicissimus* cartoon in which a pastry cook uses
the Berlin Cathedral designed by Wilhelm himself as an example
for his apprentices. "Study it carefully—you can learn a lot from
it, boys!" In the similarly ornate and tasteless restoration of the
"Friedrichsbau" at Heidelberg (completed in 1903) Thoma saw a

plot to conceal the German cultural heritage under a pompous and artificial facade.

> We feel the pressure from On High,
> The Genuine is banished,
> And Truth, amid the boastful Lie,
> Forevermore has vanished.
> But, cowards all, we still obey
> And all is done just as they say.[44]

Although in agreement in their reverence for the great works of the past, the two journals emphatically disagreed when confronted with contemporary artistic innovation. *Kladderadatsch,* which had defended the right of the artist to free expression, nonetheless voiced a thoroughly conservative skepticism about modern art and literature. As previous chapters have shown, such artistic conservatism was conveyed through its own literary style and visual format which, except for the contributions of a few younger cartoonists, remained on the whole traditional. Its reaction to contemporary styles ranged from mild amusement to undisguised hostility. For modern poets and artists *Kladderadatsch* suggested a "League of the Misunderstood" open to "any poet or artist who will swear that he himself cannot understand his own work," which would sponsor exhibitions and readings only for members and would expel any member whose work contained an intelligible idea. Far more aggressive was the response to works which challenged not only accepted aesthetic standards but traditional moral standards as well. The magazine's view of Ibsen, whose plays gained wide popularity during the 1890s, agreed essentially with those of the British critics who characterized the playwright as a "crazy, cranky being . . . not only consistently dirty but deplorably dull." Here is the comment of *Kladderadatsch* on *Hedda Gabler:*

> I don't think I'll go to the theater today,
> Hysterical Hedda's the star of the play.
> I'm not a man who feels much fear,
> But when the playbills did appear
> I looked on Ibsen's awful face
> And trembled at that owlish gaze;
> So bitterly he looked around,
> As if on earth there could be found
> Nothing at all that the heart delighted,

> As if the world were sick and blighted.
> A scoundrel and fool is every man,
> And every woman a harridan.
> And love is never fresh and sweet,
> And in the human breast doth beat
> No heart—in joy nor in despair,
> And I felt I had come from the fresh spring air
> Into a dismal, dark sickroom
> Full of medicinal smells and gloom.

The versifier, who concluded that he would rather stay home and read Goethe and Schiller, had conveniently forgotten the similarly shocking impact of some of these authors' works when they were first published.[45]

Still more unfavorable was the response to a younger playwright, Frank Wedekind, whose *Frühlingserwachen* touched upon the highly controversial topic of adolescent sexuality. Abandoning all pretense of humorous detachment, *Kladderadatsch* reacted with open hostility:

> This man's a lunatic, I guess,
> His play is not a great success,
> So dull, so sordid is this play
> The people quickly run away.

In the nostalgic spirit which had become increasingly typical, the verse concluded that forty years before, the play would have been banned and its author labelled "lascivious, impotent, and totally crazy." In the face of threatening cultural change, *Kladderadatsch* thus abandoned its cherished liberal principles and indirectly called for censorship. Such revulsion at the newest trends in German art was shared by the similarly respectable *Punch,* which reacted to Humperdinck's sugary opera *Hansel and Gretel* with astonishment that "in a squalid age, when horror, blood, and ugliness so many pens engage," such a pure work could emerge from Germany. *Kladderadatsch*'s reactions to plays challenging accepted sexual and family morals reflected the older magazine's fundamental tendency to restrict the legitimate sphere of the satirist to public life, leaving the private sphere unchallenged.[46]

To such cultural conservatism may be contrasted the modernist and avant-garde spirit of *Simplicissimus.* To be sure, *Simplicissimus* too frequently ridiculed the more precious and esoteric artistic cults of the period, as in a cartoon entitled "Misunderstood," which showed a sensitive young poet in a fit of depression. "This is the frightful destiny of the genius. I am the only person who understands me." In general, however, *Simplicissimus* aggressively supported the freedom of the artist to experiment. "*Simplicissimus* has the reputation of being revolutionary, socialistic," read the statement of purpose which appeared in its seventh issue. "But what does the poor rogue have to do with politics? To art, and art alone, we devote our feeble powers. But this art must be free to choose its own direction, wherever it wishes and will be bound neither by hypocritical morality nor by political slogans." In asserting the artist's duty to rescue his contemporaries from Philistine complacency, *Simplicissimus* foreshadowed the manifesto of the Vienna Secession of 1897, in which the young artists vowed to save culture from stagnation and decadence. Not only innovative in artistic style, *Simplicissimus* (as previous chapters have shown) committed itself to publishing new and controversial literary works by such authors as the Manns, Rilke, Dehmel, Wedekind, Mühsam, and many others.[47]

Both its critics and its admirers regarded *Simplicissimus* as an important organ of artistic modernism. "To be sure, *Simplicissimus* sometimes makes jokes about conditions in Bavaria and Munich," snarled an editorial in the *Kölnische Zeitung,* "but in general its point of view is purely artistic, with a clear French influence. Its style is that mixture of naturalism and neoromanticism known as Bohemianism. We can trace a great deal of material which we don't like to the abandoned excesses of the artists' tavern. There and in many ateliers one finds all kinds of drawings showing the grotesque imaginings of riotous hours." In a more positive vein, Gerhardt Hauptmann, among the most prominent of the period's playwrights, wrote that "the sharpest and most ruthless satirical force in Germany is *Simplicissimus.* We see both the advantages and the weaknesses of inspired satire in this brilliant art magazine." Many other artists and writers echoed Hauptmann's opinion, confirming the vital role of *Simplicissimus* as an advocate and popularizer of new artistic styles.[48]

More clearly than any other topic, modern art called forth specifically age-related reactions from the two groups of satirists, for the modernist movement of the 1890s was a self-consciously generational phenomenon in which the superiority of youth over age was constantly asserted (even by some artists who were no longer in their first youth). Schorske referred to Viennese modernism, in both literature and the visual arts, as a collective "oedipal revolt" against the conventional "fathers." "Their only common ground," he remarked of these young artists, "was rejection of the classical realist tradition of their fathers in the search for modern man's true face." This purpose was also stated by *Simplicissimus*' contemporary and rival, the satirical weekly *Jugend*, which proclaimed in 1896, "We want to name this new weekly *Jugend* [youth] for that word sums up everything! Of course we're not talking about chronological age, but about the heart." While the *Simplicissimus* staff reveled in the youth-cult, the older editors of *Kladderadatsch*, including the editor-in-chief, Trojan, now in his sixties and nearing retirement, expressed the insecurity of older men who saw their own methods—humor, satire, and irony—used to undermine the values in which they continued to believe. The appointment of Paul Warncke, an outspoken patriot and conservative, to succeed Trojan in 1909 decisively confirmed the magazine's movement not only toward artistic traditionalism but toward political conservatism as well.[49]

Kladderadatsch, Simplicissimus, and the Weimar Republic

7

AT the close of World War I both *Kladderadatsch* and *Simplicissimus* faced a major problem of readjustment. Appealing to the sense of political unity in the face of a common enemy, the *Witzblätter,* which had been widely distributed in special editions at the front, had maintained and increased their readership during the war years. But as first warweariness and then defeat plunged the nation into bitter internal strife, both magazines returned to political partisanship. The purpose of this chapter is not to analyze the humor of this period in depth (a task too complex for a short space) but merely to suggest how the humorous imagery and techniques developed during the prewar period were adapted to the changed conditions of the Weimar Republic.[1]

Both the wartime and the postwar content of *Kladderadatsch* reflected the personality and convictions of Paul Warncke, who had succeeded Johannes Trojan as editor-in-chief in 1909. Warncke, who was born in Lübz (Mecklenburg) in 1866 into a businessman's family, abandoned his commercial training for the study of sculpture at the Berlin Academy in 1894. His early literary works—a poem honoring Bismarck's birthday in 1895, and a pageant commemorating the founding of the German Empire—seem to have been conventionally patriotic. A member of the editorial staff since 1906, Warncke had changed the magazine's policy to allow for initialled rather than anonymous contributions. Among the many contributors of the Weimar period, the cartoonists—longtime members of the staff such as Ludwig Stutz and Gustav Brandt and such newcomers as the German-American artist Arthur Johnson—were the most creative. The increasing prominence given to graphic art after 1914 reflected both the belated impact of the modern style pioneered by *Simplicissimus* and the need to fill the empty space now deserted by advertisers, who withdrew their support from the declining publication. To be sure, this decline was conspicuous only after the war, for until 1915 *Kladderadatsch* maintained its approximate prewar circulation figure of 40,000. Although no figures were published during the 1920s the next available figure, 17,500 for 1934, reflects a marked decline in popularity. In the absence of yearly figures, one may speculate that the magazine's troubles were increased by postwar hyperinflation, when single issues priced at three million marks (September 20, 1923) and twelve million marks (October 7, 1923) were beyond the means of former subscribers. Financial losses forced the Hofmann Verlag, publishers of *Kladderadatsch* since the first issue of 1848, to sell the magazine to the Stinnes conglomerate, which added many newspapers and presses to its financial empire during the inflationary period. The influence of Stinnes reinforced the magazine's capitalist, right-wing, and antisocialist views. By 1925 the magazine was again sold, this time to the H. and S. Hermann publishing firm in Berlin.[2]

The hostility of *Kladderadatsch* toward the Republic was aroused primarily by anger at what it regarded as a conciliatory response to the demands of the victorious Allies. By its distorted portrayal of Germany as the innocent and "encircled" victim of foreign malice, the Wilhelmine *Kladderadatsch* had helped to lay the psychological foundation for this self-pitying and ferocious postwar chauvinism. *Kladderadatsch* joined right-wing demagogues in denouncing moderate politicians—who hoped through limited fulfillment to bring about future revision of the treaty—for their alleged betrayal of German interests. Even the mild protest against the assassination of Foreign Minister Walther Rathenau in 1922 implied almost as much hostility toward Rathenau himself as toward his murderers.

We will forget his oft-misguided life
His errors and his sins we'll not remember
Instead we mourn the fratricidal strife
Which threatens our dear country to dismember.[3]

Despite Gustav Stresemann's commitment to the policy of fulfillment, *Kladderadatsch* expressed qualified approval when he took office as chancellor in 1923, perhaps because of his reputation as a strong nationalist: "Long years have passed. Now once again we see, / A man who stands as Bismarck once stood, tall." But the Locarno Treaties of 1925, which represented Stresemann's greatest diplomatic triumph, were received with hostility or skepticism. *Kladderadatsch* expressed mistrust, not only of the Rhineland Pact negotiated with France, which guaranteed the Franco-German frontier, but of the arbitration agreements signed with Poland and Czechoslovakia, which gave no such guarantee. Thus, while not yet joining right-wing extremists in their intemperate and vicious denunciations of Stresemann, the *Kladderadatsch* staff exhibited a reluctance typical of even moderate right-wing opinion to accept the need for patience and negotiation. When Germany entered the League of Nations in 1926 the magazine likewise expressed doubt whether the French "would put new strings on their old fiddle," and complained about the continued occupation of the Rhineland and the Saar. The reaction to the Young Plan of 1929, a revised schedule of reparations negotiated by Stresemann in return for the evacuation of the Rhineland in 1930, was far more strident in tone, showing the influence of Hugenburg, a conservative leader who had steered the formerly moderate right-wing parties into an ever-closer alliance with Hitler. Accusing Stresemann of burdening future generations with crushing financial obligations, a *Kladderadatsch* cartoon showed a father, son, and grandson carrying a huge slab up a hill, urged on by a fat devil with a whip. And once again, as in 1919, the cartoonist used the figure of Saint Sebastian to symbolize Germany's helpless and victimized plight, "Ten Years in Chains." Thus throughout the Weimar period *Kladderadatsch* clung to the familiar and misleading image of Germany as innocent victim. But Germany in the 1920s was in fact not helpless. Indeed, under Stresemann's leadership she made significant progress toward power, economic recovery, and international equality. By rejecting moderation and compromise, *Kladderadatsch* and other right-wing journals encouraged extreme solutions.[4]

Like its position on international affairs, the magazine's attitude toward the internal politics of Weimar showed the persistence of prewar prejudices regardless of social change. Previous chapters have shown the refusal of *Kladderadatsch* to recognize the claims of the industrial working class to political power, even when the SPD had abandoned much of its revolutionary rhetoric and adopted evolutionary and democratic policies. The same anti-socialist passion, intensified during the war years, pervaded the

contributors' reaction to the Revolution of 1918–19. From the beginning the formerly liberal journals regarded the civil rights
granted by the Republic as a facade for left-wing dictatorship.
The wave of strikes which swept over Germany in 1919 merely
reinforced the magazine's traditional tendency to blame the nation's economic woes on the Social Democratic party and the labor unions which supported it, as in this "Song of the Class-Con-
scious Worker."

> And what if the factories all close down
> And the mines into ruins fall,
> And what if commerce comes to a halt
> And there is no money at all?
> And what if we have no foreign trade?
> And we can't break through the blockade?
> And everyone starves or freezes to death.
> . . . .
> I'VE GOT TO HAVE HIGHER WAGES.

Even during the more stable years from 1924 to 1928, *Kladderadatsch* continued to portray the SPD as a revolutionary and dis-
ruptive party and to clamor for a strong authority figure to restore
patriotic enthusiasm and national unity.[5]

The longing for political authority was by no means a new theme
in a magazine which had been an eager proponent of the Bismarck cult since 1890. To the traditional veneration of past leaders, however, the *Kladderadatsch* of the 1920s added an antici-
patory longing for a future leader who would avenge Germany's
humiliation and restore her former greatness. As early as 1919,
Warncke used imagery which showed the influence of right-wing
ideologues such as Moeller van den Bruck.

> We do not know who he may be
> Or when will be his birth,
> We know that somehow, someday he
> Will walk on German earth.
>
> And he will build again
> All that our foes destroy,
> And wakened by his noble flame,
> We'll be reborn in joy.

Thus renouncing every vestige of its liberal tradition, *Kladderadatsch* joined the substantial group of neoconservative journals
which ever more openly advocated dictatorship as the solution

to Germany's problems. To be sure, Hindenburg, elected to the presidency of the German Republic in 1925, seemed (at least according to Warncke's highly idealized vision) to embody some of the traits of the longed-for leader. But week after week the cover verses expressed the monotonous yearning for the "great and powerful one" who could put an end to party strife and "bring light after the long night." In the demoralized and anxiety-ridden political atmosphere of Weimar the Bismarck-cult had given way to a dangerous fantasy which rejected flesh-and-blood politicians in favor of a messianic dream. "Where is that stronger and wiser hand," asked Warncke in an obituary on Stresemann, "which will kill the Hydra of these days!"[6]

To be sure, the long-expected messiah was not immediately identified with that vulgar little Austrian rabble-rouser, Adolf Hitler. Reactions to Hitler's abortive *Putsch* of 1923 were mixed. While warning against destructive separatism and picturing Hitler as a fanatic (one cartoon ridiculed the volatile Bavarian political atmosphere by showing Hitler and Kurt Eisner, the leader of the left-wing coup of 1918, both jumping out of beer steins), *Kladderadatsch* responded positively to Hitler's trial in 1924 by praising the patriotic spirit which had "flamed in brilliant magnificence . . . proudly over betrayal and shame." In 1930 *Kladderadatsch* paved the way for the stunning National Socialist victory by weeks of monotonous and intemperate propaganda denouncing the Social Democrats as allies of the communists in a plot to destroy Germany. At the same time the veiled antisemitic tendency of the cartoons—which, while never specifically portraying Jews, depicted all internal and foreign enemies with typically "Jewish" features—became ever more apparent. Thus *Kladderadatsch* illustrated the tentative and shame-faced acceptance of even the most vicious National Socialist ideas by supposedly "responsible" segments of the middle-class public. But while stridently exhorting voters to support "the Right," none of the verses or cartoons ever mentioned Hitler or the Nazis by name; even the verse commenting on the party's upset victory merely alluded cryptically to the rise of "new powers" from the "long night of oppression." Such conspicuous reluctance to credit Hitler with the victory was probably prompted by the belief, common in right-wing circles, that he was an ephemeral and incompetent leader whose following could be stolen away from him and used to the advantage of the more established right-wing parties.[7]

While *Kladderadatsch* joined such moderate parties as the Center and the Democrats in endorsing Hindenburg in the presidential election of 1932, a cover verse hinted that Hitler might make a good chancellor. Earlier images of a wild-eyed demagogue had finally given way to a positive portrayal of Hitler as a bluff and simple soldier resisting the wiles of crafty politicians. In December of 1932 *Kladderadatsch,* apparently still hoping that Hitler could be "tamed," rebuked him for his failure to enter a coalition with other right-wing parties. The first issue of February 1933 celebrated Hitler's appointment as chancellor by portraying Germany as Brünhilde awakened by Siegfried:

A fragrant breath of morning wind,
Blows through our German land,
From vile humiliation free,
As men at last we stand.

Thus in 1933 as in 1914 *Kladderadatsch* did not need to be forced into political conformity but made the transition voluntarily. Indeed, the *Machtergreifung* caused little change in its customary offering of strident chauvinism, obsessive anticommunism, and ever more open antisemitism. The turnover in the editorial staff after Warncke's death in 1933 had little effect on the content.[8]

The magazine concluded its ninety-six year history in 1944. From revolutionary liberalism to National Socialism in three generations—this was the story of *Kladderadatsch* and of many of the middle-class readers whose hopes, fears, and disappointments it had reflected so faithfully. The Weimar *Kladderadatsch,* a mere shadow of its former self, is significant only as the melancholy epilogue to a long history whose outcome was already determined by decisions made decades before. The themes of the Weimar magazine were those of the prewar period. The only significant difference was in the tone, now no longer detached and ironic but shrill and hysterical. By 1890 the magazine's acceptance—first grudging, then enthusiastic, finally worshipful—of its old opponent Bismarck had become the basis of a leadership cult which spurned party politics and dreamed of a conflict-free Utopia. To change the object of this cult from a past to a future leader was a natural step for a younger generation to whom the memory of Bismarck was far more remote than to the earlier editors, some of whom had known him personally. Likewise the rejection of the Republic was justified by the same anti-socialist rhetoric with which *Kladderadatsch* had attacked the workers' movement since

the 1870s. In aesthetic as in political attitudes, the staff's hostility
to innovation had led by the 1920s to an almost total lack of creativity. The stale imagery and monotonous rhythms of Warncke's
cover verses contrasted woefully with the far more inventive contributions of Löwenstein and Trojan. The magazine thus provides
an instructive example of that intellectual bankruptcy and lack
of creativity which led many moderate conservatives of the Weimar period to accept National Socialism in the deluded hope that
they could turn the movement's crude energy to the advantage
of their own failing causes. And even the middle-class respectability of which the editors had boasted since the 1870s had become an empty pretense. To mourn the murder of Rathenau while
encouraging chauvinism, to urge votes for "the right" without
mentioning Hitler, to portray all political opponents with hooked
noses without openly advocating antisemitism—all these were
the pathetic and self-deluded compromises by which the "respectable" right played into Hitler's hands.[9]

If *Kladderadatsch* represented the right-wing oppositional view
of the Weimar Republic, *Simplicissimus* expressed that of the
Vernunftrepublikaner, the loyal but unenthusiastic citizen of a
state which commanded intellectual but not emotional support.
This ambivalent view of the new regime arose in part out of the
emotional trauma of the war years.

Particularly disturbing to his admirers was the changed attitude of Ludwig Thoma, who after a brief period of service in a
medical unit had joined the Deutsche Vaterlandspartei, a right-
wing group which advocated highly annexationist war aims. The
crisis of self-doubt and reappraisal which prompted Thoma's
wartime conversion led him to repudiate much of his work for
Simplicissimus. "I don't say *pater peccavi,*" he wrote to Haussmann in 1917, "but I have no further wish to be superior and
frivolous. The way I used to shoot my mouth off during the
'Schlemihl' years now seems immature and deplorable. Belief and
criticism are incompatible." A formerly loyal *Simplicissimus*
reader, Professor Forel of Zurich, expressed his disappointment
in an open letter to Thoma, published in the *Frankfurter Zeitung.* Recalling Thoma's earlier role as "an enemy of chauvinism,
of militarism and imperialism," he concluded, "As a psychiatrist
and psychologist, I am very concerned about this kind of war
psychosis." But Thoma's conversion arose less out of "war psychosis" than out of the deep and long-standing emotional conflicts which had emerged in his and his colleagues' work

throughout the history of *Simplicissimus.* Accusations of disloyalty and subversion which could be laughed off in the relatively secure Wilhelmine society were taken far more seriously in a demoralized and defeated nation. The Thoma withdrew completely from *Simplicissimus,* contributing only nonpolitical sections from his volume of childhood reminiscences until his death in 1921. The six owners, who were also the chief cartoonists—including the four members of the original group, Schulz, Thöny, Heine, and Gulbransson, and two younger artists, Erich Schilling and Karl Arnold—strove to recover *Simplicissimus'* original personality. But they were inhibited by their deep fear of seeming radical, subversive, or unpatriotic. Far more cautious than in the past, the *Simplicissimus* group, some now in their fifties and sixties, were less open to those iconoclastic and innovative insights which produce effective humor.[10]

To the difficulties of intellectual and emotional readjustment, financial problems were added. In desperation Karl Arnold (since 1917 a part owner of the magazine) persuaded his friend Hermann Sinsheimer, a well known Munich literary critic, to assume the editorship. Forestalling a plan to sell *Simplicissimus* to the Stinnes conglomerate, Sinsheimer preserved the magazine's traditional independence and saved it from the fate of *Kladderadatsch.* But despite the new editor's efforts, *Simplicissimus* never regained its prewar circulation. Although the drastic effects of the inflation, which in January 1923 pushed the price of a single issue up to two million marks, were somewhat remedied in the more prosperous period that followed, the average circulation never rose above 30,000 (as compared to 86,000 before the war). This decline was attributable to several trends, important both in the history of popular journalism and in that of Weimar culture as a whole.[11]

The first and most obvious reason was the competition of new styles which appealed more directly to contemporary taste. *Simplicissimus,* which had overtaken *Kladderadatsch* in its appeal to the expanding mass readership of the 1890s, was now in turn displaced by the illustrated magazines which, according to Sinsheimer, "sprang up . . . in all the big cities. . . . They were inexpensive and won the favor not only of the readers but (because of their high circulation figures) of the advertisers as well." Sinsheimer claimed that the jealous opposition of the owners, who were unwilling to share profits with younger rivals, frustrated his attempts to recruit new contributors. Although such prominent artists as George Grosz and Käthe Kollwitz contributed a few drawings (those by Grosz were among his mildest and least "offensive"), many other satirical artists and writers did not appear at all. Whatever the merits of Sinsheimer's accusation, the failure to attract new talent was also due to a change in artistic sensibility which made the *Simplicissimus* style seem as obsolete in the 1920s as did the *Kladderadatsch* style in the 1890s. The cartoon figures of the Wilhelmine period—the arrogant officer, the sanctimonious clergyman, the stern father—had represented a still-confident authority structure against which the joke could level only a disguised and indirect protest. But, much to the horror of some erstwhile iconoclasts, the war and the postwar turmoil had undermined all these traditional forms of authority. The flippant young lieutenant had disappeared into the trenches, the smug bourgeoisie had been bankrupted by inflation, and the pious morality of the pastors was now openly flaunted in the transvestite nightclubs of Berlin. The city streets portrayed by George Grosz were populated not (as were the street scenes of *Simplicissimus*) by solid citizens escaping from respectable boredom, but by pimps, murderers, black marketeers, and demagogues, "all killing, drinking, lusting, fornicating in perpetual nausea." Failing to capture the mood of the postwar generation, the magazine was regarded by younger satirists such as Kurt Tucholsky as a quaint relic of the past. "That was a wonderful time, when the incomparable *Simplicissimus*—in its old format—was really 'impertinent' as people used to say. . . . Those days are gone forever."[12]

The decline of *Simplicissimus* was due also to another important development in Weimar society, the marked cultural predominance of Berlin over provincial cities such as Munich. Gone was the free and exhilarating atmosphere of prewar Schwabing; Munich was now a center of political reaction. "The transformation of Munich into an anti-Republican bastion and a headquarters for reactionary elements completely changed its character," wrote Sinsheimer. His plan to move the headquarters of the magazine to Berlin, where he was certain he could recruit exciting younger talent, was frustrated, as he later alleged, both by the owners' jealousy of younger rivals and by their unwillingness to leave their comfortable country houses outside Munich. Sinsheimer's tendency to attribute the decline of *Simplicissimus* to the owners' artistic conservatism, financial greed, and general laziness, rather than to his own financial mismanagement (which led to his forced resignation in 1929) cannot, of course, be accepted without reservation. But it is true that, like that of *Kladderadatsch,* the history of the Weimar *Simplicissimus* was marked by a cautious clinging to tradition and a failure to innovate, whether in personnel, location, or ideas. The satirists reacted to the problems of the Weimar Republic with the system of artistic, social, and political values formed at the turn of the century and now obsolete in a radically changed society.[13]

On foreign-policy issues the ambivalence of the Wilhelmine *Simplicissimus,* which had vacillated between the cosmopolitanism of Langen and the nationalism of Thoma, gave way to a far narrower and more defensive nationalism during the Weimar period. The rapprochement with France which the prewar *Simplicissimus* had advocated was shattered by the resentment of the Versailles Treaty. The French occupation of the Rhineland and later of the Ruhr in 1923 was furiously protested in images of French officers growing fat amid a starving population and of ferocious African troops whose undisciplined behavior reinforced racial prejudice. (The hostile image of these Africans may be contrasted with sympathetic prewar portrayals of oppressed, but fortunately distant, colonial peoples.) "France will negotiate with Germany only through death and hunger," read the caption of a drawing portraying the ravages of these two grim reapers.[14]

During the Stresemann years, *Simplicissimus* expressed cautious optimism. A cartoon commenting on the negotiations at the Locarno Conference showed the Angel of Peace looking over the luggage of the arriving diplomats. "All sorts of morning coats and tuxedos! Now, if they haven't forgotten their heads, I may get some rest!" But the last achievement of Stresemann's career, the Young Plan, was stridently repudiated; Heine portrayed future generations of Germans as a procession of emaciated coolies carrying huge sacks of money up a steep slope to a fat and grinning Uncle Sam. The striking similarity between this and the *Kladderadatsch* cartoon on the same subject illustrates the dismaying emotionalism and short-sightedness of both liberal and conservative opinion. Only a few radical critics, such as Ossietsky, editor of *Die Weltbühne,* hailed the Young Plan as a victory for German diplomacy and a necessary price for the evacuation of the Rhineland. The liberal *Simplicissimus* played into the hands of the extreme right wing which it criticized by encouraging the hysterical nationalism which doomed Stresemann's policies to failure.[15]

The insecurity of a society on the defensive was nowhere more apparent than in *Simplicissimus'* gingerly treatment of its most famous traditional theme, militarism. Seemingly a change in policy, the avoidance of antimilitarist satire actually reflected the same basically patriotic attitude which had encouraged criticism of the arrogant and victorious Wilhelmine military establishment but shrank from further demoralizing the defeated and humiliated army of the Weimar years. Like the vast majority of journalists (with the exception of such brash and controversial figures as left-wing journalist Kurt Tucholsky) the *Simplicissimus* group thus shied away from the still-pressing problems caused by the influence of the military in German society. Unlike the colorful and flamboyant prewar army, moreover, the Reichswehr of the 1920s was a partially underground and secret organization. To pry into its covert operations was a task better suited to the talents of investigative reporters (such as the staff of the radical periodical *Die Weltbühne*) than to those of satirists.[16]

The disappearance of its traditional antimilitarist polemic, however, could not restore the wide popularity which the prewar *Simplicissimus* had enjoyed among young officers. "Once, in its great age," explained Sinsheimer, "one could find *Simplicissimus* in every South German and especially in every Austrian casino. . . . That was not so any more." Sinsheimer's example points up the paradoxical fact that a flourishing satirical literature reflects both the weakness (without which it would have no target) and the strength (without which it could not be tolerated) of the authority structure which it challenges. A strong and confident army could endure and even enjoy criticism; a defeated and demoralized one could not. "Power tolerates satire," Sinsheimer concluded, "weakness does not!"[17]

Universal suffrage, civil liberties, representative government, liberal-socialist cooperation—all of these goals advocated by the prewar *Simplicissimus* were fulfilled by the Weimar Republic. And yet the humorists' view of the internal politics of Weimar was predominantly disappointed rather than enthusiastic. To be sure, *Simplicissimus* defended the Republic against initial threats both from the revolutionary Left and from the separatist movements which flared up in Bavaria. The Spartacist movement was personified by a half-witted and disreputable rabble-rouser sawing off the limb on which he precariously perched and declaring, "Our object is to prove that the people can do stupid things, too!" The separatists were rebuked in a cartoon entitled "North and

South get the axe" showing two figures locked in combat on a scaffold, while a French executioner smugly looks on: "Please, Messieurs, behave yourselves properly at this solemn moment!" Such appeals, however, stressed traditional values such as order and unity rather than loyalty to the republican system.[18]

Indeed, *Simplicissimus'* picture of Republican politics emphasized not innovation but continuity in this state which Golo Mann has characterized as "a crippled and weakened Empire without an Emperor." As in Wilhelmine days, the satirists unceasingly lamented the constant and unedifying squabbling of the political parties. And again, as under the kaiser, they mourned the lack of strong, inspiring leadership. An obituary verse for Friedrich Ebert in 1925 mingled grudging praise for his political integrity with implied criticism of his colorless personality:

> The dead man was of humble birth, self made,
> And Bismarck never taught him how to ride.
> He had to walk, with tip-toe, silent stride,
> To saddle restless horses was his trade.

> To ride a bare-backed horse to death—that's better?

> You solid citizens, now tell me true,
> What did the dead man mean to me, or you?
> Another Don Quixote, as you know,
> Will come to ride us soon—away we go!

The lukewarm tone of this tribute confirmed Sinsheimer's judgment that one reason for the magazine's decline was the lack of material for the type of satire at which it excelled. The kaiser and his circle, though mediocre compared to the idealized Bismarck, had at least been flamboyant, colorful, highly visible. The sober politicians of Weimar were far more difficult to caricature. "Neither the republican nor the reactionary parties," asserted Sinsheimer, "had any really popular and striking personalities, which would have been good targets for satire. The only one was Gustav Stresemann. When there are no striking profiles, the caricaturist has no material. Mediocrities and 'decent' politicians starve him." But the boredom of which Sinsheimer complained might be attributed not only to the intrinsic dullness of the Weimar leaders but also to the humorists' traditional penchant, expressed through the prewar Bismarck cult, for heroic leadership. *Simplicissimus'* lack of enthusiasm for the politicians of the Republic was shared by the left-wing press, which snobbishly mocked their plain manners and lack of intellectual sophistication. Underlying these snide aspersions was the suspicion that democratic convictions and leadership ability were incompatible.[19]

The social commentary of the Weimar *Simplicissimus* likewise adapted familiar themes to changing times. As during the Wilhelmine period, *Simplicissimus* spoofed the political immaturity of the middle-class German. In 1919 Heine published an updated version of his famous cartoon which had depicted the solid citizen as a baby in a perambulator wheeled by a policeman over a narrow and hazardous bridge. The new version showed this same figure, again clinging to beer mug and pipe, trying to find his own way across the same bridge on foot. "Now every German can express his own opinion," read the caption, "if he only had one!" A fundamental problem of the Weimar system was the failure to reform the bureaucracy, which was still dominated by the loyally monarchist officials of Wilhelmine days. Far from supporting the Republic, they openly expressed nostalgia for the glorious past. "So what if we got a lousy salary," a cartoon showed one such decrepit official remarking to another, "at least we always got a medal at New Year." Thus although *Simplicissimus* criticized the middle class for its conservative rejection of the Republic, these comments were indeed cautious compared to those of left-wing periodicals such as *Die Weltbühne,* which constantly castigated the bourgeois parties for their failure to fulfill the goals of the November Revolution. Never wholeheartedly committed to the Republic, *Simplicissimus* sent out an ambiguous message which seemed alternately to encourage and to discourage support.[20]

Although family life and related issues such as women's rights continued to be a major focus of *Simplicissimus'* satire, a style and viewpoint which had seemed radical and shocking before the war now seemed tame by contrast with the new radicalism. The old theme of female sexual sophistication was updated in pictures of the "flapper." "At sixteen," remarks one such precocious woman of the world, "you have to have your fall from virtue and your nicotine-fit behind you." The German home was still portrayed as a hotbed of Philistine complacency. Heine's unattractive sitting rooms had now been invaded by the radio, which (or so a cartoon entitled "Radio-family" implied) had replaced the rousing family fight as a center of interest. Yet the crusading fervor of the prewar *Simplicissimus,* which had proclaimed a new and enlightened standard of sexual morality, had given way to a cautious reluctance to deal with the really controversial issues of the period, such as the legalization of abortion and homosexual activity. The frivolity of the prewar feminine stereotype was once again apparent in one of the few comments on the granting of suffrage rights to women in 1919—a titillating drawing of a woman giggling in her boudoir. "All the candidates need to do is to send their photographs to me and I'll choose which one is the handsomest." As Freud has suggested, effective sexual humor must speak the unspeakable, and in a culture where homosexuality, nudism, and free love in all its forms were openly discussed, such mildly titillating challenges to traditional mores could attract little attention.[21]

The reactions of *Simplicissimus* to the rise and eventual triumph of Hitler may only be understood in the context of the general loss of originality suffered by most contributors during the Weimar period. Still clinging to ideas and attitudes formed at the turn of the century, they were ill equipped to interpret a movement which despite its manipulative appeal to tradition was a new phenomenon, unprecedented in the history of politics. Despite their faulty understanding, however, they opposed National Socialism with an energy which, for a short while, seemed to revive the aggressive antiauthoritarian spirit of the magazine's best years.[22]

Although *Simplicissimus* opposed Hitler from the beginning, the humorists, like most of their contemporaries, at first viewed him as eccentric rather than dangerous. The reaction to Hitler's Munich *Putsch* of 1923 emphasized the responsibility of Bavarian politician Kahr and General Ludendorff, portraying Hitler as a fool. "Policeman, arrest that firebrand over there," orders a sinister cartoon figure of Kahr. Other items poked fun at the volatile politics of Munich, portraying the National Socialist leader as just another demagogue on the lunatic fringe. To be sure, many contributors, especially Heine, were aware of some of the dangerous implications of Hitler's rhetoric. One cartoon of 1924 showed Hitler in the courtroom declaring, "But I don't recognize the Weimar Constitution." "Why not?" asks the judge. "Because no one ever consulted me about it." Not allowing Hitler's imprisonment to distract his attention from the party, Heine published a very grim cartoon in 1924 depicting Nazis in Wagnerian dress roasting a Jew over an open fire. But in general the evidence confirms the impression of Franz Schoenberner that "in the first years Hitler himself seemed hardly important enough for a full-page cartoon. . . . His beer-hall demagoguery could hardly be taken seriously."[23]

Why did the satirists of *Simplicissimus* tend to trivialize Hitler? For the roots of this as of other attitudes and opinions we must look to the Wilhelmine period. Despite its frequently expressed compassion for the "common" man, the prewar *Simplicissimus* had tended to view him from above, through stereotypes either weak and pitiable (the slum dweller) or comic (the Bavarian peasant). Political power on the contrary was invariably represented by grandiose and aristocratic images, repellent but also impressive. Thus the discrepancy between these two images prevented the humorists from perceiving the real political power exercised by the lower-class Hitler. So ingrained was this misperception that close observation and even (one might speculate) some personal contact did nothing to correct it. Both the *Simplicissimus* group and the Nazis frequented the same cafe, the Osteria Bavaria, where they occupied adjoining tables. Nonetheless, Schoenberner later recalled that the cartoonists found "nothing interesting" in Hitler's "wishy-washy proletarian physiognomy," the very sight of which spoiled their appetites. (But one wonders why they did not change their cafe.) The social snobbery implied in these judgments was typical of almost all members of the social elite, whether intellectuals, politicians, or businessmen. Certainly most left-wing critics were not more perceptive; *Die Weltbühne* often portrayed the Nazis as psychopaths who were incapable of gaining the confidence of the voters. And *Simplicissimus'* theatrical or circus imagery, perceptive when applied to Wilhelm, was far less appropriate to Hitler, who was often portrayed as a circus clown or as the proprietor of a sideshow. For while Wilhelm's sabre-rattling rhetoric was indeed an empty performance, Hitler's would soon be acted out in the real world.[24]

Another barrier to an accurate analysis of the Nazi movement was the highly ambivalent picture of the Jewish community which we have already observed in the Wilhelmine *Simplicissimus.* During the Weimar period the humorists gave more attention than before to antisemitism as a social problem. Racial prejudice was often perceptively exposed as a form of psychological compensation for feelings of inferiority, as in the story of little Hans, a devoted Nazi, who reacts to a poor school report by proclaiming,"It's all the fault of the damned Jews! But we'll show them!" But the picture of the Jew often greatly blunted the impact of such criticism of his persecutors. The Jew was shown as rich, powerful, and manipulative. In 1919 Schilling commented upon the prominence of Jews in the publishing industry by depicting a Jewish editor contemplating his press empire. "What a brilliant group of newspapers! Now maybe I should found an antisemitic paper as well." Even during the years from 1930 to 1933, when the virulence of Nazi antisemitism was unmistakable, many cartoons portrayed Jews conciliating, manipulating, and controlling their persecutors. A cartoon series by Gulbransson centered on a Jewish financier, who, after warding off a Nazi tough by promising to donate one million marks to the party, breaks his promise and uses the money to build a synagogue on the site of his miraculous deliverance. Another (by Schilling) portrayed Goebbels as the guest of a celebrity-hunting Jewish hostess, and a third (by the half-Jewish Heine) depicted the Jewish-dominated stock exchange making Hitler its honorary protector. On one level, of course, this was the Wilhelmine stereotype of the assimilated Jewish *Streber* carried to its absurd extreme. But such cartoons also perpetuated the common and misleading myth of Jewish control over all aspects of German life. The contrasting images of the stupid antisemite and the all-powerful Jew combined to produce a disastrously false assessment of the Nazis' antisemitic program, for the National Socialists bore only the most superficial resemblance to the antisemitic rabble-rousers of prewar days, who were generally regarded as disreputable and ineffective. And despite the prominence of individual Jews in Weimar society, the Jewish community was not powerful but helpless in the face of Hitler's persecution.[25]

Not until 1929 did *Simplicissimus* begin to criticize the Nazi movement intensively. In that year Franz Schoenberner, formerly editor of *Jugend,* took over from Sinsheimer, who had resigned because of a dispute with the owners, and proceeded to follow "the line which seemed to me the right one for a paper with a great tradition of liberal opposition." After Hitler's great victory in 1930, *Simplicissimus* was one of the few periodicals (along with *Die Weltbühne* and *Tagebuch*) which continued to attack him, for most of the major liberal newspapers now feared the economic consequences of opposing such a popular movement. A cartoon of 1932 entitled "Autumn Lament of the Newspapermen" portrayed three publishers deliberating: "The trees are smart—they're all changing their color to brown. If we only knew what color *we* should wear this fall!" But despite the financial problems caused by the withdrawal of advertising, Schoenberner and Heine continued to insist that "the Nazi danger was the most actual, most burning question and that *Simplicissimus,* true to its tradition, was under an obligation to take a courageous stand at any cost."[26]

Although *Simplicissimus* was protected from official censorship by the Weimar Constitution, its political and social views aroused the hostility of the right-wing and National Socialist press well before the *Machtergreifung* of 1933. In 1931 Schoenberner and the proprietors of *Simplicissimus* brought a libel suit against Melitta Wiedemann, an editor of a periodical founded by Goebbels, *Der Angriff.* Offended by a mock "advertisement" entitled "Sweet-Smelling Death," which had described a painless suicide apparatus for "pensioners, unemployed persons and charity-cases" victimized by the Depression, Wiedemann had condemned what she referred to as "the Galician *Simplicissimus* of the Ullstein Press." "No mockery can be more cynical," charged the editorial, "than that of the Jewish exploiters who ridicule the classes which they have ruined. But the day will come when the aroused armies of the starving will repay this insult!" Thus despite its very ambiguous picture of Jews and the presence of only one identifiable Jew among its owners, *Simplicissimus* was again, as in prewar days, identified with the supposedly subversive and cynical "Jewish" sense of humor. As Schoenberner successfully proved, Wiedemann's identification of *Simplicissimus* with the Jewish Ullstein press showed the National Socialists' typical disregard for truth. But the National Socialist sympathies of the judge himself were reflected in the low fine which he demanded of the defendant (fifty marks) and in his own disapproving comments on *Simplicissimus'* choice of material, which he claimed had provoked "widespread outrage."[27]

Even in 1932, when Hitler and his party were on the brink of success, *Simplicissimus* continued to belittle the plebeian rabble-rouser. He was caricatured as a miniature Mussolini, as "Adolf, the Frustrated Dictator" who would never put his gory fantasies into action. In the fall of 1932 the substantial loss of electoral support and the obviously shaky financial situation of the party might have seemed to justify such a prophecy. By January of 1933, *Simplicissimus,* like *Die Weltbühne* (which during that same month characterized Hitler as "a man of missed opportunities") hailed the imminent collapse of the Nazi movement. A cartoon of January 22 showed Hitler as a shabby drummer enticing naive customers into a disreputable circus. "Come in, come in, gentlemen—this time the Third Reich is really about to begin." "But if we don't do anything," whispers Goebbels from behind a curtain, "the whole audience will run away." When Hitler was appointed chancellor eight days later, *Simplicissimus* predicted his eventual replacement in a cartoon showing Hindenburg as a magician producing a whole string of chancellors from a top hat. "So long as chancellors can be produced on the assembly line," reads the caption, "we have nothing to worry about!"[28]

But as the seizure of power proceeded with unprecedented speed and ruthlessness, this initial optimism gave way to anxiety and then to panic. Although Schoenberner and Heine (the latter prevented by Jewish ancestry as well as by convictions from making peace with the new regime) continued to urge resistance, they met with more and more opposition from the rest of the staff, now thoroughly intimidated by the accounts of Nazi reprisals against other dissenting journalists. The delayed Nazi takeover of Bavaria, where Catholic, particularist, and monarchist groups seemed for a few weeks to be capable of resistance, enabled Schoenberner and Heine to continue their anti-Nazi campaign until March 12. During these final days of freedom, as Schoenberner ironically noted, the magazine was stoutly protected by its former arch-enemy, the Center party of Bavaria. The issue of February 26 contained a scathing cartoon ridiculing the Nazis' promise of an economic "four-year plan" by showing a ragged mother responding to her child's cry for food, "Can't you wait four more years, you little brat?" Heine's lampoon on the elections of March 5 aggressively protested the arrest, beating, and intimidation of voters opposing the Nazis. But the ever more open factional rift within the staff increased the risk to the dissenters, now regarded by their colleagues as a dangerous embarrassment. When, in response to the still critical and outspoken issue of March 12, Nazi stormtroopers raided the editorial office, the owners of *Simplicissimus* held an emergency meeting at which the majority voted to dismiss Schoenberner. Schoenberner later alleged that the owners had also decided to oust Heine, who had either cast a negative vote or abstained from voting on the editor's removal. The issue of March 19, a belated response to the Reichstag fire, featured a cryptic cartoon showing a burning Reichstag building. "Will a phoenix arise from these flames?" asks the caption rhetorically. "And bring liberation from the world conflagration of Bolshevism?"[29]

Schoenberner had finally resolved to emigrate to Switzerland. Among all his erstwhile colleagues, he told only Heine of his plans for departure. "In vain I tried to convince him that he, like myself, should leave Germany, at least for a while," recollected

Schoenberner. "But he could not make up his mind to see the danger of his position. His contempt for the stupidity of the whole Nazi business was so complete that he refused to consider it anything but a silly farce. . . . With smiling confidence he assured me that the whole thing was not serious; in a few days normal conditions would be restored and he would go on publishing *Simplicissimus* as before." But as every vestige of Bavarian resistance was crushed, Nazi cultural policies, including the persecution of Jewish artists, were rigorously enforced. The next editorial meeting was invaded by three S.A. men, who ordered Heine to desist from all further artistic activity. Only then did he decide to flee, first to Prague, then to Oslo, and finally to Stockholm. Old age, persecution, and exile could not destroy his cynical, ironic, and stoically detached world view. When the Gestapo summoned him after the German invasion of Norway, they were apparently so impressed with the old man's nerve that they dismissed him with a handshake and a warning. "You just had to know how to handle them without showing any fear," he reminisced after the war. "The interrogation was pure comedy and I made fools of them . . . much to the amusement of my fellow prisoners, many of whom doubtless ended up in concentration camps."[30]

But the rest of the staff chose voluntarily to conform to the National Socialist line. Like many other policy decisions, this one was justified by a Wilhelmine precedent, the transformation of 1914. A statement published on April 16, 1933, showed how fully they had accepted Hitler's own comparison of the political crisis to a military emergency. "Once, at the beginning of and during the course of the World War, *Simplicissimus,* which was founded as an oppositional publication, proved that it could turn from negative criticism to positive support when Germany's future was at stake. The fate of Germany is again at stake—but this time not the old Germany, struggling against the entire world, but the new Germany, awakened after long years of turmoil and sorrow. To serve the new Germany will be the goal of *Simplicissimus,* which has just completely reorganized its editorial staff." The exiled Heine bitterly remarked, "All my colleagues enthusiastically shouted, 'Heil Hitler!' "[31]

The histories of *Kladderadatsch* and *Simplicissimus* during the Weimar years thus suggest both the variation and the underlying agreement among left- and right-wing segments of middle-class opinion. To be sure, *Simplicissimus'* opposition to Hitler contrasts strikingly with the half-hearted and self-deluded support accorded him by *Kladderadatsch*. However faulty, the liberal journalists' understanding of the National Socialist movement somewhat surpassed that of their younger and more innovative left-wing colleagues, who were inclined to trivialize Hitler either as a raving maniac or as the unwitting tool of capitalist interests. More effective than an eleventh-hour campaign against a movement approaching the height of its power, however, would have been a consistent policy of support for the Republic, for democratic institutions, and for a sane and constructive foreign policy. Not only the reactionary opposition of right-wing organs such as *Kladderadatsch* but also the lukewarm and condescending support of liberal journals such as *Simplicissimus* had undermined Germany's democratic experiment. Moreover the *Gleichschaltung* of the journals, both of which survived in Nazified form, illustrated the ease and rapidity (surprising even to Hitler himself) with which the National Socialist party consolidated its dictatorial power. Not only the conservative *Kladderadatsch* staff but the traditionally liberal owners of *Simplicissimus* finally yielded, cooperating with the new masters in the purge of undesirable or Jewish colleagues. As in 1914, one senses a tangle of motives— fear for physical safety and livelihood, patriotic enthusiasm, and positive relief at this opportunity to slough off the uncomfortable role of social critic.

The story of both journals during the Weimar period was marked by decreasing circulation and influence. This failure may best be explained with reference to the Freudian and Koestlerian functions of humor as protest and as creative impulse. Though rabid in their protest against foreign powers, both journals were cautious and inhibited in their criticism of domestic politics and society. Though hostile to Republican politicians, *Kladderadatsch* left truly powerful groups such as business, the army, and the aristocracy virtually unscathed. *Simplicissimus'* tentative support of the Republic forced it (in the words of Sinsheimer) "to aim both to right and to left, at both rightist and leftist extremism, and thus to occupy the political center—for a *Witzblatt* the only impossible position." Both journals had largely lost their innovative energy and clung to the political ideas and artistic styles of a bygone age. It is this atrophy of the creative impulse which in large measure explains their failure to understand the politics of the Weimar era, especially the rise of National Socialism. And yet a survey of the contemporary press produces few examples of more perceptive, constructive, or courageous journalism. Certainly the left-wing publications such as *Die Weltbühne,* though far more innovative in style, must also bear their share of blame for the destruction of the Republic, which they too often regarded with contempt. Thus the decline of the two famous *Witzblätter* may be seen as one sign of a more widespread malaise—a failure of courage and of creative energy—which afflicted the Weimar press.[32]

Protest and Innovation: Satire and Social Change

8

I N all Germany," wrote historian Friedrich Meinecke, "one can detect something new around 1890, not only politically, but also spiritually and intellectually." Meinecke's intuitive sense of cultural transition has been borne out by most historians of the period. "It was as if the world were teetering on the brink," states one recent work, "uncertain whether it ought to climb higher still or descend, an epoch in the true sense of the word. *Fin de siècle*: the great turning point." Most analyses of this cultural and intellectual "revolution" have focused either upon the high culture produced by the intellectual elite—a "vocal if not necessarily representative segment" of the population, in the words of one historian—or upon specific groups such as middle-class young people or women. Its more general impact upon the climate of opinion, as reflected by the popular culture of the period, has been far less thoroughly examined. Many accounts, indeed, tend to stress the alienation of the questioning intellectual from the allegedly complacent and self-satisfied majority culture.[1]

The two *Witzblätter, Kladderadatsch* and *Simplicissimus,* provide an instructive case-study in changing popular taste during this period of cultural transition. We have seen that these periodicals, though produced predominantly by members of an artistic or literary elite, were at the same time genuinely popular, appealing to a diverse readership. Though lower than those of the illustrated weeklies, the circulation figures of both *Kladderadatsch* and *Simplicissimus,* which were far higher than those of more intellectual periodicals of specifically political content, suggest the important role of the satirical press in shaping the political awareness of a wide segment of the public. Thus the decline of *Kladderadatsch* and the success of its competitor *Simplicissimus* reflect a significant change in both political attitudes and aesthetic taste among the consumers of political satire. But the continued existence of *Kladderadatsch* suggests that the change was neither universal nor precipitate.

Having examined both the contrasting styles and the impact upon contemporary readers of *Kladderadatsch* and *Simplicissimus*, we are now in a position to return to the question raised in the introductory chapter. To what extent did these satirical periodicals reflect public opinion, and to what extent did they form or change it? The admittedly speculative answer to this question will shed light on the more general function of humor in society.

Both sides of the question, of course, were vehemently argued by contemporary readers. Especially when protesting their "innocence" in court, both the satirists themselves and their supporters characterized satire as a mere outlet or lightning rod for already formed public opinion. Indeed, its beneficial, even tranquillizing, effects were often stressed. "A sharply worded editorial provokes anger," testified Munich publisher Georg Hirth at the trial of Heine and Linnekogel in 1904, "and forces the reader to commit himself. By contrast a satirical magazine contains so much humor that it leaves the reader in a good mood. Thus I view satirical illustrations as much less harmful than serious articles." Opponents of the *Witzblätter*, however, tended to burden them with major responsibility for the declining respect for traditional authority figures and values. By his challenge to *Kladderadatsch* editor Polstorff, Kiderlen-Wächter indicated just how seriously he regarded the magazine's attack on his reputation. War Minister von Heeringen alluded to *Simplicissimus* as "the bacillus which kills all our ideals." "In every number of *Simplicissimus* authority is undermined in a most dangerous way—the monarchy, the ministers, the government—all are degraded!" stormed a clerical delegate to the Bavarian Landtag. The large number of lawsuits brought against *Simplicissimus* by governments, interest groups, and private citizens suggested that at least some segments of the population regarded satire as an effective, even dangerous force for social change.[2]

The Freudian view of humor as a release for already existing tension certainly described the major and central function of the

Witzblätter. As an expression of frustration, satire was very important in a system which despite its democratic and parliamentary appearance allowed citizens very little direct control over the actions of an authority structure effectively insulated from public opinion. The confrontation between this political establishment, an inflexible bulwark of the status quo, and the large and vocal segment of the public which demanded democratization became the central political issue of the Wilhelmine period. Both *Witzblätter* joined in protesting arbitrary and anachronistic authority, *Kladderadatsch* in the 1890s through its attacks on irresponsible court cliques, and *Simplicissimus* in the early twentieth century through its ever more wide-ranging advocacy of political and social reform.[3]

Even more important was the broadening of the scope of dissent reflected in the transition from the traditional style of *Kladderadatsch* to the avant-garde style of *Simplicissimus*. Many historians have identified a newly skeptical and analytical view of society, as expressed through achievements in the social sciences, as a major aspect of the "intellectual revolution." The same awakened critical sense pervaded *Simplicissimus'* social and cultural commentary, which transgressed the limits set by the respectable *Kladderadatsch* (and by other traditional humor magazines such as the *Fliegende Blätter* and the British *Punch*), to ridicule not only public but private institutions such as the family. Although by no means a new phenomenon—for the dissection of bourgeois private life had been a literary theme throughout the nineteenth century—such frank and open criticism gained increased acceptance, even respectability at the turn of the century. *Simplicissimus* was often openly displayed on drawing-room tables. The success of such humor in the prewar years was one sign of the decay of long-standing systems of political, social, and religious authority which was accelerated, but not caused, by the war. The contrast between *Kladderadatsch* and *Simplicissimus* was alluded to by many contemporary readers as a sign of increasing disrespect for authority. "Hitherto we've enjoyed the innocent, delightful jokes of the *Fliegende Blätter* and the ruthless but witty mockery of *Kladderadatsch,*" stated an editorial in the *Hamburger Nachrichten*. "But now *Simplicissimus,* which from year to year becomes more conspicuous, more biting, and more obscene, has gained such an unhealthy popularity, and is so widely praised, that it is necessary to publicize the opinions of those who speak out against this harmful and immoral publication."[4]

The supporters of *Simplicissimus* tended to identify it as the symptom rather than the cause of this increasing public disenchantment. "Who would deny that the Munich *Witzblatt* has published jokes which are more effective then one hundred editorials?" asked Conrad Haussmann. "And who does not understand that the magazine has become a great power only because the *Simplicissimus-Stimmung* is already present in Germany like latent electricity which is discharged through these artistic, sometimes very artistic caricatures?"[5]

But conservatives' view of satire not simply as a discharge for antiauthoritarian protest but as an active force promoting and encouraging such protest was not a mere paranoid delusion. The active or formative role of such publications as *Kladderadatsch* and *Simplicissimus* may be understood both through Koestler's theory of creative incongruity and through Clifford Geertz's general observations on ideology as a form of symbolic discourse. Interpreting political ideologies not primarily as literal statements but as sets of images or symbols enabling the individual to understand the new and bewildering conditions produced by social change, Geertz went on to emphasize the importance to ideology of the devices used by humor. "The head-on clash of literal meanings, the irony, the hyperbole, the overdrawn antithesis," he asserted, provide "novel symbolic frames against which to match the myriad 'unfamiliar somethings' that, like a journey to a strange country, are produced by a transformation in political life." As the most widely popular political journals appealing to the middle class, both *Kladderadatsch* and *Simplicissimus* created and popularized the symbolic images which shaped the political consciousness of their readers.[6]

The striking contrast between the imagery of *Kladderadatsch* and that of *Simplicissimus* reflected the development of a new symbolic "blueprint" for the understanding of a new era. The imagery of *Kladderadatsch*, based on the classics, student songs, opera, literature, and mythology, drew on the heritage of nineteenth-century culture. *Simplicissimus* itself was not wholly without such traditionalism, as its acceptance of the popular Bismarck cult indicated. But much of its imagery—risqué, violent, grotesque, even apocalyptic—emphasized the obsolescence of nineteenth-century cultural symbols and jolted, titillated, charmed, or frightened the reader into a confrontation with new realities. The newer journal's images of the lieutenant as an idol or a bayonet-quilled porcupine, of the modern woman as a vampire, of the kaiser as a peacock, a Crusader, or a sea monster, of the Junker as a pig, all revealed familiar social types in an unfamiliar light. All of these examples show the use of metaphor, hyperbole, or caricature to short-circuit (to use the Freudian term) the inhibitions imposed by the rational mind and to give concrete form to an uncomfortable, subversive, or liberating insight.

Though not, of course, the originators of new cultural or political insights, the satirists thus played an influential role in their dissemination by translating them into appealing and widely recognized symbols. Many contemporary observers noted, with approval or with anger, that *Simplicissimus* provided a vocabulary of protest for the previously passive and inarticulate. "A phenomenon such as *Simplicissimus*," stated one editorial, "which is an exceptionally clear sign of the times, must be taken seriously. The German reader, more than most, is always ready to let 'his' opinions about art and politics be suggested to him by professional journalists." The average reader, continued this writer, finally comes "so much under the influence of 'his' paper that— unconsciously—he forms all his opinions from it." "For some years," complained another critic, "the average German has had a cheap source of complaints . . . a kind of discount shop selling all kinds of impertinent remarks against authority, God, and the world. He knows that every Monday he can buy such biting jokes for twenty *Pfennig.* He no longer has to make them up himself— they are made up for him and delivered to his table." The most familiar symbol of all was *Simplicissimus* itself, whose journalistic personality was sometimes said to provide a role-model for would-be dissenters. "The *Simplicissimus* German has become a type, as has the morally loose *Jugend* type," insisted the Catholic *Augsburger Post,* "and both these types are represented in thousands among the so-called educated elite of the Empire." The conservative *Kreuzzeitung* accused *Simplicissimus* of imposing its distorted vision upon the entire culture. "Is there nothing more that can inspire enthusiasm?" lamented an editorial. "Or has *Simplicissimus* infected all of us so that we see everything in the distorted mirror of satire?"[7]

Without giving unqualified credence to these exaggerated visions of the *Simplicissimus-Stimmung* as a universal blight upon bourgeois culture, we may speculate that these right-wing critics correctly perceived the magazine as a stimulus to a new sense of political identity among its readers. Many contemporary readers noted the appeal of *Simplicissimus* to the most respectable, indeed prominent people. The conservative periodical *Die Garten-laube* observed that "the poisonous malice of *Simplicissimus* against Throne and Altar provokes laughter even in high society. But in public those same people will express the conventional patriotic sentiments." Thus the existence of a shared and recognizable body of humorous symbolism provided even cautious people with a vocabulary for expressing dissenting opinion within a private social circle. Such private jesting can be more than a simple Freudian release of tension. Psychologist Edmund O. Wilson speculated that the joke also provides a safe means for testing out the feelings of an audience. "The ambiguity of the joke," explained Wilson, "in being both serious and trivial, allows the joker to test for fellow feelings of rebelliousness. If others signal their approval, in smiling or laughter, the joker can reassure himself that he is amongst like-minded people, and he and the group may graduate to the more satisfying expression of direct disparagement."[8]

Contemporary perceptions of the *Simplicissimus-Stimmung* as an undercurrent of dissatisfaction and restlessness beneath the respectable surface of Wilhelmine bourgeois culture attest to the crucial role of the new sense of humor in shaping the "pre-political" shifts in attitudes and awareness which precede political reorientation. The popularity of *Simplicissimus* indicated not only the disenchantment of a considerable segment of the middle-class public with a ruling elite whose prestige had been seriously eroded, but their tentative search for a new political ideology. *Simplicissimus* became the organ *par excellence* of that "renewal on the left" which (in the words of Hans-Günther Zmarzlik) "by means of a thousand and one groups (such as free-thinkers, women's organizations, the peace movement, workers' sport clubs, etc.) structured the pre-political realm of society." The transition from the traditionalism of *Kladderadatsch* to the modernism of *Simplicissimus,* moreover, suggests movement toward the liberal-socialist alliance upon which the Weimar political system was later based. By its almost equally hostile images of both upper and lower classes, *Kladderadatsch* had maintained the political isolation which condemned the progressive elements of the middle class to impotence, while *Simplicissimus,* through its increasingly positive (though still patronizing) picture of the moderate socialist and labor movements, attempted to overcome that isolation through an opening to the left. Including trade-union members as well as artists, intellectuals, politicians, liberal elements within the civil service and the professions, and young people generally, the readership of *Simplicissimus* represented a cross-section of progressive opinion in Wilhelmine Germany. The widespread attention attracted by the editors' court appearances reflected the magazine's increasing status as a symbol of dissent.[9]

Not only in Germany but in other nations as well, *Simplicissimus* served as a symbol of daring modernity. In France, Russia, and the United States, socially committed artists imitated the *Simplicissimus* style. The French periodical *L'Assiette au Beurre* combined antiestablishment satire with social protest. Like its German counterpart and model, *L'Assiette* also specialized in striking and colorful cartoons. Pictures, remarked its editor, "constitute the best weapon. They have the advantage of not tiring a mind occupied by everyday worries and of offering relaxation, while at the same time reaching out to more people than do the best newspaper articles, which often leave the most serious reader indifferent." A group of young contributors to the American radical sheet *The Liberator* pioneered a style of "sharp linear caricature," distinguished by its "thin, tight nervous outline" and its "microscopic attention to detail" which was directly influenced by *Simplicissimus.* And the short-lived Russian *Zhupel,* founded during the 1905 Revolution, was produced almost entirely by artists who had studied in Munich and who stayed in contact with their German colleagues. Thus, as Sinsheimer noted, *Simplicissimus* voiced not just a Bavarian or German but "a European rejection of bureaucracy and class oppression, of snobbery and orthodoxy, religious and otherwise. . . . Many of its contributors, especially the cartoonists, became figures of European stature."[10]

Whether cause or symptom of cultural change, the satire of the Wilhelmine period was indeed a sign of the times. The French philosopher Henri Bergson defined the laugh as the response to any behavior—whether an accidental slip on a banana peel, an obsessive ritual, or a meaningless but still widely observed social custom—which appeared puppetlike, rigid, or mechanistic. "There remains," Bergson concluded, "a certain rigidity of the body, of the mind, or of the character which society still aims to eliminate in order to obtain the greatest possible elasticity and the most highly developed sociability. . . . Rigidity is thus funny, and laughter is its punishment." *Simplicissimus'* pervasive images of political and social life as theatrical spectacle, complete with costumes, mock-heroic poses, bombastic speeches, and the tawdry trappings of a bygone age, expressed just such a Bergsonian perception of puppetlike rigidity inhibiting healthy progress. *Simplicissimus,* observed an editorial in the Berlin newspaper *Der Tag,* was "a joker who only aims to find the moth-holes in old costumes; whether by 'costume' we mean the arrogance of a certain caste, or the fat bourgeois respectability which covers inner callousness. . . . When the mature adults of today are called upon to respect the faded glory of yesterday, they are moved to ridicule." Thus the sense of humor acted as a creative force, breaking down rigid ideologies, traditions, and mores, affirming the freedom of individuals and cultures to grow, change, and develop.[11]

The decline of both magazines—*Kladderadatsch* during the Wilhelmine period, *Simplicissimus* during the Weimar period—was due to the atrophy of their editors' creative energies. In postwar Germany, moreover, the humorists' optimistic faith in the "assault of laughter" as a force for social change was finally destroyed, for one significant symptom of the generally demoralized and despairing atmosphere of Weimar society was the decline of the sense of humor. "Whenever someone makes a good political joke, half of all Germany sits on the sofa and complains of a belly ache," wrote Kurt Tucholsky. "The satire of a courageous artist . . . does not deserve the puritanical contempt and outraged condemnation which it receives in this country." "If ridicule kills," reflected the rueful Schoenberner, "then the whole attitude of the Nazis was simply suicidal. We should have known that this, like almost any proverb, was wrong, at least for Germany." During their best days both *Kladderadatsch* and *Simplicissimus* had exuded the confidence of the liberal that age-old prejudice could be destroyed by the power of reasoned argument. "Satirists are characterized by their naively fundamentalist faith in reason as a sort of moral principle," wrote Schoenberner. "Laughing St. Georges, armed only with a pointed pen, they bravely and constantly slay the monstrous dragon of absurdity, which unfortunately refuses to know it is slain. . . . Their noble misconception of incommensurable forces is the secret of their courage." Just how baseless this confidence was, the Weimar years showed.[12]

Notes

Abbreviations used in the notes:

K   *Kladderadatsch*
S   *Simplicissimus*
BHStA   Bayerische Hauptstaatsarchiv
MJu   Justizministerium

In the early years of both *Simplicissimus* and *Kladderadatsch*, no dates appeared on individual issues. Early volumes of both also lack continuous pagination. I therefore decided on a uniform system of citation: volume number, year, issue number, and page (where page numbers are given).

1 A Playful Judgment

1 Kuno Fischer, *Über den Witz*, quoted in Sigmund Freud, *Wit and Its Relation to the Unconscious*, in *Basic Writings of Sigmund Freud*, trans. and ed. A.A. Brill (New York, 1938), 634. Leszek Kolakowski is quoted from Barbara Fultz, *The Naked Emperor: An Anthology of International Political Satire*, by Victor S. Navasky (New York, 1970), xvi. Malcolm Muggeridge is quoted in Arthur P. Dudden, ed., *The Assault of Laughter: A Treasury of American Political Humor* (New York, 1962), 21.
2 Several dissertations have been written on the history of the German *Witzblatt*: Christian Gehring, *Die Entwicklung des politischen Witzblattes in Deutschland* (Leipzig, 1927), and Gustav Bald, "Die politisch-satirische Lyrik: Ein publizistisches Kampfmittel" (Ph.D. diss., Univ. of Erlangen, 1936), are two early treatments of the subject. More recent works include Hasso Zimdars, "Die Zeitschrift *Simplicissimus:* Ihre Karikaturen" (Ph.D. diss., Univ. of Bonn, 1972); Klaus Schulz, *Kladderadatsch: Ein bürgerliches Witzblatt von der Märzrevolution bis zum Nationalsozialismus, 1848–1944* (Bochum, 1975); Ruprecht Konrad, "Nationale und internationale Tendenzen im *Simplicissimus*, 1896–1933" (Ph.D. diss., Univ. of Munich, 1975); and my own dis-

sertation, Ann Allen Jobling, " 'A Playful Judgment:' Satire and Society in Wilhelmine Germany" (Ph.D. diss., Columbia Univ., 1974).

3 The history of the German press and its relation to society has been perceptively explored in many works, most notably Kurt Koszyk, *Geschichte der deutschen Presse*, 2 vols. (Berlin, 1966); and Rolf Engelsing, *Massenpublikum und Journalistentum im 19 Jahrhundert in Nordwestdeutschland* (Berlin, 1966); and Engelsing's article "Die Zeitschrift in Nordwestdeutschland," in *Archiv für die Geschichte des Buchwesens* 4 (1964): 937–1036.

4 Engelsing, *Massenpublikum*, 26. For statistics on founding of new periodicals see Engelsing, "Zeitschrift," 1021.

5 For a discussion of circulation figures for *Kladderadatsch*, see Schulz, *Kladderadatsch*, 169; for the *Münchener Fliegende Blätter* see Joachim Kirchner, *Das Deutsche Zeitschriftenwesen: Seine Geschichte und seine Probleme*, 2 vols. (Wiesbaden, 1962), 2: 348–49; for *Jugend* see Engelsing, "Zeitschrift," 938; for *Der Wahre Jakob* see Koszyk, *Geschichte der Presse*, 209.

6 William Cohn, "Popular Culture and Social History," *Journal of Popular Culture* 11 (Summer 1977): 30–41 (quotation is from p. 30). For some remarks on the social function of the periodical, see Engelsing, "Zeitschrift," 938. For suggestions for interpretation of popular materials see Gregory H. Singleton, "Popular Culture or the Culture of the Populace," *Journal of Popular Culture* 11 (Summer 1977): 117–28; and Cohn's article.

7 Engelsing, "Zeitschrift," 938; Mark Twain quoted from Dudden, *Assault of Laughter*, 523.

8 Robert C. Elliot, *The Power of Satire: Magic, Ritual, Art* (Princeton, 1960). Nicholas Boileau-Despreaux, *Satires*, 8, 252; Juvenal, Saturae 1, 79.

9 Jeffrey H. Goldstein and Paul E. McGhee, eds., *The Psychology of Humor: Theoretical Perspectives and Empirical Issues* (New York, 1972), xiii.

10 For a general account of early theories of humor, including those of Hobbes and Plato, see Patricia Keith-Spiegel, "Early Conceptions of Humor: Varieties and Issues," in Goldstein and McGhee, *Psychology of Humor*, 5–7.

11 Freud, *Wit*, 697.

12 Henri Bergson, *Le Rire: Essai sur la Signification du Comique* (Paris, 1900; rpt., 1967), 15; Christopher P. Wilson, *Jokes: Form, Content, Use and Function* (London and New York, 1979), 226; Antonin Obrdlík, "Gallows Humor: A Sociological Phenomenon," *American Journal of Sociology* 47 (1942): 712.

13 Arthur Koestler, *The Act of Creation* (New York, 1964), 27–100. See also Edward L. Galligan, "The Usefulness of Arthur Koestler's Theory of Jokes," *South Atlantic Quarterly* 75 (Spring 1976): 145–59.

14 Herbert Block, *The Herblock Book* (Boston, 1952), 25, quoted from Carroll Emerson Word, "Freudian Theories of Wit and Humor as Applied to Certain Theories of Social Conflict" (Ph.D. diss., Boston Univ., 1960), 275; Clifford Geertz, "Ideology as a Cultural System," in his *The Interpretation of Cultures: Selected Essays* (New York, 1973), 218–19. For some other interpretations of the history and social significance of caricature see Lawrence H. Streicher, "On a Theory of Political Caricature," *Comparative Studies in Society and History* 9 (1966–67): 428–45; idem, "David Low and the Sociology of Caricature," ibid., 8 (1965–66): 1–23; and W.A. Coupe, "Observations on a Theory of Political Caricature," ibid., 11 (1969): 79–95.

15 Barrington Moore, *Social Origins of Dictatorship and Democracy: Lord and Peasant in the Making of the Modern World* (Boston, 1966), 438.

232 / Notes to pages 10–15

16 Kaiser Wilhelm is quoted in Koszyk, *Geschichte der deutschen Presse*, 2: 258; on censorship policies during this period see R.J.V. Lenman, "Art, Society and Law in Wilhelmine Germany: The *Lex Heinze*," *Oxford Studies Review* 8 (1973): 86–113; idem, "Politics and Culture: The State and the Avant-Garde in Munich, 1886–1914," in Richard J. Evans, ed., *Society and Politics in Wilhelmine Germany* (London, 1978), 90–111; and Gary D. Stark, "Pornography, Society and the Law in Imperial Germany," *Central European History* 14 (Sept. 1981): 200–229.

17 For a fuller discussion of the careers of Thoma and Quidde, see pp. 37–38.

18 Circulation figures of *Simplicissimus* and *Kladderadatsch* are in Engelsing, "Zeitschrift," 938; and Schulz, *Kladderadatsch*, 169. For other figures see Kirchner, *Deutsche Zeitschriftenwesen*, 2: 348–49.

19 *Zwanzig Jahre S.M.: Heitere Bilder zu ernsten Ereignissen*, ed. Harold Morré, preface by Maximilian Harden (Berlin, 1909), 5.

20 Hans-Ulrich Wehler, *Das deutsche Kaiserreich, 1871–1918* (Göttingen, 1973), 134. For opposing views of Wilhelmine culture see Hans-Günter Zmarzlik, "Das Kaiserreich in neuer Sicht?" *Historische Zeitschrift* 222 (1976): 105–26; Thomas Nipperdey, "Wehlers 'Kaiserreich': Eine kritische Auseinandersetzung," *Geschichte und Gesellschaft* 1 (1975): 539–60; and Richard J. Evans, "Introduction: Wilhelm II's Germany and the Historians," in Evans, ed., *Society and Politics in Wilhelmine Germany* (London, 1978), 11–39.

21 For an account of the arts as an oppositional force in Wilhelmine Germany, see Ludwig Leiss, *Kunst im Konflikt: Kunst und Künstler im Widerstreit mit der Obrigkeit* (Berlin, 1971). A discussion of the Social Democratic victory of 1912 is contained in Carl E. Schorske, *German Social Democracy, 1905–1917: The Development of the Great Schism* (Cambridge, Mass., 1955). An informative bibliographical essay on the development of a middle bourgeois opposition is James C. Hunt, "The Bourgeois Middle in German Politics," *Central European History* 11 (Mar. 1978): 83–106. *Der Untertan* appears in *S* 16 (1911–12), no. 35: 600–607; and *S* 17 (1912–13), no. 14: 216–17.

2 *Kladderadatsch, Simplicissimus,* and German History

1 Albert Hofmann, ed., *Der Kladderadatsch und seine Leute* (Berlin, 1898), 104–8; *K* 1 (1848), no. 1: cover.

2 *K* 2 (1848), no. 3: 10. For the best general history of *Kladderadatsch*, see Schulz, *Kladderadatsch*. Also very useful is Liesel Hartelstein, ed., *Facsimile Querschnitt durch den Kladderadatsch*, intro. by Hans Rothfels (Munich, 1965)(hereafter cited as *Facsimile-Kladderadatsch*). For a discussion of the significance of the year 1848 in the history of periodical literature see Rolf Engelsing, "Die Perioden der Lesergeschichte in der Neuzeit," in *Zur Sozialgeschichte deutscher Mittel- und Unterschichten* (Göttingen, 1973), 168.

3 Hofmann, *Kladderadatsch und seine Leute*, 118. For names of periodicals and circulation see Kirchner, *Deutsche Zeitschriftenwesen*, 2: 113. The role of humor in the 1848 revolution is discussed in Eugen Kalkschmidt, *Deutsche Freiheit und deutscher Witz: Ein Kapitel Revolutions-Satire aus der Zeit von 1830–1850* (Berlin, 1928); and in W.A. Coupe, "The German Cartoon and the Revolution of 1848," *Comparative Studies in Society and History* 9 (1966–67): 138–67.

4 For a general discussion of the staff, see Hofmann, *Kladderadatsch und seine Leute*, 8–9. See also Max Ring, *David Kalisch, der Vater des Kladderadatsch* (Berlin, 1873). For biographical information on Löwenstein, see his autobiographical statement, published in Karl Lembach, ed., *Die deutschen Dichter der Neuzeit und Gegenwart*, 5 vols. (Leipzig, 1893), 5: 447–50; and Kurt Stephenson, "Redakteure des *Kladderadatsch:* Ihr Echo im Studentenlied," in *Darstellungen und Quellen zur Geschichte der deutschen Einheitsbewegung im neunzehnten und zwanzigsten Jahrhundert* (Heidelberg, 1967), 7: 9–48.

5 For a discussion of the Berlin style in humor see Gerhard Masur, *Imperial Berlin* (New York, 1970), 148. For comments on the social status of Jewish journalists see Engelsing, *Masssenpublikum*, 48.

6 *K* 1 (1848), no. 10: cover. For a general account of the style and political message of *Kladderadatsch* in 1848 see Kalkschmidt, *Deutsche Freiheit;* and *Facsimile-Kladderadatsch*, 36.

7 *K* 1 (1848), no. 15: 60; *K* 2 (1849), no. 2: cover. All translations from *Kladderadatsch* and *Simplicissimus* are my own.

8 *K* 1 (1848), no. 30: 119; *K* 2 (1849), no. 4: 14; *K* 3 (1850), no. 3: cover. For a history of the magazine during this period see *Facsimile-Kladderadatsch*, 37.

9 *K* 2 (1849), no. 1: cover. For a general account of German liberalism during the 1850s see Theodore S. Hamerow, *The Social Foundations of German Unification: Ideas and Institutions* (Princeton, 1969), 135–80.

10 *K* 14 (1862), no. 6: 24. For general information on German liberalism during the constitutional crisis see Otto Pflanze, *Bismarck and the Development of Germany* (Princeton, 1963), 151; and Leonard Krieger, *The German Idea of Freedom* (Boston, 1957), 413.

11 *K* 15 (1862), no. 18: 70; *K* 18 (1865), no. 22: 86; no. 41: 162.

12 "Chassepot-Lied" in *K* 23 (1870), no. 34: cover. The Müller-Schulze dialogue is from *K* 23 (1871), no. 59–60 (double issue): 239.

13 *K* 25 (1873), no. 30: 120. For an account of the official reaction to the *Kladderadatsch* campaign see *Facsimile-Kladderadatsch*, 13.

14 The magazine's changing response to Bismarck is graphically illustrated in *Bismarck-Album des Kladderadatsch* (Berlin, 1890), a collection of verses and Scholz cartoons from three decades. Because the *Album* was published in honor of the retired chancellor it left out some of the more hostile reactions and thus creates a somewhat misleading impression.

15 *K* 22 (1869), no. 49: 196; *K* 31 (1878), no 56, 222; *K* 37 (1884), no. 24, 96. For a discussion of the humorists' attitude toward the social question see Stephenson, "Redakteure," 64; *Facsimile-Kladderadatsch*, 13.

16 Löwenstein quoted from Lembach, *Deutschen Dichter der Neuzeit*, 5: 450. For another discussion of the magazine's change in policy, see *Facsimile-Kladderadatsch*, 14.

17 See Trojan, *Erinnerungen* (Berlin, 1912), *passim*. See also "Johannes Trojan" in Stephenson, "Redakteure," 49–93.

18 Julius Stinde, "Der Dichter des Fröhlichen Gemüts," *Schorers Familienblatt* 13 (1892): 427–29.

19 For biographical information on the *Kladderadatsch* staff in the 1890s see Hofmann, *Kladderadatsch und seine Leute*, 268–70. See also Schulz, *Kladderadatsch*, 183–92.

20 Trojan, *Erinnerungen*, 130–35.

21 For the history of *Punch,* see R.C.G. Price, *A History of Punch* (London, 1957). The cartoon is reprinted in R.E. Williams; ed., *A Century of Punch* (London, 1956), 8.

22 Price, *Punch,* 47, 48.

23 For circulation figures see Gerhard Muser, *Statistische Untersuchungen über die Zeitungen Deutschlands, 1885–1914* (Leipzig, 1914), 59–61; and Schulz, *Kladderadatsch,* 170. Hamerow comments on the magazine's wide circulation in *Social Foundations,* 284–86. Further comments on readership may be found in Harry Barthel, "Der *Kladderadatsch* im Kampf um die Sozial- und Wirtschaftsordnung des Bismarckschen Reiches" (Ph.D. diss., Univ. of Munich, 1954), 67.

24 Barthel ("*Kladderadatsch,*" 62–67) agrees that the magazine's style appealed to educated people. For a general discussion of journalistic style at mid-century, see Engelsing, *Massenpublikum,* 117–18.

25 For a discussion of the diverse liberal constituency see James J. Sheehan, "Liberalism and Society in Germany, 1815–1848," *Journal of Modern History* 45 (Dec. 1973): 583–604.

26 For advertisements see the *Beiblätter* of issues from 1866 to 1914.

27 Price, *Punch,* 30. Hofmann, *Kladderadatsch und seine Leute,* 230.

28 On the image of Bismarck, see *Facsimile-Kladderadatsch,* 5. For the comparison to *Punch,* see Price, *Punch,* 10.

29 For circulation statistics see Muser, *Statistische Untersuchungen,* 59–61; and *Facsimile-Kladderadatsch,* 15. For the study of Bremen see Engelsing, "Zeitschrift," 1013–14. See also Isolde Rieger, *Die wilhelminische Presse im Uberblick, 1888–1918* (Munich, 1957), 154.

30 *K* 50 (1898), no. 48: 196. For a more detailed discussion of the magazine's relationship to Bismarck, see Chapter 3. Johannes Trojan's account of his imprisonment is in his *Zwei Monate Festung* (Berlin, 1898). For the history of *Kladderadatsch* in the early twentieth century see *Facsimile-Kladderadatsch,* 12; and Schulz, *Kladderadatsch,* 183–223.

31 Hofmann, *Kladderadatsch und seine Leute,* 233. For another account of the competition between *Simplicissimus* and *Kladderadatsch* see Stephenson, "Redakteure," 55.

32 The best of several accounts of the beginnings of *Simplicissimus* is Eugen Roth, *Simplicissimus: Ein Rückblick auf die satirische Zeitschrift* (Hannover, 1955), 1–20. Other good historical accounts may be found in Konrad, "Nationale und internationale Tendenzen, 1–46; and in Anton Sailer, "Glanz und Elend des *Simplicissimus,*" in *Simplicissimus: Eine satirische Zeitschrift, München 1896–1944* (Munich, 1977), 23–34. (This article appears in the catalog of an exhibition held in Munich from November 1977 to January 1978).

33 Viktor Mann, *Wir waren Fünf: Bildnis der Familie Mann* (Konstanz, 1964), 71; and Thomas Mann, "Gladius Dei," in *Der Tod in Venedig und andere Erzählungen* (Frankfurt, 1960), 171. For a further discussion of Bavarian and Prussian values in *Simplicissimus* see Konrad, "Nationale und internationale Tendenzen," 69.

34 For personal reminiscences of the early days of *Simplicissimus* see Jakob Wassermann, *Gesammelte Reden und Studien* (Leipzig, 1928), 326; and Thoma, *Erinnerungen,* 25.

35 Holitscher is quoted from Sailer, "Glanz und Elend," 36. For a thorough account of Langen and his career see Ernestine Koch, *Albert Langen: Ein Ver-*

leger in München (Munich, 1969). For more biographical information see Hansludwig Geiger, *Es war um die Jahrhundertwende* (Munich, 1953); and Hermann Sinsheimer, *Gelebt im Paradies* (Munich, 1953).

36 Thoma wrote an autobiography, *Erinnerungen*. His collected correspondence is held in the Handschriften-Abteilung of the Stadtbibliothek München (which also holds letters and papers of some other prominent staff members and contributors, such as Frank Wedekind, Korfiz Holm, Otto Julius Bierbaum, and Thomas Theodor Heine). A good selection of Thoma's letters has been published as *Ein Leben in Briefen, 1875–1921* (Munich, 1963). Biographical work on Thoma has been extensive; a few examples are: Roland Ziersch, *Ludwig Thoma* (Stuttgart, 1964); Walter L. Heilbronner, "Ludwig Thoma as a Social and Political Critic and Satirist" (Ph.D. diss., Univ. of Michigan, 1955); Friedl Brehm, *Ludwig Thoma und der Simplicissimus: Immer gegen die Machthaber* (Feldaffing, 1966); Peter Haage, *Ludwig Thoma: Mit Nagelstiefeln durchs Kaiserreich* (Munich, 1975); and Helmut Ahrens, *Ludwig Thoma: Sein Leben, sein Werk, seine Zeit* (Pfaffenhofen, 1983).

37 Albert Haas, *Das moderne Zeitungswesen in Deutschland* (Berlin, 1914). For a discussion of the caricature art of this period see Georg Hermann Borchardt, *Die deutsche Karikatur im neunzehnten Jahrhundert* (Bielefeld, 1901); and Jean Adhémar, *Twentieth-Century Graphics*, trans. A. Hart (New York, 1971), 43.

38 For brief biographical sketches of the *Simplicissimus* group see Golo Mann, introduction to Christian Schütze, ed., *Facsimile Querschnitt durch den Simplicissimus* (Stuttgart, 1963), 11–12.

39 Hermann Esswein, *Moderne Illustratoren* (Munich, 1905), 47; Sinsheimer, *Gelebt im Paradies*, 237. Thomas Theodor Heine wrote a short autobiographical sketch which was published in an anthology: Hans Lamm, ed., *An und über Juden: Aus Schriften und Reden (1906–1963)* (Dusseldorf, 1964). A biographical sketch may be found in *Th. Th. Heine: Aus dem Nachlass: Ausstellung städtischer Galerie*, the catalog to an exhibition held in Munich from February 29 to April 24, 1960, 3–5. Some of Heine's unpublished correspondence is held in the Handschriften-Abteilung of the Munich Stadtbibliothek. His novel, *Ich warte auf Wunder* (Hamburg, 1941), contains sóme autobiographical material.

40 Max Halbe, *Jahrhundertwende* (Danzig, 1935), 211–12. For Thoma's reactions to Reznicek's drawings, see Thoma to Langen, Aug. 23, 1900, in Thoma, *Leben in Briefen*, 59.

41 For an account of this incident see Sailer, "Glanz und Elend," 45.

42 For participants' reactions to the "Palestine" incident see Korfiz Holm, *Farbiger Abglanz* (Munich, 1940), 61–66 (Holm's comment is from p. 75); and Thoma, *Erinnerungen*, 145–49. For Heine's feelings about prison life see especially Heine to Langen, Apr. 18, 1899, in the Handschriften-Abteilung of the Stadtbibliothek München. See also Thoma to Langen, May 4, 1901, in Thoma, *Leben in Briefen*, 76–77. Wedekind's career is more fully discussed in Peter Jelavich, "Art and Mammon in Wilhelmine Germany: The Case of Frank Wedekind," *Central European History* 12, no. 3 (Sept. 1979): 203–36.

43 A newspaper clipping file is in the Hamburg Staatsarchiv, "Politische Polizei S 5458," vols. 1 and 2. An account of clerical attempts at censorship is in Thoma, *Erinnerungen*, 160. The Woermann suit is discussed in *Hamburger Echo*, Jan. 28, 1907.

44 Thoma, *Erinnerungen*, 160. For details of the jurisdictional dispute between

Munich and Stuttgart see the many documents held in the Conrad Haussmann *Nachlass* in the Stuttgart Staatsarchiv. For a general discussion of press censorship in Bavaria see Robin Lenman, "Politics and Culture: The State and the Avant-Garde in Munich, 1896–1914," in Evans, *Society and Politics*, 90–112. An account of the acquittal of the Hamburg bookseller is in *Generalanzeiger*, Nov. 8, 1905.

45 See Haussmann to Thoma, Jan. 15, 1904, in the Handschriften-Abteilung at the Stadtbibliothek München; memorandum from Staatsrat K. von Dandl to the King of Bavaria, May 14, 1914. This and other documents related to the history of *Simplicissimus* may be found in the BHStA, MJu 17354.

46 Sinsheimer, *Gelebt in Paradies*, 227; Freud, *Wit*, 699. Hirth's testimony may be found in the transcript of the trial, entitled "Protokoll geführt in der öffentlichen Sitzung des Schöffengerichts München, June 4, 1903," in BHStA, MJu, 17352.

47 The significance of *Simplicissimus* in the history of twentieth-century graphic art is discussed in Adhémar, *Twentieth-Century Graphics*, 43. A general discussion of the Berlin Secession and its historical background is Peter Paret, *The Berlin Secession: Modernism and Its Enemies in Imperial Germany* (Cambridge, Mass., 1980); for the inclusion of *Simplicissimus* artists in the Exhibition of 1898, see Paret, p. 84.

48 Nikolaus Pevsner, *Pioneers of Modern Design from William Morris to Walther Gropius* (Harmondsworth, Middlesex, 1960), 108. Further discussion of *Simplicissimus* as a proponent of the *Jugendstil* is in Werner Haftmann, Alfred Hentzen, and William S. Lieberman, *German Art of the Twentieth Century* (New York, 1957), 27; and Franz Roh, *German Art in the Twentieth Century*, trans. Catherine Hutter (New York, 1968), 35–43.

49 Thoma to Langen, May 12, 1901, in Thoma, *Leben in Briefen*, 78–79.

50 Viktor Mann, *Wir waren Fünf*, 160; *Augsburger Postzeitung*, Sept. 19, 1903; *Stenographische Berichte über die Verhandlungen der bayerischen Kammer der Abgeordneten*, Jan. 14, 1904; *Allgemeine Rundschau*, Oct. 16, 1909.

51 *Augsburger Postzeitung*, Mar. 15, 1912; June 18, 1903.

52 *Allgemeine Rundschau*, Oct. 16, 1909; *Stenographischer Bericht über die Verhandlungen der bayerischen Landtags, Kammer der Abgeordneten*, Jan. 14, 1904; "Protokoll geführt in der öffentlichen Sitzung des Schöffengerichts München, June 4, 1903." An account of socialist *Simplicissimus* evenings, including quotations from the *Chemnitzer Volksstimme* and the *Frankfurter Volksstimme*, is in *Die Post*, Sept. 11, 1904.

3 Politics as Theater

1 *K* 66, no. 24, *Beiblatt*. Quotations from Wilhelm in Erich Eyck, *Das persönliche Regiment Wilhelms II: Politische Geschichte des deutschen Kaiserreiches von 1890 bis 1914* (Zurich, 1948), 61; and from Johannes Hohlfeld, ed., *Dokumente der deutschen Politik und Geschichte: von 1848 bis zur Gegenwart: Ein Quellenwerk für die politische Bildung und staatsbürgerliche Erziehung* 6 vols. (Berlin, 1951–53), 2: 65.

2 James J. Sheehan, "Conflict and Cohesion among German Elites in the Nineteenth Century," in James J. Sheehan, ed., *Imperial Germany* (New York, 1976), 60; Max Weber, "Das Nationalstaat und die Volkswirtschaftspolitik," in his

Gesammelte politische Schriften (Tübingen, 1958), 20. There are many perceptive overall analyses of the Wilhelmine political system. A few of the most interesting are: Karl Erich Born, "Structural Changes in German Social and Economic Development at the End of the Nineteenth Century," in Sheehan, *Imperial Germany*, 16–38; Arthur Rosenberg, *Die Entstehung der Weimarer Republik*, 2 vols. (1928; rpt., Frankfurt, 1961), 1–55; and Wehler, *Deutsche Kaiserreich*, 60–77.

3   A.J.P. Taylor, "The Ruler in Berlin," in his *From Napoleon to Lenin: Historical Essays* (New York, 1966), 103. Personal characteristics of the kaiser are described in many sources, among which are Walter Rathenau, *Der Kaiser: Eine Betrachtung* (Berlin, 1919); and Michael Balfour, *The Kaiser: His Life and Times* (New York, 1972). On the political and ideological foundation for the German monarchy see Elisabeth Fehrenbach, *Wandlungen des deutschen Kaisergedankens, 1871–1918* (Munich, 1969).

4   Baroness Hildegard Amalie Henriette Maria von Sptizemberg, *Das Tagebuch der Baronin Spitzemberg: Aufzeichnungen der Hofgesellschaft des Hohenzollernreiches* (Göttingen, 1960), 284. On the position of the Junkers in imperial Germany, see (among many sources) Karl-Erich Born, "Structural Changes," 48–55; Hans Rosenberg, "Die Pseudodemokratisierung der Rittergutsbesitzerklasse," in *Moderne Deutsche Sozialgeschichte*, ed. Hans-Ulrich Wehler (Berlin, 1966), 304; and Alexander Gerschenkron, *Bread and Democracy in Germany* (Berkeley, 1943).

5   On the feudalization of the bourgeoisie see especially Eckart Kehr, "Das soziale System der Reaktion in Preussen," in Hans-Ulrich Wehler, ed., *Der Primat der Innenpolitik: Gesammelte Aufsätze zur preussisch-deutschen Sozialgeschichte im 19 und 20 Jahrhundert* (Berlin, 1965) (quotation is from p. 35); and Sheehan, "Conflict and Cohesion," 77–84. On the development of left wing liberalism and liberal-socialist alliances see Peter Gilg, *Die Erneuerung des demokratischen Denkens* (Wiesbaden, 1965); James J. Sheehan, *German Liberalism in the Nineteenth Century* (Chicago, 1978), 221–72; Beverly Heckart, *From Bassermann to Bebel: The Grand Block's Quest for Reform in the Kaiserreich, 1900–1914* (New Haven, 1974); and the bibliographical article by James C. Hunt, "The Bourgeois Middle in German Politics, 1871–1933," *Central European History* 11 (Mar. 1978): 83–106.

6   Wehler, *Deutsche Kaiserreich*, 78. For the development of the Social Democratic party during this period see Vernon Lidtke, *The Outlawed Party: Social Democracy in Germany, 1878–1890* (Princeton, 1966), 291–333; and Schorske, *German Social Democracy*.

7   Ludwig Quidde, *Caligula: Eine Studie über römischen Cäsarenwahnsinn* (Leipzig, 1894), 4. A complete account of Quidde's life and work may be found in Utz-Friedebert Taube, *Ludwig Quidde: Ein Beitrag zur Geschichte des demokratischen Denkens in Deutschland* (Kallmünz, 1963).

8   Maximilian Harden, "König Phaeton," *Die Zukunft* 13 (June 18, 1898): 495–502. For a thorough account of Harden's career see Harry Young, *Maximilian Harden, Censor Germaniae: The Critic in Opposition from Bismarck to the Rise of Nazism* (The Hague, 1959).

9   *S* 2. (1897/98), no. 40: cover. Two delightful anthologies of caricatures are John Grand-Carteret, *"Lui" devant l'objectif caricatural* (Paris, 1905); and Harold Morré, ed., *Zwanzig Jahre S.M.: Heitere Bilder zu ernsten Ereignissen* (Berlin, 1909). See also Eduard Fuchs, *Die Karikatur de europäischen Völker*

vom Altertum bis zur Neuzeit (Berlin, 1901). For a description of Wilhelm as an intellectual and artistic dilettante see Eyck, *Persönliche Regiment*, 60–62. Another discussion of Wilhelm as a cartoon figure is E.A. Coupe, "Kaiser Wilhelm II and the Cartoonists," *History Today* 30 (Nov. 1980): 16–23.

10   *S* 2 (1897/98), no. 40: 313. For the editors' reaction to these punitive measures see *S* 2 (1897/98), no. 41: 320.

11   *S* 3 (1898/99), no. 29: 229.

12   *S* 11 (1906/07), no. 28: 436.

13   Baroness von Spitzemberg, *Tagebuch*, 488–89; *S* 13 (1908/09), no. 35: 576; verse from *S* 13 (1908/09), no. 33: 545. For the reactions of *Kladderadatsch* see *K* 61 (1908), no. 45: 178. For a thorough account of the *Daily Telegraph* affair see Wilhelm Schüssler, *Die Daily-Telegraph Affäre: Fürst Bülow, Kaiser Wilhelm und die Krise des zweiten Reiches* (Göttingen, 1952).

14   Rathenau, *Der Kaiser*, 27; Balfour, *Kaiser*, 89. For another psychological interpretation of Wilhelm's personality see Donald Dietrich, "Kaiser Wilhelm II: Crisis and the Failure of Leadership," *Journal of Psychohistory* 8 (Spring 1981): 465–83.

15   *S* 14 (1909/10), no. 25: 424; *Das Bayerische Vaterland*, Apr. 29, 1909.

16   Cartoon and verse from *S* 18 (1913/14), no. 7: cover and 115.

17   The transcript of the trial, sentencing, and subsequent pardon are in BHStA, MJu, 17354. An account of the Wittelsbach dynasty during this period is contained in Ernst Rudolf Huber, *Deutsche Verfassungsgeschichte seit 1789*, 5 vols. (Stuttgart, 1957–69), 4: 385–400. For Thoma's reaction to the trial see Thoma to Haussmann, June 10, 1914, in Thoma, *Leben in Briefen*, 263.

18   *K* 61 (1908), no. 45: 178; Thoma, "Die Reden Kaiser Wilhelms II: Ein Beitrag zur Geschichte unserer Zeit," in *Gesammelte Werke* 7, 347–48; Harden is quoted from Young, *Harden*, 61.

19   Pross, *Literatur*, 55; Quidde, *Caligula*, 9; Young, *Harden*, 61. For some of Harden's other comments on the law against *Majestätsbeleidigung* see *Die Zukunft* 6 (June 16, 1894): 483–86. For a more general account of press campaigns against prominent men see Koszyk, *Geschichte der deutschen Presse*, 2: 250–54.

20   See Helmuth Rogge, "Die Kladderadatschaffäre: Ein Beitrag zur inneren Geschichte des Wilhelminischen Reiches," *Historische Zeitschrift* 195 (1962): 90–130; and Norman Rich, *Friedrich von Holstein: Politics and Diplomacy in the Era of Bismarck and Wilhelm II*, 2 vols. (Cambridge, England, 1965), 2: 403–10. *K* 46 (1893), no. 52: 206. See also Isabel V. Hull, *The Kaiser's Entourage, 1888–1918* (New York, 1982), 102–3.

21   *Die Zukunft* 7, no. 1 (April 7; 1899): 1–5. For Harden's role in the *Kladderadatsch* affair see Young, *Harden*, 78–79.

22   On the political implications of the *Kladderadatsch* affair see Rich, *Friedrich von Holstein*, 404–08; J. Alden Nichols, *Germany after Bismarck: The Caprivi Era, 1890–1894* (Cambridge, Mass., 1958), 288–99; and J.C.G. Rohl, *Germany without Bismarck: The Crisis of Government in the Second Reich, 1890–1900* (Berkeley, 1967), 100–109.

23   *K* 47 (1894), no. 3: 10; 47 (1894), no. 8: 40.

24   Rich, *Friedrich von Holstein*, 410.

25   For a more extensive evaluation of *Kladderadatsch* and its political significance see *Facsimile-Kladderadatsch*, 5–16.

26 *S* 12 (1907/08), no. 33: 519. A thorough account of the Eulenburg affair is in Young, *Harden*, 100–112.
27 Young, *Harden*, 124.
28 *K* 47 (1894), no. 9: 34; *S* 18 (1913/14), no. 4: 51; *K* 56 (1903), no. 18: 71. Max Weber's opinion was expressed in his essay "National Character and the Junkers," in *From Max Weber: Essays in Sociology*, ed. H.H. Gerth and C. Wright Mills (New York, 1958), 386.
29 *K* 52 (1899), no. 17: 67.
30 *S* 12 (1907/08), no. 15: 242. Rosenberg, "Pseudodemokratisierung," 53.
31 *K* 65 (1912), no. 14: 2 *Beiblatt*; *S* 11 (1906/07), no. 35: cover. On attitudes toward minority nationalities see Wehler, *Deutsche Kaiserreich*, 110–18.
32 *S* 11 (1906/07), no. 35: cover. On attitudes toward minority nationalities see Wehler, *Deutsche Kaiserreich*, 110–18.
33 Weber, "National Character," 394.
34 *S* 5 (1900/01), no. 3: cover.
35 *S* 6 (1901/02), no. 39: 307. For further discussion of this theme in satirical literature see Harry Pross, *Die Zerstörung der deutschen Politik: Dokumente 1871–1933* (Frankfurt, 1959), 54.
36 *S* 16 (1911/12), no. 22: 379; *K* 66 (1913), no. 36: 3 *Beiblatt*: *S* 10 (1905/06), no. 5: *Beiblatt*. For a further discussion of the economic role of the middle class see Born, "Social and Economic Developments," 52.
37 For the political attitudes of the professional class see (among many sources) Sheehan, "Elites and Institutions," 72–84.
38 *K* 51 (1898), no. 49: 199.
39 *S* 10 (1906/07), no. 37: 434–35; Thoma, *Erinnerungen*, 163. For various views of the Puttkamer system and its effects, see Kehr, "Das soziale System der Reaktion in Preussen," in Wehler, *Primat der Innenpolitik*, 35; 131–33; and Margaret Lavinia Anderson and Kenneth Barker, "The Myth of the Puttkamer Purge," *Journal of Modern History* 54 (Dec. 1982): 647–86.
40 *S* 12 (1907/08), no. 47: 775; Max Weber, *Gesammelte Aufsätze zur Sozial-und-Wirtschaftsgeschichte* (Tübingen, 1924), 386; a further discussion of Weber's ideas on the political and economic role of the Prussian aristocracy is in Reinhard Bendix, *Max Weber: An Intellectual Portrait* (London, 1960), 258.
41 Rathenau, *Der Kaiser*, 24. For another description of the kaiser cult see Pross, *Zerstörung*, 18–22.
42 *S* 12 (1907/08), no. 27: 427.
43 This chapter from *Der Untertan* appears in *S* 17 (1912/13), no. 24: 377–79.
44 Heinrich Mann, *Der Untertan* (Leipzig, 1918; rpt. Berlin, 1958), 213. Two modern interpretations of the novel are Friedrich Carl Scheibe, "Rolle und Wahrheit in Heinrich Manns *Der Untertan*," *Literaturwissenschaftliches Jahrbuch* 7 (1966): 209–21; and Klaus Schröter, *Heinrich Mann* (Stuttgart, 1971), 9–21. Quotations from Rathenau are from his *Kritik der Zeit* in *Gesammelte Schriften*, 3: 72.
45 *S* 12 (1907/08), no. 5: 23; no. 52: cover. Friedrich Naumann, "1848/1908," in *Werke*, 6 vols. (Cologne, 1964), 5: 309.
46 *K* 60 (1907), no. 26: cover; *S* 12 (1908/09), no. 26: 414; no. 44: cover; *K* 62 (1909), no. 28: cover. For a further discussion of the attitudes of liberals toward the Bülow bloc see Heckart, *Bassermann to Bebel*, 44–91.
47 Stern, "Political Consequences of the Unpolitical German," 3–25; *K* 47 (1894),

no. 2: cover; Wehler, *Deutsche Kaiserreich*, 134. Naumann is quoted from Pross, *Zerstörung*, 27.

48 *S* 13 (1908/09), no. 33: 540.

49 *K* 61 (1908), no. 46: cover. On the character of Bülow see Gordon Craig, *From Bismarck to Adenauer: Aspects of German Statecraft* (New York, 1965), 33–39.

50 *S* 13 (1908/09), no. 36: 599.

51 *S* 10 (1906/07), no. 18: *Beiblatt*. For a perceptive general treatment of liberal-socialist relationships see Gilg, *Erneuerung*, 138–78.

52 *K* 44 (1891), no. 16: 62. For liberal ideas on free enterprise see Gilg, *Erneuerung*, 223. For an account of Stumm's labor policies see G.A. Ritter, *Die Arbeiterbewegung im wilhelminischen Reich: Die sozialdemokratische Partei und die freien Gewerkschaften, 1890–1900* (Berlin, 1959), 16–26.

53 *K* 43 (1890), no. 23: 2 *Beiblatt*. *Punch* cartoons are anthologized in *A Century of Punch*, ed. R.E. Williams (London, 1956), 250, 25. For an account of protective legislation see Lidtke, *Outlawed Party*, 294–98.

54 *K* 43 (1890), no. 1: 3; no. 5: *Beiblatt*. For an account of the effects of tariffs see Hans Rosenberg, "Political and Social Consequences of the Great Depression of 1873–1896 in Central Europe," in Sheehan, *Imperial Germany*, 39–60.

55 *K* 47 (1894), no. 34: cover. For an account of the increasing patriotism among workers see Schorske, *German Social Democracy*, 66–69.

56 *K* 43 (1890), no. 12: *Beiblatt*.

57 *K* 47 (1894), no. 7: 26; *K* 43 (1890), no. 23: 1 *Beiblatt*. For a summary of Richter's book see Günther Roth, "Die kulturellen Bestrebungen der Sozialdemokratie," in Wehler, *Moderne Deutsche Sozialgeschichte*, 358.

58 *S* 2 (1897/98), no. 6: 5; *S* 9 (1904/05), no. 45: 450; *S* 16 (1911/12), no. 21: cover; *S* 12 (1907/08), no. 46: 764.

59 *S* 12 (1907/08), no. 38: 453; *S* 10 (1906/07), no. 34: cover. For the French reaction to the authoritarian discipline of the SPD see Wehler, *Deutsche Kaiserreich*, 133. For a discussion of the conflict between socialist and liberal views of the state see Lidtke, *Outlawed Party*, 325–26.

60 For another opinion on liberal-socialist cooperation see Naumann, *Werke*, 5: 18. Liberal-socialist cooperation is discussed in detail in Gilg, *Erneuerung*, 178–218; and in Heckart, *From Bassermann to Bebel*, 211–88.

61 *S* 7 (1904/05), no. 43: cover; *S* 8 (1904/05), no. 41: *Beiblatt*. Confiscation is discussed in Konrad, "Nationale und Internationale Tendenzen," 76. For a historical account of the Zwickau-Crimmitschau lockout see Schorske, *Social Democracy*, 30.

62 *S* 9 (1904/05), no. 47: 461; *S* 14 (1909/10), no. 10: cover. An account of Gulbransson's trial is in *Frankfurter Zeitung*, Feb. 21, 1910.

63 For the reaction of *Kladderadatsch* to the Russian Revolution see *K* 58 (1905), no. 29: cover. *Simplicissimus'* reaction (including the cartoon mentioned) is in *S* 9 (1904/05), no. 48: 475–76. The influence of *Simplicissimus* on *Zhupel* is described in Robert C. Williams, *Artists in Revolution: Portraits of the Russian Avant-garde, 1905–1925* (Bloomington, 1977), 120–21. The incident in Dresden is described in *Vorwärts*, Feb. 14, 1905.

64 *K* 62 (1909), no. 17: *Beiblatt*; *S* 14 (1909/10), no. 28: cover. A historical account of the socialist campaign against the three-class system may be found in Schorske, *Social Democracy*, 171–96.

65 *S* 14 (1909/10), no. 52: cover; *S* 15 (1910/11), no. 29: cover; no. 28: cover. For an account of the tactical struggle within the SPD see Peter Nettl, *Rosa Luxemburg*, abridged ed. (Oxford, 1969), 282–86.

66 Friedrich Meinecke, "Politische Schriften," in *Ausgewählte Werke*, ed. H. Herzfeld 6 vols. (Munich, 1957–62), 2: 43; *K* 65 (1912), no. 1: cover; *S* 16 (1911/12), no. 52: 834. Liberal defection is further discussed in Heckart, *From Bassermann to Bebel*, 211–21.

67 *S* 19 (1914/15), no. 5: 103. See also the very laudatory tribute to Bebel in *S* 18 (1913/14), no. 2: 370.

68 *Kölnische Zeitung*, Dec. 28, 1908. For a discussion of the attempt of the *Simplicissimus* editorial board to appeal to socialist readers, see above, pp. 46–47.

69 Max Weber, "Der Nationalstaat und die Volkswirtschaftspolitik," in *Politische Schriften*, 21.

70 *K* 43 (1890), no. 13: cover. For a more general discussion of the Bismarck image in the Wilhelmine era see Franz Schnabel, "The Bismarck Problem," in Hans Kohn, ed., *German History: Some New German Views* (Boston, 1954), 65–66.

71 Quoted in *Bismarck-Album des Kladderadatsch* (Berlin, 1890), 84.

72 For an account of Bismarck's retirement see Erich Eyck, *Bismarck: Leben und Werk*, 3 vols. (Zurich, 1941–44), 2: 600–605. Bismarck's use of the press is extensively described in Koszyk, *Geschichte der deutschen Presse*, 251–55.

73 *Bismarck-Album*, preface.

74 An account of the response to the birthday verse may be found in Hofmann, *Kladderadatsch und seine Leute*, 226. Bismarck's speech is quoted in Hohlfeld *Dokumente*, 12.

75 *K* 61 (1908), no. 45: cover.

76 Thoma, *Erinnerungen*, 155; Young, *Maximilian Harden*, 37.

77 *S* 3 (1898/99), no. 21: 164.

78 *S* 3 (1898/99), no. 22: 170.

79 *S* 11 (1906/07), no. 32: 512; *S* 13 (1908/09), no. 15: 254.

80 *S* 5 (1900/01), no. 38: 304. For an evaluation of Bülow's character and influence see Craig, *From Bismarck to Adenauer*, 39.

81 Naumann is quoted from Pross, *Zerstörung*, 72; Taube, *Ludwig Quidde*, 83.

4 Köpenick Revisited

1 Walther Rathenau, *Der Kaiser: eine Betrachtung*, in *Gesammelte Schriften*, 6 vols. (Berlin, 1925–29), 6: 25; Ludwig Thoma, *Stadelheimer Tagebuch*, in *Gesammelte Werke*, 1: 308–9.

2 For another discussion of *Simplicissimus'* view of military life see Hasso Zimdars, "Die Zeitschrift *Simplicissimus*," 150–53. See particularly the comparison between the images of the military in *Punch* and those in *Simplicissimus.*

3 Alfred Vagts, *A History of Militarism* (New York, 1959), 17. For a classical discussion of the political role of the German army see Gerhard Ritter, *Staatskunst und Kriegshandwerk: Das Problem des "Militarismus" in Deutschland*, 4 vols. (Munich, 1954–68), 2: 148.

4 The characterization of Wilhelm is from Gordon Craig, *The Politics of the*

Prussian Army, 1640–1945 (Oxford, 1955), 239. This is still the best overall treatment of German militarism. Another penetrating analysis is in Wehler, *Deutsche Kaiserreich*, 149–71.

5   The Turkish diplomat is quoted from Ritter, *Staatskunst*, 2: 125. The quotation from Treitschke is from Heinrich von Treitschke, *Politics*, ed. Hans Kohn (New York, 1963), 243. Attitudes toward war during this period are explored in Roger Chickering, *Imperial Germany and a World without War: The Peace Movement and German Society* (Princeton, 1975).

6   Sinsheimer, *Gelebt im Paradies*, 29.

7   Karl Liebknecht, *Ausgewählte Reden, Briefe, und Aufsätze* (Berlin, 1952), 60. For the social basis of militarism see Wehler, *Deutsche Kaiserreich*, 159–60; and Martin Kitchen, *The German Officer Corps, 1890–1914* (Oxford, 1968).

8   For a further discussion of the social composition of the officer corps see Craig, *Prussian Army*, 233; Ritter, *Staatskunst*, 2: 120, and Eckart Kehr's classic essay "Zur Genesis des königlich-preussischen Reserveoffiziers," in Hans-Ulrich Wehler, ed., *Primat der Innenpolitik: Gesammelte Aufsätze zur preussisch-deutschen Sozialgeschichte im 19. und 20. Jahrhundert* (Berlin, 1965), 53–84.

9   See Joachim Remak, "The Third Balkan War: Origins Reconsidered," *Journal of Modern History* 43 (1971): 353–66.

10   For another incomparable portrait of Wilhelmine militarism and the culture which supported it see Karl Zuckmayer's famous play *Der Hauptmann von Köpenick* (Berlin, 1928).

11   *S* 3 (1898/99), no. 49: cover. On social attitudes of the officer corps toward civilians cf. Kitchen, *Officer Corps*, 120.

12   *S* 3 (1898/99), no. 1: 1; *K* 50 (1897), no. 19: 67. On extravagance in the army see Craig, *Prussian Army*, 238.

13   *S* 5 (1900/01), no. 3: 19. On educational requirements for the officer corps see Kitchen, *Officer Corps*, 30–31. The lawsuit of the Deutzer Cuirassiers against the *Simplicissimus* editorial board is described in *Hamburger Nachrichten*, Apr. 8, 1908.

14   *S* 10 (1905/06), no. 4: cover; *S* 16 (1910/11), no. 14: 239; *S* 9 (1904/05), no. 13: 123. The technological incompetence of the officer corps is discussed in Vagts, *Militarism*, 231.

15   *K* 52 (1899), no. 2: 12. A discussion of the implications of the reserve officer status is found in Kehr, "Zur Genesis des königlich-preussischen Reserveoffiziers," 59–61.

16   The chapter of *Der Untertan* entitled "Die Mächtigen" was published in *S* 17 (1912/13), no. 14: 216–17. For other comments on the effects of military values on civilian life see *S* 3 (1898/99), no. 13: 100.

17   *K* 50 (1897), no. 48: 193; *K* 64 (1911), no. 10: 1 *Beiblatt*. The problems of Jewish Reserve officers are discussed in Werner T. Angress, "The Prussian Army and the Jewish Reserve Officer Controversy before World War I," in Sheehan, *Imperial Germany*, 93–152.

18   *K* 62 (1909), no. 4: 4 *Beiblatt*. Kitchen (*Officer Corps*, 47) mentions that some officers even hoped that their own families would be exempted from Nazi antisemitic measures.

19   *K* 50 (1897), no. 2: 10; *S* 9 (1904/05), no. 52: 521. For an account of the controversy over duelling see Kitchen, *Officer Corps*, 51–53. For another example of protest against duelling see *S* 6 (1901/02), no. 43: 338.

20 For socialist denunciation of the army as an instrument of class oppression see Liebknecht, *Ausgewählte Reden*, 95. For Luxemburg's role in the prosecution of abusive officers see Peter Nettl, *Rosa Luxemburg*, 320–23.

21 *S* 15 (1910/11), no. 23: 383. Other examples are in *S* 6 (1901/02), no. 27: 212; *S* 9 (1904/05), no. 25: 242–43. For an example from *Kladderadatsch* see *K* 46 (1893), no. 2: 6. Verse from *Der Wahre Jakob*, July 2, 1903.

22 *S* 19 (1914/15), no. 9: cover; *S* 15 (1910/11), no. 21: cover. On the domestic function of militarism and war as conservative "Flucht nach vorn" see Wolfgang J. Mommsen, "Domestic Factors in German Foreign Policy," in Sheehan, *Imperial Germany*, 223–68.

23 *K* 59 (1906), no. 43: cover; *S* 11 (1906/07), no. 33: 515. For another contemporary reaction see the editorial by Maximilian Harden in *Die Zukunft*, Oct. 6, 1906.

24 *Punch*, Jan. 14, 1914.

25 *K* 66 (1913/14), no. 50: cover; *S* 18 (1913/14), no. 35: 576; *S* 18 (1913/14), no. 36: *Beiblatt*. On the political dimensions of the Zabern affair see David Schoenbaum, *Zabern 1913: Consensus Politics in Imperial Germany* (London, 1982).

26 Sinsheimer, *Gelebt in Paradies*, 230; Friedrich Naumann, "Reichstagsrede zur Zabern-Interpellation," in his *Werke*, 6 vols. (Cologne, 1964), 5: 504–5; Rathenau, *Der Kaiser*, 26.

27 Liebknecht, *Ausgewählte Reden*, 111; Thoma, *Erinnerungen*, 159; Otto Erich Hartleben, *Rosenmontag*, in *Ausgewählte Werke*, 3 vols. (Berlin, 1913), Act 1, sc. 5; *Hamburger Fremdenblatt*, May 20, 1910. See also Thoma's article "Der Simplicissimus und unser Heer," in *Zweites Morgenblatt der Frankfurter Zeitung*, June 17, 1904.

28 *S* 8 (1905/06), no. 52: *Beiblatt*. The inadequacy of traditional ideas of warfare to the new conditions is discussed in Theodore Ropp, *War in the Modern World* (Durham, 1959), 215–35.

29 *S* 10 (1906/07), no. 20: cover. For one of the many social analyses of nationalism during the Wilhelmine period see Wehler, *Deutsche Kaiserreich*, 107–10.

30 For an account of the "Palestine" affair and its effect on the participants and on *Simplicissimus* itself see above, pp. 39–40.

31 *S* 3 (1898/99), no. 31: cover, 249.

32 *Punch*, Oct. 15, 1898. An excerpt from the French satirical journal *Le Rire* was published in English as *The All-Highest Goes to Jerusalem: Being the Diary of the German Emperor's Journey to the Holy Land*, trans. Frank A. Dearborn (New York, 1918), 5. For more reactions to the Palestine trip see *Zwanzig Jahre S.M.: Heitere Bilder zu ernsten Ereignissen* (Berlin, 1909), *passim;* Thoma to Haussmann, Aug. 27, 1911, in Thoma, *Leben in Briefen*, 235. See also the comments of Max Weber in *Max Weber: Werk und Person*, ed. Eduard Baumgarten (Tübingen, 1964), 487.

33 *K* 59 (1906), no. 31: cover; *S* 9 (1904/05), no. 6: 55. For a discussion of the background to German imperialism see Hans-Ulrich Wehler, "Bismarck's Imperialism, 1862–1890," in Sheehan *Imperial Germany*, 180–222.

34 *S* 5 (1900/01), no. 15: cover. See also the similarly outraged reaction of Maximilian Harden, quoted in Harry Young, *Maximilian Harden*, 61.

35 *K* 64 (1911/12), no. 32: 2 *Beiblatt; S* 13 (1908/09), no. 29: 478; *S* 16 (1911/12), no. 26: 444; Thoma, *Erinnerungen*, 212–13.

244 / Notes to pages 128–139

36 *K* 49 (1896), no. 45: cover.
37 The response of *Harper's Weekly* and a general account of the crisis appear in Thomas A. Bailey, *A Diplomatic History of the American People* (New York, 1940; rpt., New York, 1969), 501–3. A transcript of the trial of Heine and Linnekogel is in BHStA, MJu, 17352. The trial was reported by many newspapers; the best of these accounts may be found in *Münchener Neueste Nachrichten*, June 5, 1903. See also an account of the case in Leiss, *Kunst im Konflikt*, 142–51.
38 Thoma's initial misgivings were expressed in Thoma to Langen, Sept. 14, 1900, in Thoma, *Leben in Briefen*, 55; his letter to the *Wiener Arbeiter-Zeitung* is quoted in *Hamburger Echo*, Nov. 11, 1908.
39 *K* 57 (1904), no. 22: cover; *S* 6 (1901–02), no. 32: cover.
40 *S* 5 (1901/02), no. 32: cover. Barth's remarks are quoted in Pauline R. Anderson, *The Background of Anti-English Feeling in Germany, 1890–1902* (Washington, D.C., 1939), 320–40. For an account of the confiscation see *Volkszeitung*, Apr. 27, 1900. Thoma's reaction to this is in Thoma to Dagny Langen, Apr. 20, 1900, in Thoma, *Leben in Briefen*, 41.
41 For examples of anti-Slavic humor see *S* 12 (1907/08), no. 33: 540; *S* 19 (1914/15), no. 16: cover; and *S* 9 (1904/05), no. 1: *Beiblatt*. For a discussion of the domestic purposes served by such hostility see Wehler, *Deutsche Kaiserreich*, 107–10.
42 Freud, *Wit and Its Relation to the Unconscious*, 697. Thoma to Langen, July 11, 1900, in Thoma, *Leben in Briefen*, 49. See also the debate on this issue by another group of artists, the Werkbund, described in Joan Campbell, *The German Werkbund: The Politics of Reform in the Applied Arts* (Princeton, 1978), 57–82.
43 *S* 9 (1904/05), no. 33: cover; *S* 18 (1913/14), no. 20: cover; *S* 16 (1911/12), no. 37: 664; *S* 10 (1905/06), no. 3: 52. For a discussion of violence in Expressionist art see Walter Sokel, *The Writer in Extremis: Expressionism in Twentieth-Century German Literature* (Stanford, 1959), 45. The apocalyptic theme is treated in Frederick S. Levine, *The Apocalyptic Vision: The Art of Franz Marc as German Expressionism* (New York, 1979).
44 Thoma to Haussmann, Aug. 27, 1911, Thoma, *Leben in Briefen*, 234.
45 *K* 67 (1914), no. 32: cover; see also *K* 67 (1914), no. 27: 2 *Beiblatt*. For a discussion of *Kladderadatsch* during the war years see Schulz, *Kladderadatsch*, 197–98.
46 An account of this meeting is found in Sinsheimer, *Gelebt im Paradies*, 230; and Thoma, *Erinnerungen*, 212–13. Thoma's own feelings about the outbreak of war are expressed in several letters; for example, Thoma to Haussmann, Aug. 7, 1914, Thoma, *Leben in Briefen*, 266.
47 Klaus Vondung, "Deutsche Apokalypse, 1914," in Vondung, ed., *Das wilhelminische Bildungsbürgertum: Zur Sozialgeschichte seiner Ideen* (Göttingen, 1978), 153–71.
48 Thoma, *Erinnerungen*, 212–13.

5 Sex and Satire

1 Holbrook Jackson, *The Eighteen Nineties* (New York, 1966), 30.
2 For another view of the political significance of *Kladderadatsch*'s avoidance of family and sexual issues see Schulz, *Kladderadatsch*, 53–54.

3 The relationship of this new style in caricature to deepened sociological insight is discussed in Borchardt, *Deutsche Karikatur.*
4 General trends in family history during this period are outlined in Edward Shorter, *The Making of the Modern Family* (New York, 1975), 227–54.
5 Heinrich von Treitschke, *Politics*, ed. Hans Kohn (New York, 1963), 109; Wilhelm Heinrich Riehl, *Die Familie* (Stuttgart, 1855; rpt., 1882), 343–51.
6 For the socialist critique of the family see August Bebel, *Die Frau und der Sozialismus* (Stuttgart, 1893), originally published in 1878. For discussions of the impact, readership, and influence of Bebel's book see Günther Roth, "Die kulturellen Bestrebungen der Sozialdemokratie," in Wehler, *Moderne Deutsche Sozialgeschichte*, 358. For a more general view of German socialist views on the status of women within the family see R.P. Neumann, "The Sexual Question and Social Democracy in Imperial Germany," *Journal of Social History* 7 (Spring 1974): 271–86. Compare the account of similar developments in England in Samuel Hynes, *The Edwardian Turn of Mind* (Princeton, 1968), 132–72; and in America in John C. Burnham, "The Progressive Era: Revolution in American Attitudes toward Sex," *Journal of American History* 59 (Mar. 1973): 885–909.
7 Press laws are discussed in Leiss, *Kunst im Konflikt*, 81–142; and Lenman, "Art, Society and the Law," 86–113.
8 A transcript of the 1904 "Gesandtenerziehung" trial is in BHStA, MJu 17354; *S* 1 (1896/97), no. 7: 3. For a general discussion of attitudes toward pornography see Stark, "Pornography, Society and the Law."
9 Stefan Zweig, *The World of Yesterday* (London, 1941; rpt., Lincoln, Neb., 1964), 83. On the portrayal of sexual themes in the visual arts, see (among many sources) Dolf Sternberger, "Sinnlichkeit um die Jahrhundertwende," in Jost Hermand, ed. *Jugendstil* (Darmstadt, 1971), 100–106; and Carl Schorske, *Fin-de-Siècle Vienna: Politics and Culture* (New York, 1980), 208–36. For information on prostitution in German cities see Richard J. Evans, "Prostitution, State and Society in Wilhelmine Germany," *Past and Present* 70 (Feb. 1976): 106–29.
10 Laura Marholm, *Wir Frauen und unsere Dichter* (Berlin, n.d.), 13. On the German feminist movement and its attitudes toward the family see Richard J. Evans, *The Feminist Movement in Germany, 1894–1933* (London, 1976), 115–44.
11 Rosa Mayreder, *A Survey of the Woman Problem*, trans. Hermann Schiffauer (New York, 1908), 180; Ellen Key, *Die Frauenbewegung* (Frankfurt, 1909), 175. On expanding job opportunities for women see Evans, *Feminist Movement*, 231–45.
12 Key, *Frauenbewegung*, 193.
13 *S* 3 (1898/99), no. 49: 389; *S* 2 (1897/98), no. 6: cover.
14 *S* 3 (1898/99), no. 3: 37.
15 *S* 3 (1898/99), no. 16: cover; *S* 3 (1898/99), no. 22: 176; Mayreder, "Family Literature," in her *Survey of the Woman Problem*, 180; Zweig, *World of Yesterday*, 78.
16 *S* 9 (1904/05), no. 7: 62–63; Zweig, *World of Yesterday*, 80.
17 On Heine's relationship to the *Jugendstil*, see Borchardt, *Deutsche Karikatur*, 109–15; and Helmut Seling, *Jugendstil—Der Weg ins 20. Jahrhundert* (Heidelberg, 1959), 104.
18 *S* 9 (1904/05), no. 18: *Beiblatt.*

19 *S* 1 (1896/97), no. 3: 8.

20 *S* 1 (1896/97), no. 36: 138; *S* 12 (1907/08), no. 47: 779; *S* 3 (1898/99), no.
1: 4. For a description of the portrayal of the *nouveau riche* in *Punch* see
Price, *History of Punch*, 133.

21 For a study of the theme of social mobility in German literature see Ernest
Kohn Bramsted, *Aristocracy and the Middle Classes in Germany: Social Types
in German Literature* (Chicago, 1964).

22 *S* 6 (1901/02), no. 28: 219; *S* 12 (1908/09), no. 52: 858; *S* 6 (1901/02), no.
48: 378; no. 17: 133.

23 *S* 5 (1900/01), no. 28: 301; Thoma to Langen, Dec. 16, 1900, in Thoma, *Leben
in Briefen*, 66.

24 Bebel, *Die Frau*, 110; George Bernard Shaw, *Pygmalion*, in *The Bodley Head
Bernard Shaw: Collected Plays with Their Prefaces*, 7 vols. (London, 1972),
vol. 4, act 4.

25 *S* 5 (1900/01), no. 9: 76. On laws regulating sales of alcohol to minors see
E.S. Turner, *Roads to Ruin: The Shocking History of Social Reform* (London,
1950; rpt. 1966), 202–27.

26 *S* 18 (1913/14), no. 27: 436. On the transition from patriarchal to more egalitarian family patterns see Shorter, *Modern Family*, 227–53.

27 *S* 16 (1911/12), no. 35: 600–607. See Theodore W. Adorno *et al., The Authoritarian Personality* (New York, 1950). On recent theories see Peter Loe-
wenberg, "Psychohistorical Perspectives on Modern German History," *Journal of Modern History* 47 (June 1975): 229–79.

28 *S* 12 (1907/08), no. 37, 59; *S* 1 (1896/97), no. 38: cover; *S* 2 (1897/98), no.
14: 108. For a general discussion of family life among the urban poor see
Louise A. Tilly and Joan W. Scott, *Women, Work and Family* (New York,
1978), 61–147. For the relationship of Naturalist art to the socialist movement see Vernon L. Lidtke, "Naturalism and Socialism in Germany," *American Historical Review* 79 (Feb. 1974): 14–37.

29 *Die Zukunft*, Jan. 8, 1898; Hermann Esswein, *Moderne Illustratoren* (Munich,
1905), 47. The Landtag deputy's remarks are in *Stenographischer Bericht über
die Verhandlungen des bayerischen Landtags Kammer der Abgeordneten* 428
Sitzung (Jan. 14, 1904).

30 On changes in family relationships during this period see Shorter, *Modern
Family*, 269–82; and Wehler, *Deutsche Kaiserreich*, 122–23 (a short but useful summary).

31 Mayreder, *Survey of the Woman Problem*, 181; Irma von Troll-Borostanyi in
"Edward Hartmanns neue Offenbarung über die Frauenfrage," *Die Gesellschaft* 1 (1885), no. 20: 362. Victorian stereotypes of feminine behavior are
discussed by many authors, for example by Walter Houghton, *The Victorian
Frame of Mind* (New Haven, 1957), 341–48.

32 Friedrich Nietzsche, *Beyond Good and Evil: Prelude to a Philosophy of the
Future*, vol. 12 of *The Complete Works of Friedrich Nietzsche*, trans. Helen
Zimmern (Edinburgh, 1909), 190; Key, *Frauenbewegung*, 199; Philip Rieff,
Freud: The Mind of the Moralist (New York, 1964), 203.

33 *S* 3 (1898/99), no. 13: 102; *S* 19 (1914/15), no. 1: 3; *S* 2 (1897/98), no. 24:
186; *S* 5 (1900/01), no. 41: 351. For a general discussion of women's changing work roles during this period see Tilly and Scott, *Women, Work and
Family*, 147–76. On women in the professions see Evans, *Feminist Movement*, 239–42. A heartfelt complaint about the inaccessibility of dignified

employment for middle-class women is in Fanny Lewald, *Für und wieder die Frauen: Vierzehn Briefe* (Berlin, 1870), 13.

34 Hilaire Belloc, "Ladies and Gentlemen," in his *Cautionary Verses* (London, 1961), 361; *S* 6 (1901/02), no. 39: 306; *S* 5 (1900/01), no. 22: 177; *S* 3 (1898/99), no. 11: 84. For the social impact of the bicycle see S.S. Wilson, "Bicycle Technology," *Scientific American* 228 (Mar. 1973): 85.

35 For discussion of the highly controversial topic of changing sexual behavior see Edward R. Shorter, "Illegitimacy, Sexual Revolution and Social Change in Modern Europe," *Journal of Interdisciplinary History* 2 (Fall 1971): 237–72. An interesting treatment of sexual attitudes of American women during this same period is Carl Degler, "What Ought To Be and What Was," *American Historical Review* 79 (Dec. 1974): 1467–90.

36 *S* 7 (1902/03), no. 5: 52.

37 Thoma to Rothmaier, May 20, 1902, in Thoma, *Leben in Briefen*, 126–27.

38 *S* 1 (1897/98), no. 3: 7. For a discussion of the confiscation of this issue see Leiss, *Kunst im Konflikt*, 143–44.

39 *S* 6 (1901/02), no. 28: 220; *S* 5 (1900/01), no. 37: 295; *S* 7 (1902/03), no. 24: 172. For the image of the "femme fatale" see Sternberger, "Sinnlichkeit," in Hermand, *Jugendstil*, 100–106.

40 *S* 2 (1897/98), no. 37: 295; *S* 5 (1900/01), no. 2: 100; *S* 1 (1896/97), no. 41: cover; no. 27: 8. On the activities of the Bund für Mutterschütz see Evans, *Feminist Movement*, 115–45.

41 The first three comments on prostitution are in a special issue devoted to the subject, *S* 11 (1906/07), no. 36: 561–70. The editorial is from *S* 10 (1905/06), no. 52: 118; the final cartoon is from *S* 14 (1909/10), no. 3: 25. For an account of the feminist campaign against prostitution see Evans, *Feminist Movement*, 35–70.

42 Thoma, *Erinnerungen*, 1: 137; *Kölnische Zeitung*, Dec. 28, 1908.

43 Thoma's verse (along with a cartoon by Gulbransson) is in *S* 9 (1904/05), no. 31: *Beiblatt*. The quotations from Bernstein, Haussmann, and Thoma are in the unpublished typescript, held in the Stadtbibliothek München, of a documentary produced for the Bavarian Radio: Otto Gritschneder, "Bei Durchsicht gewisser Akten: Der Strafprozess gegen Ludwig Thoma" (Bayerischer Rundfunk, 1976), 26, 33, 17.

44 For a perceptive account of nineteenth-century child rearing in Europe see Priscilla Robertson, "Home as Nest: Middle Class Childhood in Nineteenth-Century Europe," in Lloyd de Mause, ed., *The History of Childhood* (New York, 1974), 407–31. For a general overview of the history of childhood see the introductory chapter to the same volume: Lloyd de Mause, "The Evolution of Childhood," 1–73.

45 *S* 7 (1902/03), no. 9: 70; *S* 10 (1905/06), no. 2: cover; *S* 1 (1896/97), no. 28: 8.

46 *S* 19 (1914/15), no. 1: 4; *S* 3 (1898/99), no. 44: 348. For a chart demonstrating the falling birthrate in Germany in the years 1880–1914 see E.A. Wrigley, *Population and History* (New York, 1969), 182; and for a discussion of socialist ideas on birth control see Neumann, "Sexual Question," 280–82.

47 *S* 2 (1897/98), no. 11: cover; no. 46: 368. For many additional examples see Jobling, "Playful Judgment," Chapter VI.

48 Viktor Mann, *Wir waren Fünf*, 160; for a discussion of Freud's ideas see Stephen Kern, "Freud and the Discovery of Childhood Sexuality," *History of Childhood Quarterly* 1 (Summer 1973): 136–38.

49 *Kölnische Zeitung*, Dec. 8, 1906.
50 *S* 1 (1896/97), no. 13: 6.

6 The Assault of Laughter

1 The quotation from the kaiser's speech is in R.H. Samuel and Hinton Thomas, *Education and Society in Modern Germany* (London, 1949), 120. For further background on the German educational system during this period see (among many works) Friedrich Paulsen, *German Education Past and Present*, trans. T. Lorenz (London, 1908); Fritz K. Ringer, *Education and Society in Modern Europe* (Bloomington, 1979), 32–113; and James C. Albisetti, *Secondary School Reform in Germany* (Princeton, 1983).
2 *K* 52 (1900), no. 41:162.
3 *S* 18 (1914/15), no. 6:51. The documents are in BHStA, MJu 17354. On the policies of the Bavarian police in regard to confiscation see Konrad, "Nationale und internationale Tendenzen," 82.
4 *K* 51 (1898), no. 20:78; *K* 44 (1891), no. 2: cover. For a general discussion of the arguments about classical vs. modern curriculum see Paulsen, *German Education*, 206–21; and Stern, *Politics of Cultural Despair*, 329–61.
5 *S* 8 (1902/03), no. 12:98. For a similarly grotesque portrait of a schoolmaster see the well-known novel by Heinrich Mann, *Professor Unrat, oder das Ende eines Tyrannen* (Leipzig, 1918), 3. For an autobiographical account of school experiences see Zweig, *World of Yesterday*, 28–66; other contemporary school literature is discussed in Albisetti, *Secondary School Reform*, 42–56.
6 *S* 9 (1904/05), no. 23: 228; *S* 13 (1908/09), no. 5: 8.
7 *S* 13 (1908/09), no. 5: 81. For explanation of this humorous technique see Freud, *Wit and Its Relation to the Unconscious*, 665.
8 *S* 18 (1913/14), no. 49: 831. For background on the German Youth Movement see Walter Laqueur, *Young Germany: A History of the German Youth Movement* (New York, 1962). For a dramatic portrayal of schoolboy suicide see Frank Wedekind, *Frühlingserwachen* in *Ausgewählte Werke*, 6 vols. (Munich, 1924), vol. 1.
9 Reasons for this high dropout rate are discussed in Ringer, *Education and Society*, 72.
10 The chapter from *Der Untertan* is in *S* 17 (1912/13), no. 4: 55–57. For a contemporary comment on the duelling ritual see Max Weber, "National Character and the Junkers," in Gerth and Mills, *From Max Weber*, 390–91.
11 *S* 5 (1900/01), no. 6: cover. For a thorough account of the Arons case see Ernst Rudolf Huber, *Deutsche Verfassungsgeschichte seit 1789*, 5 vols. (Stuttgart, 1954–59), 4: 950–51.
12 *K* 52 (1899), no. 9: 35; *K* 45 (1892), no. 3: 18; *S* 7 (1902/03), no. 13: 99; *S* 16 (1911/12), no. 29: 499. Background on the struggle of German feminists to open educational opportunities to women may be found in Katharine Anthony, *Feminism in Germany and Scandinavia* (New York, 1915), 31; and in Evans, *Feminist Movement in Germany*, 1–71.
13 Theodor Fontane, *Frau Jenny Treibel*, in *Gesammelte Werke*, 7 vols. (Berlin, 1915), 3: 57. The protest against the insult to the teaching profession is in *Berliner Neueste Nachrichten*, Nov. 24, 1913. The Kiel incident is reported in

Notes to pages 179–187 / 249

Vorwärts, July 7, 1902. Viktor Mann is quoted from Roth, *Simplicissimus*, 36.

14 Friedrich Paulsen, *Geschichte des gelehrten Unterrichts auf deutschen Schulen und Universitäten* (Leipzig, 1897), 650.

15 For a thorough discussion of the image of the Catholic church in the German satirical press, see Friedheim Jürgensmeister, *Die katholische Kirche im Spiegel der Karikatur der deutschen Tendenzeitschriften von 1848 bis 1900* (Trier, 1969). For a discussion of the political role of the Catholic church during this period see especially Ronald J. Ross, *Beleaguered Tower: The Dilemma of Political Catholicism in Wilhelmine Germany* (Notre Dame, 1976); and John K. Zeender, *The German Center Party, 1890–1906* (Philadelphia, 1976).

16 *K* 45 (1892), no. 5: cover; no. 8: *Beiblatt*. For a discussion of the conflict over the Zedlitz-Trützschler School Bill see J.C.G. Röhl, *Germany without Bismarck: The Crisis of Government in the Second Reich, 1890–1900* (Berkeley, 1967), 79; and Huber, *Verfassungsgeschichte*, 4: 888–99.

17 For the effect of the liberal press campaign see Röhl, *Germany*, 84.

18 *K* 54 (1901), no. 6: cover. For a discussion of the Jesuit laws see Ross, *Tower*, 18–21. For a more detailed discussion of Bismarck's abandonment of the Kulturkampf see Gordon A. Craig, *Germany, 1866–1945* (New York, 1978), 74–75. For the reaction of other satirical periodicals see Jürgensmeister, *Katholische Kirche*, 210–16.

19 The Bavarian political situation during this period is discussed in Huber, *Verfassungsgeschichte*, 4: 391–401.

20 *S* 8 (1904/05), no. 42: 332, 330. For statistics on the educational level of German Catholics see Wehler, *Deutsche Kaiserreich*, 120–22.

21 Thoma to Haussmann, Jan. 9, 1904, in Thoma, *Leben in Briefen*, 145; *Münchener Neueste Nachrichten*, Jan. 13, 1904; *Frankfurter Zeitung*, Jan. 15, 1904. For a general discussion of antiobscenity laws during this period see Lenman, "Art, Society and the Law," 86–113; Leiss, *Kunst im Konflikt*, 81–88; and Stark, "Pornography, Society and the Law."

22 *Stenographischer Bericht über die Verhandlungen des bayrischen Landtags Kammer der Abgeordneten, 428 Sitzung*, Jan. 14, 1904. A report on the constitutional crisis and an account of the protest against cooperation with Bavarian authorities is in *Deutsches Volksblatt*, Jan. 16, 1904. For more material on this case, including correspondence and a newspaper clipping file, see the *Nachlass* of Conrad Haussman held in the Stuttgart Hauptstaatsarchiv, E 151 c II, Bü 203, and Q 1/2, Bü 254a. On the right to jury trial in Bavarian censorship cases see Robin Lenman, "Politics and Culture: The State and the Avant-Garde in Munich," in Evans, *Society and Politics*, 90–111.

23 Haussmann to Thoma, Jan. 15, 1904; Thoma, *Nachlass*, Handschriften-Abteilung, Stadtbibliothek München; Ludwig Thoma, "Das Verfahren gegen den *Simplicissimus*," *Münchener Neueste Nachrichten*, Mar. 18, 1904; Haussmann to Thoma, Apr. 25, 1904, in Thoma, *Nachlass;* Thoma, *Erinnerungen*, 208. For the legal background of the censorship proceeding see Leiss, *Kunst im Konflikt*, 81–88.

24 *S* 6 (1904/05), no. 42: cover. The most complete descriptions of this trial are given by Otto Gritschneder in a program of the Bayerischer Rundfunk entitled "Bei Durchsicht gewisser Akten: Der Prozess gegen Ludwig Thoma, nach den bisher verschollenen Dokumenten dargestellt" (Nov. 7, 1977; the unpublished typescript is held in the Munich Stadtbibliothek); and idem, *An-*

geklagter Ludwig Thoma: Unveröffentlichte Akten (Munich, 1978). For a description of the audience, quotations from the arguments for the defense, and Haussmann's arguments, see Gritschneder, "Bei Durchsicht," 25–29, 35–36. For a general discussion of Thoma's attitude toward censorship see Friel Brehm, *Sehnsucht nach Unterdrückung: Zensur und Presserecht bei Ludwig Thoma* (Feldaffing, 1957).

25 The quotations are from Gritschneder, "Bei Durchsicht," 39, 31. Thoma's recollections of prison life are recorded in his *Stadelheimer Tagebuch*, in *Gesammelte Werke*, vol. 1.

26 Thoma, *Erinnerungen*, 160. For an appraisal of the lasting effects of the Kulturkampf see Ross, *Beleaguered Tower*, 1–5.

27 For a general discussion of antisemitism and its social causes during this period, see (among many sources) Fritz Stern, "Money, Morals and the Pillars of Society," in his *Failure of Illiberalism*, 26–57; P.C.G. Pulzer, *The Rise of Political Anti-Semitism in Germany and Austria* (New York, 1964), 75–127; and George Mosse, *Germans and Jews* (New York, 1970).

28 *K* 3 (1850), no. 3: cover.

29 *K* 46 (1893), no. 1: 3; *K* 49 (1896), no. 14: 1 *Beiblatt*. For a description of Ahlwardt's pamphlet see Pulzer, *Rise of Political Anti-Semitism*, 113. Pulzer also discusses the fears provoked by an influx of Eastern Jews (p. 261).

30 *K* 51 (1898), no. 16: 62; *K* 46 (1893), no. 42: 1 *Beiblatt*. On class differences among Jews see Pulzer, *Rise of Political Anti-Semitism*, 14. For an example of the antisemitic literary criticism mocked by *Kladderadatsch* see Adolf Bartels, *Heinrich Heine: Auch ein Denkmal* (Dresden, 1906).

31 The impact of antisemitism on culture during the late nineteenth century is analyzed in Mosse, *Germans and Jews*.

32 Thoma to Langen, July 18, 1900, in Thoma, *Leben in Briefen*, 50–51. Fritz Stern, in *Gold and Iron: Bismarck, Bleichröder, and the Building of the German Empire*, describes the social-climbing Jew as "the *arriviste* who never arrived." For Wassermann's opinions on Jewish "character" see "Der Jude als Orientale," 173–77. A general discussion of the status of Jews in Wilhelmine Germany may be found in Peter Gay, *Freud, Jews and other Germans* (New York, 1978), 93–168.

33 *S* 5 (1900/01), no. 9: cover; *S* 7 (1902/03), no. 39: cover; *S* 2 (1898/99), no. 15: 118. For another analysis of the Bruno Paul cartoon see Gay, *Freud*, 204. See also Stern, *Gold and Iron*, 461–93.

34 *S* 7 (1904/05), no. 10: 75; *S* 15 (1911/12), no. 19: cover; Heinrich von Treitschke, *Politics*, ed. Hans Kohn (New York, 1963), 133; Wassermann, "Der Jude als Orientale," 176. For a general discussion of these views of Jewish "character" see Gay, *Freud*, 184.

35 Gay, *Freud*, 100. For another example of a Jew's acceptance of prevailing racial theories see James Joll's short biography of Rathenau in his *Three Intellectuals in Politics* (New York, 1960), 65–67.

36 *S* 10 (1906/07), no. 35: cover. The reaction of German Jews to Russian antisemitism is discussed in Howard Morley Sachar, *The Course of Modern Jewish History* (New York, 1958), 382.

37 Gay, *Freud*, 205; *Augsburger Postzeitung*, June 18, 1903.

38 Two very enlightening discussions of Jewish attitudes toward German culture may be found in Gay, *Freud*, 131–54; and Stern, *Gold and Iron*, 461–70.

39 Gay comments on the Jews' false sense of security in *Freud*, 162–68.

40 General treatments of artistic trends during this period include (among many sources) Leiss, *Kunst im Konflikt;* Hermand, *Jugendstil;* and Paret, *Berlin Secession.*

41 Wilhelm II is quoted from Gerhard Masur, *Imperial Berlin* (New York, 1970), 147. The official view of the arts is discussed in Marion Deshmukh, "Rinnsteinkunst: German Artists and Writers, 1880–1900" (paper delivered at the annual meeting of the Western Association for German Studies, Snowbird, Utah, 1978). On the Lex Heinze see Lenman, "Art, Society and the Law," 86–113.

42 *K* 47 (1894), no. 52: 205; *S* 4 (1899/1900), no. 24: 391.

43 *S* 2 (1897/98), no. 11: 82; *S* 7 (1902/03), no. 8: 59.

44 *K* 50 (1897), no. 43: 170; *S* 7 (1902/03), no. 8: 59; Egon Friedell, *A Cultural History of the Modern Age: The Crisis of the European Soul from the Black Death to the World War,* 3 vols. (New York, 1954), 3: 299.

45 *K* 53 (1900), no. 19: 73; *K* 51 (1898), no. 13: 51. For comparable British reactions to Ibsen see George Bernard Shaw, "The Quintessence of Ibsenism," in *Selected Non-Dramatic Writings of George Bernard Shaw,* ed. D. Lawrence (Boston, 1965), 252–54 (critical reactions to *Ghosts*); and Michael Egan, ed., *Ibsen: The Critical Heritage* (London, 1972).

46 *K* 51 (1898), no. 13: 51; *Punch,* Dec. 17, 1913. See also *Kladderadatsch's* reaction to Hermann Bahr's *Die Mütter, K* 44 (1891), no. 2: 7.

47 *S* 9 (1905/06), no. 30: 295; *S* 1 (1896/97), no. 7: 3. For a more general discussion of comparable developments in the visual arts see Carl Schorske, "Gustav Klimt: Painting and the Crisis of the Liberal Ego," in his *Fin de Siècle Vienna: Politics and Culture* (New York, 1980), 215–18. The artistic significance of *Simplicissimus* was also celebrated in an exhibition, "*Simplicissimus*: Eine satirische Zeitschrift, München 1896–1944," held in the Haus der Kunst from November 19 to January 15, 1978. The catalog is published by the Ausstellungsleitung, Haus der Kunst, Munich. The artistic credo of the *Simplicissimus* staff is also discussed in Konrad, "Nationale und Internationale Tendenzen," 72–73.

48 *Kölnische Zeitung,* Dec. 28, 1908; Hauptmann's reaction is quoted in Thoma to Langen, Aug. 16, 1900, in Thoma, *Leben in Briefen,* 58.

49 Schorske, *Fin-de-Siècle Vienna,* 215. The quotation from Jugend is in Harry Pross, ed., *Literatur und Politik: Geschichte und Programme der politisch-literarischen Zeitschriften im deutschen Sprachgebiet seit 1870* (Freiburg, 1963), 53.

7 *Kladderadatsch, Simplicissimus,* and the Weimar Republic

1 For a discussion of the wartime role of *Simplicissimus* see Ruprecht Konrad, "Politische Zielsetzung und Selbstverständnis des *Simplicissimus*," in "*Simplicissimus: Eine satirische Zeitschrift,*" 98–103. A general discussion of postwar mood is in Peter Gay, *Weimar Culture: The Outsider as Insider* (New York, 1968). An overview of the German press in wartime is given in Isolde Rieger, *Die wilhelminische Presse,* 152.

2 For brief historical accounts of *Kladderadatsch* during the Weimar years, see

the introduction by Hans Rothfels to *Facsimile-Kladderadatsch*, 15–16; and Schulz, *Kladderadatsch*, 195–201.

3 *K* 72 (1919), no. 32: cover; *K* 75 (1922), no. 75: cover. For a discussion of fulfillment policy see Klaus Epstein, *Matthias Erzberger and the Dilemma of German Democracy* (Princeton, 1959), 284–328. The prohibition of *Kladderadatsch* in the occupied Ruhr is mentioned in *Facsimile-Kladderadatsch*, 15. A general overview of reactions of the German satirical press to the Versailles Treaty is in E.A. Coupe, "German Cartoonists and the Peace," *History Today* 32 (Jan. 1982): 46–54.

4 *K* 76 (1923), no. 35: cover; *K* 81 (1928), no. 38: cover; *K* 82 (1929), no. 26: cover. For a general discussion of the anti-Young Plan campaign see Erich Eyck, *A History of the Weimar Republic*, 2 vols. (Cambridge, Mass., 1963; rpt., 1967), 2: 203–13.

5 *K* 71 (1918), no. 48: n.p. For an analysis of the social consequences of the Weimar revolution see (among many sources) Wehler, *Deutsche Kaiserreich*, 218–26.

6 *K* 72 (1919), no. 21: cover; *K* 78 (1925), no. 18: cover; *K* 79 (1926), no. 23: cover; *K* 82 (1929), no. 41: cover. The background on authoritarian theory during this period is covered in Klemens von Klemperer, *Germany's New Conservatism: Its History and Its Dilemma in the Twentieth Century* (Princeton, 1957; rpt., 1968), 92–133.

7 *K* 77 (1924), no. 11: cover. For examples of protest against the alleged suppression of Hitler's activities see also *K* 76 (1923), no. 45: n.p.; and *K* 79 (1926), no. 22: cover. Examples of electoral propaganda may be found in *K* 88 (1930), nos. 37–40. A general discussion of the reactions of "respectable" conservatives of the Weimar period to the rise of Hitler may be found in Walter Laqueur, *Weimar: A Cultural History* (New York, 1975), 78–109; and Klemperer, *Conservatism*, 197–201.

8 Hitler is urged to join the coalition in *K* 85 (1932), no. 49: cover. The verse is from *K* 86 (1933), no. 7 n.p. For other accounts of the *Gleichschaltung* of *Kladderadatsch* see Schulz, *Kladderadatsch*, 197–210; and *Facsimile-Kladderadatsch*, 16.

9 For another summary and analysis of the magazine's history see Schulz, *Kladderadatsch*, 201–7.

10 Thoma to Haussmann, Aug. 13, 1917, and Oct. 4, 1917, in Thoma, *Leben in Briefen*, 302, 308. A great deal of correspondence and some other documents from this period are held in the Thoma *Nachlass*, Handschriften-Abteilung, Stadtbibliothek München, including the letter from Forel.

11 Sinsheimer, *Gelebt im Paradies*, 246. Because of Sinsheimer's quarrel with the owners of *Simplicissimus*, the hostile picture of their personalities and actions which he presented in this memoir must be taken with a grain of salt. For a brief account of this dispute see Otto M. Nelson, "*Simplicissimus* and the Rise of National Socialism," *Historian* 40 (May 1978): 444. For another discussion of the change of orientation after the war, see Konrad, "Politische Zielsetzung," 103–4.

12 Sinsheimer, *Gelebt im Paradies*, 232; Gay, *Weimar Culture*, 138. For a discussion of Grosz's contributions see John Willett, *Art and Politics in the Weimar Period* (New York, 1978), 188. An example of Kollwitz's contributions is her "Eine deutsche Mutter," *S* 27 (1924), no. 43: 527. For a more complete treatment of Grosz see Beth Irwin Lewis, *George Grosz: Art and Politics in the Weimar Republic* (Madison, Wis. 1971). The dark and chaotic aspects of

Weimar culture are discussed in (among many sources) Alex de Jonge, *The Weimar Chronicle: Prelude to Hitler* (New York, 1978).

13 Sinsheimer, *Gelebt im Paradies*, 234. For an account of Berlin and its role in Weimar culture see Wolf von Eckhardt, *Bertolt Brecht's Berlin* (New York, 1975).

14 *S* 28 (1924), no. 34: 420. On French occupation of the Ruhr see de Jonge, *Weimar*, 75–93.

15 *S* 31 (1925–26), no. 30: cover; *S* 34 (1928/29), no. 1: 29; no. 19: cover. For Ossietzky's views see Istvan Deak, *Weimar Germany's Left-Wing Intellectuals: A Political History of the Weltbühne and Its Circle* (Berkeley, 1968), 172.

16 For a discussion of attitudes toward the military among Weimar intellectuals see Laqueur, *Weimar Culture*, 44–48. The antimilitarist activities of *Die Weltbühne* are discussed in Deak, *Intellectuals*, 112–21.

17 Sinsheimer, *Gelebt im Paradies*, 246.

18 *S* 22 (1918), no. 40: cover; *S* 28 (1923/24), no. 33: 408. Other reactions to the founding of the Weimar Republic are discussed in Laqueur, *Weimar*, 9–23.

19 *S* 29 (1924/25), no. 51: 730. The characterization of the Weimar Republic is from Golo Mann, *Deutsche Geschichte des 19. und 20. Jahrhunderts* (Frankfurt, 1958), 804. Sinsheimer, *Gelebt im Paradies*, 235. For a discussion of left-wing intellectuals' attitudes toward Social Democratic leadership see Laqueur, *Weimar Culture*, 69.

20 *S* 23 (1918/19), no. 38: 474; *S* 28 (1923/24), no. 40: 499. A discussion of the left-wing campaign against conservative bureaucracy is in Deak, *Intellectuals*, 122–29.

21 *S* 29 (1924/25), no. 7: 124; *S* 23 (1919/20), no. 23: 43; *S* 22 (1918/19), no. 43: 528. The campaign for sexual reform waged by *Die Weltbühne* is discussed in Deak, *Intellectuals*, 129–35. Sexual mores are described in de Jonge, *Weimar*, 125–94; and Laqueur, *Weimar*, 224–53.

22 The following account of the reaction of *Simplicissimus* to the rise of Hitler relies heavily on the thorough and well-researched article of Otto M. Nelson, "*Simplicissimus* and the Rise of National Socialism," which draws on archival materials as well as the magazine's contents.

23 *S* 28 (1923/24), no. 51: cover, 632. Franz Schoenberner's opinion is expressed in his *Reflections of a European Intellectual* (New York, 1946), 305.

24 Schoenberner, *Reflections*, 305. For the initial attitudes of other groups toward Hitler see Klemperer, *Conservatism*, 193: Laqueur, *Weimar*, 260–65; and Deak, *Intellectuals*, 180–81, 204–5.

25 *S* 28 (1923/24), no. 7: 107; *S* 23 (1918/19), no. 29: 357; *S* 35 (1930/31), no. 36: 429. The Weimar myth of the "Jewish parnassus" is described in Laqueur, *Weimar*, 71–77. Further discussion of the position of Jews in Weimar Germany is in Peter Gay, "The Berlin-Jewish Spirit: A Dogma in Search of Some Doubts," in *Freud, Jews and Other Germans*, 168–87. For another analysis of *Simplicissimus*' picture of the Jewish community see Nelson, "*Simplicissimus* and the Rise of National Socialism," 451.

26 *S* 37 (1932/33), no. 31: 364; Schoenberner, *Reflections*, 2, 310.

27 A typescript of the charge and sentence in this case is held in the BHStA, MJu 17354 (date of transcript, Dec. 19, 1931), which also holds the transcript of another libel suit brought against Schoenberner by party official Gottfried Feder (Nov. 29, 1930).

28 *S* 37 (1932/33), no. 43: 507; *S* 37 (1932/33), no. 46: 544. The quotation from *Die Weltbühne* is in Deak, *Intellectuals*, 213. Schoenberner discusses the policies followed during those years in *Reflections*, 310.

29 *S* 37 (1932/33), no. 49: cover; no. 51: cover. An account of Nazi reprisals is in Schoenberner, *Reflections*, 9–12. National Socialist press policies are discussed in Kurt Koszyk, *Das Ende des Rechtstaates 1933/34 und die deutsche Presse* (n.p., 1959). Nazi cultural policies are discussed in Karl Dietrich Bracher and Wolfgang Sauer, *Die nationalsozialistische Machtergreifung* (Cologne, 1962), 288, 308. For this account of *Simplicissimus'* final days I am greatly indebted to Nelson, "*Simplicissimus* and the Rise of National Socialism," 456–61, which presents some archival evidence not available to me.

30 Schoenberner, *Reflections*, 10; Heine to Seemann, July 2, 1946, in *Nachlass* Thomas Theodor Heine, Handschriften-Abteilung, Stadtbibliothek München. See also Otto Nelson, "T.T. Heine: His Expatriate Correspondence," *Library Chronicle* 8 (Fall 1974): 41–47.

31 *S* 40 (1933/34), no. 1: 26.

32 Sinsheimer, *Gelebt im Paradies*, 235.

8 Protest and Innovation

1 Friedrich Meinecke, *Erlebtes, 1862–1901* (Leipzig, 1941), 167–68; C. Swart, *The Sense of Decadence in Nineteenth-Century France* (The Hague, 1964), 139; Jan Romein, *The Watershed of Two Eras: Europe in 1900* (Middletown, Conn., 1978), 25.

2 Von Heeringen is quoted from *Hamburger Fremdenblatt*, Apr. 5, 1910; the Bavarian Landtag deputy is quoted from *Stenographischer Bericht über die Verhandlungen des bayerischen Landtags, Kammer der Abgeordneten*, 428 Sitzung, Jan. 14, 1904.

3 A discussion of the struggle for democratization is in Wehler, *Deutsche Kaiserreich*, 78–79.

4 For a general analysis of the intellectual climate of this period see H. Stuart Hughes, *Consciousness and Society: The Reorientation of European Social Thought* (New York, 1958), 125–53. The quotation is from *Hamburger Nachrichten*, Dec. 29, 1903.

5 Conrad Haussmann, "Satire und *Simplicissimus*," *Frankfurter Zeitung*, Jan. 19, 1904.

6 Clifford Geertz, "Ideology as a Cultural System," in *The Interpretation of Cultures*, 220.

7 *Neue Hamburger Zeitung*, Nov. 11, 1905; *Allgemeine Zeitung*, Dec. 20, 1903; *Augsburger Postzeitung*, Mar. 15, 1912.

8 *Die Gartenlaube*, 1908, 641; Wilson, *Jokes*, 227.

9 Zmarzlik, "Das Kaiserreich in neuer Sicht?" 120.

10 On *L'Assiette au Beurre* see Stanley Appelbaum, ed., *French Satirical Drawings from L'Assiette au Beurre* (New York, 1978), v–vii. On the American magazines see Richard Fitzgerald, *Art and Politics: Cartoonists of the Masses and the Liberator* (Westport, Conn., 1973), 30–31. On *Zhupel* see Williams, *Artists in Revolution*, 111–48.

11 Bergson, *Le Rire*, 16; *Der Tag*, Jan. 5, 1904.

12 Schoenberner, *Reflections*, 2.

Bibliographical Essay

Primary Sources

Apart from a few letters, no manuscript or archival sources exist for *Kladderadatsch*, whose main archive was apparently destroyed by bombs. Many documents pertaining to the history of *Simplicissimus* are preserved in the Bayerische Hauptstaatsarchiv in Munich. Files are entitled "Innenministerium: Uberwachung der Presse 1903–1909" and "Justizministerium 17353–17355." These files contain transcripts of trials, police reports, official memoranda, and a collection of miscellaneous newspaper clippings.

The Münchener Stadtbibliothek, Handschriften-Abteilung holds unpublished letters from and to the following *Simplicissimus* staff members and contributors: Otto Julius Bierbaum, Thomas Theodor Heine, Korfiz Holm, Albert Langen, Ludwig Thoma, Donald and Frank Wedekind. Some of these collections contain letters from many other *Simplicissimus* contributors. The Thoma *Nachlass* is very complete, containing a variety of documents and newspaper clippings in addition to his handwritten letters. Thoma's most important letters have been published in the excellent collection, Ludwig Thoma, *Ein Leben in Briefen, 1875–1921* (Munich, 1963). The *Handschriften-Abteilung* also holds the "Brief-Kopierbuch," a day-to-day record of Holm's correspondence during the years of Langen's exile. The Stadtbibliothek München also holds an excellent collection of secondary literature, much of which is noted in the bibliography of secondary sources which follows.

Some documents pertaining to *Simplicissimus'* tangles with the police may be found in the *Nachlass* of Conrad Haussmann, Ludwig Thoma's attorney and close friend. The collection, which also contains some of the Haussmann-Thoma correspondence and a newspaper clipping file, is held in the Hauptstaatsarchiv Stuttgart (Files E 151 and Q 1/2).

A very useful newspaper clipping file was compiled on *Simplicissimus* by the Political Police of Hamburg. The file, "Politsche Polizi S 5452," vols. 1 and 2, contains newspaper clippings from all over Germany pertaining both to the legal proceedings against *Simplicissimus* and to the reactions of individuals and groups to the magazine in general and to specific items. It is held in the Hamburg Staatsarchiv.

Autobiographical materials on the editors of *Kladderadatsch* include Rudolf Löwenstein's autobiographical statement in Paul Lembach, ed., *Die deutschen Dichter der Gegenwart*, 5 vols. (Leipzig, 1893), 5: 447–50 and Johannes Trojan's autobiographical works, *Erinnerungen* (Berlin, 1912) and *Zwei Monate Festung* (Berlin, 1899). Many memoirs deal with the history of *Simplicissimus* from the often highly biased points of view of editorial board members and readers. Among these are: Eugen Roth, *Simplicissimus: Ein Rückblick auf das satirische Zeitschrift* (Hannover, 1955); Jakob Wassermann, *Lebensdienst: Gesammelte Studien und Reden aus drei Jahrzehnten* (Zurich, 1968); Ludwig Thoma, *Erinnerungen*, vol. 1 of his *Gesammelte Werke*, 7 vols. (Munich, 1933); Korfiz Holm, *Farbiger Abglanz* (Munich, 1940); Viktor Mann, *Wir waren Fünf: Bildnis der Familie Mann* (Konstanz, 1964); Franz Blei, *Erzählung eines Lebens* (Leipzig, 1930); Hans-Ludwig Geiger, *Es war um die Jahrhundertwende* (Munich, 1953); Max Halbe, *Jahrhundertwende: Geschichte meines Lebens* (Danzig, 1935); Arthur Holitscher, *Lebensgeschichte eines Rebellen: Meine Erinnerungen* (Berlin, 1924); and Hans Brandenburg, *München Leuchtete: Jugenderinnerungen* (Munich, 1953). Such sources as these offer a wealth of anecdotal material but are often idiosyncratic and impressionistic in their evaluation of the magazine, its milieu, and its impact on public opinion. The memoirs of the two editors of the Weimar period, Hermann Sinsheimer, *Gelebt im Paradies* (Munich, 1953), and Franz Schoenberner, *Confessions of a European Intellectual* (New York, 1946), must be interpreted with particular caution, since both contain rather one-sided and apologetic accounts of disputes between the owners and the editors, and among the editors themselves.

Secondary Sources

Many sources providing general historical background, most of them well known to the specialist, have been cited in the notes. The present bibliographical essay is therefore restricted to sources pertaining directly to *Kladderadatsch* and *Simplicissimus* and to two related themes, the interpretation of humor and the history of journalism and public opinion. Only the most important and helpful sources are included.

Two book-length histories of *Kladderadatsch* are Harry Barthel, "Der *Kladderadatsch* im Kampf um die Sozial- und-Wirtschaftsordnung des Bismarckischen Reiches" (Ph.D. diss., Univ. of Munich, 1951); and Klaus Schulz, *Kladderadatsch: Ein bürgerliches Witzblatt von der Märzrevolution bis zum Nationalsozialismus, 1848–1944* (Bochum, 1975). Barthel presents a detailed and rather plodding account of the magazine's response to the political issues of the Bismarck years. Schulz focuses chiefly on the financial and administrative bases of editorial policy—in the absence of archival material, a difficult and problematic task. A useful anthology is Liesel Hartenstein, ed., *Facsimile Querschnitt durch den Kladderadatsch* (Munich, 1965); the historical introduction by Hans Rothfels is particularly valuable.

Biographical material on the editorial staff of the magazine includes Albert Hofmann, ed., *Der Kladderadatsch und seine Leute* (Berlin, 1898), a *Festschrift* published to commemorate the periodical's fiftieth anniversary; Max Ring, *David Kalisch, der Vater des Kladderadatsch* (Berlin, 1873); and the rather extensive accounts given in Kurt Stephenson, "Redakteure des *Kladderadatsch:* Ihr Echo im Studentenlied," in *Darstellungen und Quellen zur Geschichte der deutschen Einheits-bewegung im neunzehnten und zwanzigsten Jahrhundert,* 7 vols. (Heidelberg, 1967), 7: 9–48. A biographical article on Trojan is Julius Stinde, "Der Dichter des froh-lichen Gemuts," *Schorers Familienblatt* 13 (1892): 427–29.

Several books and articles explore various episodes in the history of *Kladder-adatsch*. Eugen Kalkschmidt, *Deutsche Freiheit und deutscher Witz: Ein Kapitel Revolutions-Satire aus der Zeit von 1830–1850* (Berlin, 1928), places *Kladdera-datsch* in the context of the numerous other satirical periodicals which appeared in 1848. Another analysis of *Kladderadatsch* as a product of the 1848 revolution is W.A. Coupe, "The German Cartoon and the Revolution of 1848," *Comparative Studies in Society and History: An International Quarterly* 9 (1966–67): 138–76. The magazine's satirical attack on the Catholic Church is discussed in Friedheim Jürgensmeister, *Die katholische Kirche im Speigel der deutschen Tendenzzeit-schriften von 1848 bis 1900* (Trier, 1969). The *"Kladderadatsch* affair" of 1893–94 is analyzed in detail in Helmuth Rogge, "Die Kladderadatsch-Affäre: Ein Bei-trag zur inneren Geschichte des wilhelminischen Reiches," *Historische Zeit-schrift* 195 (1962): 90–130. It is also described in its historical context in Rogge, *Holstein und Harden: Politisch-publizistisches Zusammenspiel zweier Aussen-seiter des wilhelminischen Reiches* (Munich, 1959); and in Harry F. Young, *Max-imilian Harden, Censor Germaniae: The Critic in Opposition from Bismarck to the Rise of Nazism* (The Hague, 1959).

Several dissertations have been written on *Simplicissimus:* Ruprecht Konrad, "Nationale und internationale Tendenzen im *Simplicissimus:* Der Wandel künstlerisch-politischen Bewusstseinsstrukturen im Spiegel von Satire und Kari-katur in Bayern, 1896–1937" (Ph.D. diss., Univ. of Munich, 1975), concentrates rather narrowly on political issues, largely ignoring the magazine's social and cultural criticism. Hasso Zimdars, "Die Zeitschrift *Simplicissimus:* Ihre Karika-turen" (Ph.D. diss., Univ. of Bonn, 1972), is rather lightweight. My own disser-tation, Ann Allen Jobling, " 'A Playful Judgment:' Satire and Society in Wilhel-mine Germany" (Ph.D. diss., Columbia University, 1974), formed the basis for the present study, but lacks the archival evidence which I have since added. Several articles have also appeared, including Gerhard Bennecke, "The Politics of Out-rage: Social Satire in *Simplicissimus,* 1896–1914," *Twentieth Century Studies* 13/14 (December 1975): 92–109; Otto M. Nelson, *"Simplicissimus* and the Rise of National Socialism," *Historian* 40 (May 1978): 440–62; and Ann Taylor Allen, "Sex and Satire in Wilhelmine Germany: *Simplicissimus* Looks at Family Life," *Journal of European Studies* 7 (March 1977): 19–40. A catalog entitled *"Simpli-cissimus:" Eine satirische Zeitschrift, München, 1896–1944* was published by the Ausstellungsleitung (Exhibitions Department) of the Haus der Kunst in Munich, 1977. Besides numerous reproductions of cartoons, this extensive catalog con-tains many articles on various aspects of the magazine's history, including the useful narrative of Anton Sailer, "Glanz und Elend des *Simplicissimus."* Other anthologies which contain useful historical and biographical material are: Chris-tian Schütze, ed., *Facsimile-Querschnitt durch den Simplicissimus* (Stuttgart, 1963), which also has a perceptive preface by Golo Mann; *Simplicissimus, 1896–1944,* ed. Richard Christ (Berlin, 1978); *Simplicissimus: Satirical Drawings from the Famous German Weekly,* ed. Stanley Appelbaum (New York, 1963); and *Der Gute Ton: Aus dem Simplicissimus 1896–1932* (Munich, 1963).

Biographies of individual *Simplicissimus* contributors are numerous and un-even in quality. Among the many biographical and critical works on Ludwig Thoma, a few examples are: Roland Ziersch, *Ludwig Thoma* (Stuttgart, 1964); Walter L. Heilbronner, "Ludwig Thoma as a Social and Political Critic and Satirist" (Ph.D. diss., Univ. of Michigan, 1955); Peter Haage, *Ludwig Thoma: Mit Nagelstiefeln durchs Kaiserreich* (Munich, 1975); and three pamphlets by Friedl Brehm, *Ludwig Thoma und der Simplicissimus: Immer gegen die Machthaber* (Feldaffing, 1966), *Sehnsucht nach Unterdrückung: Zensur und Presserecht bei Ludwig Thoma* (Feldaffing, 1957), and *Zehn haben neun Meinungen: Kritik und Kritiker bei Ludwig Thoma* (Feldaffing, 1958). Two works by Otto Gritschneder give a thorough account of the trial of Ludwig Thoma for insults to the Protestant pastorate in 1905; an unpublished radio play, "Bei Durchsicht gewisser Akten: Der Prozess gegen Ludwig Thoma nach den bisher verschollenen Dokumenten dargestellt," produced by the Bayerischer Rundfunk on November 7, 1977 (the unpublished typescript is held in the Munich Stadtbibliothek) and *Angeklagter Ludwig Thoma: Unveröffentlichte Akten* (Munich, 1978). A recent and very comprehensive biography of Thoma is Helmut Ahrens, *Ludwig Thoma: Sein Leben, sein Werk, seine Zeit* (Pfaffenhofen, 1983).

A thorough account of Langen's career in publishing is Ernestine Koch, *Albert Langen, Ein Verleger in München* (Munich, 1969). On Thomas Theodor Heine, one semiautobiographical source is his novel *Ich Warte auf Wunder* (Hamburg, 1948). More biographical information is found in exhibition catalogs such as *Th. Th. Heine: Aus dem Nachlass: Ausstellung Städtischer Galerie* (Munich, 1960); and in anthologies such as *Der Zeichner Thomas Theodor Heine* (Freiburg i.B., 1955), and Hermann Esswein, *Moderne Illustratoren: Thomas Theodor Heine* (Munich, 1905). An account of Heine's career after 1933 based on his unpublished correspondence is Otto M. Nelson, "T.T. Heine: His Expatriate Correspondence," *Library Chronicle* 8 (Fall 1974): 41–47. A brief biographical sketch of Rudolf Wilke is in the exhibition catalog *Rudolf Wilke: Centennial Anniversary of His Birth* (Iowa City, 1973). One of Karl Arnold is in *Karl Arnold, Drunter, Drüber, Mittenmang: Karikaturen aus dem Simplicissimus,* introduction by Hermann Kesten (Munich, 1974). Information on individual cartoonists may also be found in general works on caricature; see particularly Ralph E. Shikes, *The Indignant Eye: The Artist as Social Critic in Prints and Drawings from the Fifteenth Century to Picasso* (Boston, 1969).

The analysis of popular humor must draw heavily on general works on satire and its social and historical significance. Works on the German satirical tradition tend to fall into three categories. Among anthologies with historical introductions, the best is Ludwig Hollweck, *Karikaturen von den Fliegenden Blättern bis zum Simplicissimus* (Munich, 1973). Two rather pedestrian dissertations are Gustav Bald, "Die politisch-satirische Lyrik: Ein publizistisches Kampfmittel," (Ph.D. diss., Univ. of Erlangen, 1936); and Christian Gehring, *Die Entwicklung des politischen Witzblatts in Deutschland* (Leipzig, 1927). There are also a number of works concentrating on satire as a literary tradition, such as Klaus Lazarowicz, *Verkehrte Welt: Vorstudien zu einer Geschichte der deutschen Satire* (Tubingen, 1963), which are of limited use to a study of popular sources. Among general works on caricature and the graphic arts, the most helpful were: Georg Hermann Borchardt, *Die deutsche Karikatur im neunzehnten Jahrhundert* (Bielefeld, 1901); Ralph E. Shikes, *The Indignant Eye* (see above); and Ann Gould, ed., *Masters of Caricature from Hogarth and Gillray to Scarfe and Levine* (New York, 1981). Lively and informative are the two articles by E.A. Coupe, "Kaiser Wilhelm II and the Cartoonists," *History Today* 30 (November 1980): 16–23; and "German Cartoonists and the Peace," *History Today* 32 (January 1982): 46–54. All of these contain at least brief references to *Simplicissimus,* as does Franz Roh, *German Art in the Twentieth Century* (New York, 1957).

On general psychological and sociological theories of humor, only the most important for the present study can be mentioned here. Sigmund Freud, *Wit and Its Relation to the Unconscious,* most conveniently found in the Modern Library volume *The Basic Writings of Sigmund Freud,* trans. and ed. A.A. Brill (New York, 1938), is particularly valuable because it arose out of the same cultural milieu as did the Wilhelmine *Simplicissimus* and *Kladderadatsch.* Other relevant works are: Arthur Koestler, *The Act of Creation* (New York, 1964); Henri Bergson, *Le Rire: Essai sur la Signification du Comique* (Paris, 1900; rpt., 1967); Antonin Obrdlík, "Gallows Humor: A Sociological Phenomenon," *American Journal of Sociology* 47 (1942): 710–20; Christopher P. Wilson, *Jokes: Form, Content, Use and Function* (London and New York, 1979); and Robert C. Elliot, *The Power of Satire: Magic, Ritual, Art* (Princeton, 1960).

An invaluable general survey of the subject is Jeffrey H. Goldstein and Paul E. McGhee, eds., *The Psychology of Humour: Theoretical Perspectives and Empirical Issues* (New York, 1972). A well reasoned and interesting sociological interpretation of Freud's theory is Carroll Emerson Word, "Freudian Theories of Wit and Humour as Applied to Certain Theories of Social Conflict" (Ph.D diss., Boston University, 1960). An aid to the interpretation of Koestler's rather complex theory of humor is Edward L. Galligan, "The Usefulness of Arthur Koestler's Theory of Jokes," *South Atlantic Quarterly* 75 (Spring 1976): 145–49. Martin Grotjahn, *Beyond Laughter: Humor and the Subconscious* (New York, 1957), offers an elaborated version of Freud's basic theory. Although Clifford Geertz, "Ideology as a Cultural System," included as a chapter in his *The Interpretation of Cultures: Selected Essays* (New York, 1973), does not directly mention satire, it offers a stimulating interpretation of the role of metaphorical and symbolic discourse in forming political ideology. There are several sources on comparable satirical literature in other countries; some examples are *French Satirical Drawings from L'Assiette au Beurre,* ed. Stanley Appelbaum (New York, 1978); R.C.G. Price, *A History of Punch* (London, 1957); Robert C. Williams, *Artists in Revolution: Portraits of the Russian Avant-Garde* (Bloomington, 1977); and Richard Fitzgerald, *Art and Politics: Cartoonists of the Masses and the Liberator* (Westport, Conn., 1973).

Other interesting analyses of the relationship of caricature to the social and political history of various periods are Lawrence H. Streicher, "On a Theory of Political Caricature," *Comparative Studies in Society and History* 9 (1966–67): 428–45; and idem, "David Low and the Sociology of Caricature," *Comparative Studies in Society and History* 8 (1965–66): 1–23; W.A. Coupe, "Observations on a Theory of Political Caricature," *Comparative Studies in Society and History* 11 (1969): 79–95; and Charles Press, "The Georgian Political Print and Democratic Institutions," *Comparative Studies in Society and History* 19 (1977): 216–38.

Another important general topic is the history of journalism and of public opinion. Robin Lenman has done valuable research on the censorship laws and general intellectual climate of Wilhelmine Germany; his dissertation, "Censorship and Society in Munich, 1890–1914, with Special Reference to *Simplicissimus* and the plays of Frank Wedekind" (Ph.D. diss., Oxford Univ., 1975), and his two articles, "Art, Society and the Law in Wilhelmine Germany: The *Lex Heinze,*"

Oxford Studies Review 8 (1973): 86–113, and "Politics and Culture: The State and the Avant-Garde in Munich," in *Society and Politics in Wilhelmine Germany,* ed. Richard J. Evans (London, 1978), 90–111, provide excellent analyses of the various controversies over freedom of the press which occurred during this period. Ludwig Leiss, *Kunst im Konflikt: Kunst und Künstler im Widerstreit mit der Obrigkeit* (Berlin, 1971), similarly uses some of the legal cases in which *Simplicissimus* was involved in his general account of the debate over the permissible limits of sexual frankness in the arts. Gary D. Stark has discussed general attitudes toward pornography in his recent article, "Pornography, Society and the Law in Imperial Germany," *Central European History* 14 (Sept. 1981): 200–229. I would like to thank Peter Jelavich for allowing me to read his unpublished paper, "The Censorship of Literary Naturalism, 1885–1895: Bavaria," presented at the Seventh Annual Conference of the Western Association for German Studies, October 1, 1983.

Harry Pross, *Literatur und Politik: Geschichte und Programme der politisch-literarischen Zeitschriften im deutschen Sprachgebiet seit 1870* (Freiburg i.B., 1963), gives an overall view of political periodicals during this period. On the history of journalism in imperial Germany, the works of Rolf Engelsing, *Massenpublikum und Journalistentum im 19 Jahrhundert in Nordwestdeutschland* (Berlin, 1966), and "Die Zeitschrift in Nordwestdeutschland, 1850–1914," *Archiv für die Geschichte des Buchwesens* 4 (1964): 937–1036, give important general background, particularly on changes in readership of newspapers and periodicals. A valuable study of reading habits is Rudolf Schenda, *Volk ohne Buch: Studien zur Geschichte der populären Lesestoffe, 1770–1900* (Frankfurt, 1970). Some general histories of the press in Wilhelmine Germany are: Kurt Koszyk, *Geschichte der deutschen Presse,* 2 vols. (Berlin, 1966); Isolde Rieger, *Die wilhelminische Presse im Überblick, 1888–1918* (Munich, 1957); and Joachim Kirchner, *Das deutsche Zeitschriftenwesen: Seine Geschichte und seine Probleme,* 2 vols. (Wiesbaden, 1962). Various accounts of the responses of the press to certain specific events are interesting for comparative purposes; for example, Paul Gruschinske, *Kiderlen-Wächter und die deutschen Zeitungen in der Marokkokrise des Jahres 1911* (Cologne, 1913); Otto Friedrich Ris, *Das Verhältnis der deutschen Presse zur offiziellen deutschen Politik wahrend der ersten Marokkokrise, 1904–1905* (Cologne, 1949), and Ursula Koch, *Berliner Presse und europäisches Geschehen 1871: Eine Untersuchung über die Rezeption der grossen Ereignisse im ersten Halbjahr 1871 in den politischen Zeitungen der deutschen Reichshauptstadt* (Berlin, 1978).

Index